VIGILANCE

VIGILANCE

My Life Serving America and
Protecting Its Empire City

RAY KELLY

NEW YORK   BOSTON

Hachette Books
Hachette Book Group
1290 Avenue of the Americas
New York, NY 10104

www.HachetteBookGroup.com

Printed in the United States of America

RRD-C

First Edition: September 2015
10 9 8 7 6 5 4 3 2 1

Hachette Books is a division of Hachette Book Group, Inc.
The Hachette Books name and logo are trademarks of Hachette Book Group, Inc.

The publisher is not responsible for websites (or their content) that are not owned by the publisher.

Library of Congress Cataloging-in-Publication Data has been applied for.

For Veronica

CONTENTS

I yman Faris was perfectly positioned to deliver the follow-up attack to 9/11.

If you had asked his neighbors in Columbus, Ohio, they would have described Faris as a quiet, hardworking family man. He held down a regular job as a long-haul trucker, delivering chemicals and other flammable materials to airport cargo depots across the United States. He married a preacher's daughter from Kentucky and doted on his teenage stepson. He'd even become a U.S. citizen, swearing allegiance to his newly adopted homeland. That's the man almost everyone knew. But Iyman Faris was living a double life. A thirty-three-year-old native of Pakistan, he had spent time at terrorist training camps in Afghanistan and was now an al-Qaeda sleeper agent. Using disguised e-mail accounts, he was trading frequent messages with top terror operatives overseas. Late in 2002, Khalid Sheikh Mohammed, the principal architect of the 2001 World Trade Center attack, directed Faris to drive his tractor-trailer to New York City.

He wasn't coming just to see the Brooklyn Bridge. He was coming to destroy it.

By the time Faris left Ohio, he already had a detailed plan. Using a gas-powered blowtorch, he would slice several of the bridge's heavy suspension cables. It really wouldn't be that difficult, he was convinced. If the right cables were severed, the integrity of the 120-year-old span could be swiftly undermined, causing the mile-long bridge deck to collapse 275 feet into the East River below. Depending on the time of day, the death toll could be comparable to 9/11, easily reaching thousands of lives.

* * *

I took over as New York City police commissioner at the beginning of 2002, three months and twenty-six days after the worst terrorist attack ever executed on American soil. For the next twelve years, I had an immense responsibility: making sure that nothing remotely like the terrible events of September 11, 2001, ever happened again. Every day, I asked myself the same question: What can we do to tilt the odds a little more in our favor? My job was to keep finding ways. The pressure was enormous. The resources were never sufficient. The terrorists had many advantages. The critics were everywhere. But I had an incomparable organization behind me—the New York City Police Department—and a daunting threat hanging over my head. I knew that if we failed even once, the consequences would be devastating. If the terrorists succeeded again after their triumph on 9/11, something vital and irreplaceable would certainly be lost.

Stopping terror wasn't the only thing I had to contend with when the city's new mayor, Michael Bloomberg, put me in charge of the world's greatest police department. We had to lock up street criminals, extending the crime drop that had started in the early 1990s under Mayor David Dinkins, when I served as NYPD commissioner the first time, and had accelerated through the Rudy Giuliani years. We had to maintain order and protect the quality of life in New York. We also had to improve the department's strained relations with some of the diverse communities we served. But none of that, important as it was, was more urgent than protecting America's largest city, which was also America's ripest target, from another deadly terror attack.

Our enemies kept coming at us, over and over again, sixteen

times in all. That's the number of serious terror plots launched against New York City and the number of plots that were foiled. With our federal partners and some luck, we didn't fail once in those twelve years. The terrorists went 0 for 16.

How did we do it?

It took leadership. It took teamwork. It took extraordinary expertise, inside and outside the police department, from some of the smartest and most dedicated people I've ever met. It took effective relationships with the FBI, the CIA, and many other organizations.

But more than anything, the post-9/11 terror fight required vigilance—constant, relentless, tireless, and creative vigilance. This was no responsibility that could be assumed halfheartedly. There was no going through the motions here. The terrorists never let up, and neither did we.

*   *   *

We had known for months that the Brooklyn Bridge was a prime target for al-Qaeda terrorists.

"The bridge in the *Godzilla* movie," they called it in e-mails and text messages intercepted by U.S. and foreign intelligence agencies overseas. With sufficient planning and a little bit of luck, the terror schemers were confident, they could wreck at least as many New York landmarks as the famous movie monster had.

It was easy to see why the bridge was such an enticing target. It was massive. Iconic. Almost as well-known as the toppled towers. Another feature of the downtown skyline recognized the world over. And best of all, the bridge was right out in the open and busy all the time, carrying 120,000 vehicles a day—plus another 8,000 runners, walkers, skaters, and bikers—between lower Manhattan and Brooklyn.

How could the local police possibly protect a structure as large and open as that?

The minute I was briefed on the Godzilla chatter, during my

second month on the job, I ordered security stepped up on the bridge. "I want radio cars on the Brooklyn side and the Manhattan side," I said to David Cohen, NYPD deputy commissioner of intelligence, who had previously run clandestine operations at the CIA.

"And let's put a boat in the water below the bridge," I added.

In the months and years that followed, we would activate similar strategies at high-profile locations around the city as we rolled out our comprehensive post-9/11 antiterror campaign. We flooded the zone with uniformed police officers and established our own extensive undercover intelligence and counterterrorism operations, something no other local police department had ever attempted before. We hired top people from the upper ranks of the FBI, the State Department, the military, and, in Cohen's case, the CIA—far beyond the normal recruitment pool for local law enforcement. We initiated Operation Hercules, a unique Demographics Unit, and the Lower Manhattan Security Initiative. High-visibility critical response vehicles cruised the streets. We stationed full-time New York City police detectives in terror hot spots overseas. Some of these measures didn't always sit well with the federal agencies that had long considered terror fighting their exclusive purview. But leaving the city's security entirely in federal hands hadn't worked out so well for New York. Twice already, once in 1993 and again in 2001, the terrorists had struck us. Twice was more than enough. Now it was time for America's top target to face an unavoidable reality of the modern terror age: no one would ever protect New York as well as New Yorkers would.

*   *   *

I took 9/11 very personally, as did many New Yorkers. Two thousand, seven hundred and fifty-three people were killed at the World Trade Center that day, including 343 New York City firefighters, 23 New York City police officers, and 37 Port Authority police officers. I had friends and colleagues among the victims, quite a few of them. My wife, Veronica, and I lived two blocks from the site, which was now a giant pile of rubble on the other side of West Street. This wasn't just our city. It was our neighborhood. It took eight weeks before Veronica and I were allowed back in our apartment, which had to be cleaned by HAZMAT specialists.

The whole city was having real trouble getting back on its feet. Hundreds of local companies still hadn't returned to their offices. Manhattan's vibrant nightlife was so quiet, you could get a restaurant reservation anywhere. Taxi traffic breezed through Midtown even at rush hour. These were all troubling signs. Wall Street, tourism, retail, and real estate—the powerful pillars of the city's economy were a series of giant question marks. Corporate CEOs were starting to ask if it still made sense to maintain large operations in the city, with its sky-high rents and inherent vulnerabilities.

And then there was this—if we suffered another attack, I was convinced, we really did risk losing something crucial: The New York that people everywhere knew and loved. The New York that was the center of global commerce. The New York where talented and ambitious people came to realize their dreams. The New York that was a diverse and powerful font of media, entertainment, culture, and the arts.

If people no longer felt secure living and working here, how could New York be any of those?

*   *   *

When Iyman Faris finally arrived at the Brooklyn Bridge, he didn't like what he saw.

An NYPD radio car was parked at the Manhattan end of the roadway, where the bridge cables were most readily accessible. A uniformed police officer was inside, sitting there, watching. A second police car was at the Brooklyn end of the bridge, the other point of vulnerability. An officer was inside that car as well, scanning everything. In the water below, a boat from the NYPD Harbor Unit was patrolling near the bridge supports.

I don't believe Faris caught sight of the extra security cameras that were sending live video feeds of the bridge to 1 Police Plaza, two short blocks away. He never even made it to the small machine sheds at either end of the bridge. They sheltered some of the bridge's key cable connections and other machinery. Prior to 9/11, anyone with a crowbar could have busted inside and gone to work in total privacy. Now those cable sheds are like little vaults.

Faris took in the scene. He weighed his options. And something almost miraculous occurred. The sleeper-agent truck driver from Ohio listened to his own second thoughts. After carefully surveying the bridge and our new intensified security measures, he concluded that his bridge plot was unlikely to succeed.

He sent a coded message to his al-Qaeda handlers back in Pakistan.

"The weather is too hot," he wrote.

Aren't those great words?

They showed, very early on, that our measures were having a real impact on the safety of New York, dissuading would-be terrorists who were intent on mass murder in the city we were sworn to protect.

It was one mind changed, but it was also a huge victory for law enforcement, local and federal alike—the first of many, thank God—and a major catastrophe avoided for the people of America and New York. In the years to come, those measures and countless others would continue paying dividends.

*　　*　　*

Much of the Faris plot was revealed after Khalid Sheikh Mohammed's arrest in Pakistan in March 2003, showing how intelligence activities overseas can be intimately tied to security at home in America. When Faris was confronted the following month in

Ohio by the FBI and quickly pleaded guilty to providing material support to al-Qaeda, I wanted to see for myself just how secure the bridge cables were. So I rounded up David Cohen and Mike Sheehan, our deputy commissioner for counterterrorism. With a couple of uniformed officers, the three of us took a ride.

We left police headquarters and went to the foot of the bridge. Traffic was roaring in both directions. Horns were honking. Limos were heading out to the airport. Taxis and private cars were creeping past. Runners, walkers, and bikers were streaming by. I'd crossed that bridge thousands of times before. But I had never looked at it quite like this.

I climbed over a waist-high railing that separated the roadway from the understructure of the bridge. I was wearing a suit, and I couldn't help but notice how filthy everything down there was. With Cohen and Sheehan behind me, I stepped into a dark, cramped room. I saw where the bridge's thick cables split into several thinner cables and were anchored to the shore.

As my eyes adjusted to the darkness, I could hear the traffic rumbling nearby, just a few feet from where we stood. But there was no way anyone on the outside could possibly see us in there.

I thought to myself: Someone could sit in here for hours or days without being discovered. And it wouldn't take nearly that long. Had our units not been on the scene to spook Faris when he arrived, had the bridge facilities not been hardened yet, he could easily have entered this room and cut or weakened the cables of the bridge. He was a truck driver. He knew how to handle tools. He had the practical skills of a working American and the endless zeal of the committed jihadist—a deadly combination if there ever was one.

Shocking as it was to contemplate, had we not been in a position to deter him, he could well have taken down the bridge.

I know the two deputy commissioners were thinking the same thing I was. "Thank God we put our cops where we put them," I said. "Where else should they go?"

CHAPTER ONE

City Kid

I was born September 4, 1941, at the French Hospital on Manhattan's West Thirtieth Street, three months and three days before the attack on Pearl Harbor. My parents, James and Elizabeth Kelly, already had three sons and a daughter. My brother Donald, the one immediately ahead of me, was seven years old. My mother was forty-two, my father nearly forty-five, ancient to be having a baby in those days. I was named after my father's brothers, Raymond and Walter Kelly.

I arrived in a New York that was big and bustling and loud, and the Kellys fit right in. In the middle of this frenetic city, we had our own close-knit world on the Upper West Side. We lived in a five-story walk-up apartment at 636 Columbus Avenue between West Ninetieth and West Ninety-First Streets with six spacious rooms. Living room, dining room, eat-in kitchen, and three bedrooms.

I used to lie on the living room floor, drawing pictures, which I was pretty good at, and showing my artwork to anyone who would look. We had an upright piano, though I never learned to play it, and large, creaky windows that looked down on the avenue. The landlord was Mr. Averett. To us, his name was a dirty word: "Averett, ugh," like he was the worst possible person in the world. Nobody ever admits to liking his landlord in New York, then or now. The building isn't there anymore. It was torn down to make way for a McDonald's, which was then replaced by a luxury high-rise. In today's crazy Manhattan real estate market, I wouldn't be surprised if a Wall Street couple and their one baby are now occupying the space that seven raucous Kellys once did. Today, forty-eight dollars would barely cover a night in the parking garage.

Even the crime back then reflected an earlier time. When I was almost two, my mother left me in my carriage on Amsterdam Avenue while she ran into the supermarket, tucking her purse snugly behind my head. Today, this would be called *asking for trouble*—if not *felonious child neglect*. It seemed perfectly normal in early-1940s New York. So my mother was both surprised and angry when she came outside just in time to see a man reach into the carriage, push me aside, grab her handbag, and take off down the avenue.

"Hey!" she called out indignantly. But she was too late, and he was too fast. To me, the trust that story implies is as telling as the crime it reports.

My father, who'd served as a private in France during World War I, worked as a milkman, delivering dairy products in the predawn hours to people's apartments, first by horse and cart and then in a boxy refrigerator truck. But in 1943, the Office of Defense Transportation ordered a skip-a-day milk delivery schedule to conserve home front resources. Mayor Fiorello La Guardia engineered a change in city regulations that made it cheaper to buy a quart of milk at the corner grocery, and the city's milkmen became economic dinosaurs almost overnight. My dad wasn't out of work for long. World War II was raging. The city's defense plants were humming around the clock. He quickly caught on at Atlantic Basin Iron Works, a shipyard on the Brooklyn waterfront that was converting the 9,500-ton passenger steamship *Rio Parana* into the British Royal Navy escort carrier HMS *Biter.* The shipyard job paid well and lasted as long as the war did. But in 1945, after the Germans and Japanese surrendered and the emergency defense contracts all dried up, my father was out of work again. The postwar boom hadn't started yet. Returning veterans were scooping up what few jobs there were. A forty-nine-year-old, second-generation Irish American like my father—high school diploma, basic blue-collar skills—wasn't much in demand. But with five children and a wife depending on him, he couldn't just wait around for his luck to change. He hit the pavement, picking up whatever work he could find. On Saturday afternoons, he started "shaping up," as the union men called it, as a day laborer at the *New York Times*, tossing fat bundles of Sunday papers onto trucks at the loading dock on West Forty-Third Street. It wasn't quite a living, but he was grateful for the shifts.

As a kid, I had no sense that any of this was cause for hardship. I certainly didn't want for anything. Our family seemed on par with the other families in the neighborhood, a mix of first- and second-generation immigrants from different parts of Europe— dockworkers, tradesmen, shop owners, lots of stay-at-home moms. Our building had eight families and six or seven different ethnic groups, totally typical for the time. Next door to us on the fifth floor was Mo Bernstein from Mo and Joe's Candy Store. Before Mo, the Kajandas from Norway lived there. Mrs. Kajanda was friendly with my mother. A floor down was the Waters family, the only other Irish Americans in the building. Next to them were the Collelas, Italian Americans. Their two sons both fought in World War II and flew B24s. It went on like that. On the third floor were a Czechoslovakian family and a French family. On the second floor were the Rothbergs, German Americans. Mr. Rothberg was the grumpy neighbor, impatient and nasty. Next to the Rothbergs were Dr. Kieve, a philosophy professor at Columbia University, and his wife. On the ground floor was Mr. Irving's hardware store.

All the stores on Columbus Avenue were owned by people we knew. The Childcraft store. Mrs. Eagan's music and candy shop. (The combination didn't strike me as odd at the time. My sister,

Mary, worked there after school.) The Mulaskis had a glazier business. They sold picture frames and fixed broken windows. There was Old Nick's Bar. No one seemed rich. No one seemed poor. Everyone was climbing into the middle class or hoping to.

In early September 1947, the week of my sixth birthday, my mother walked me around the corner to St. Gregory's, our local Catholic school. Four hundred kids, thirty-five in a class, far more nuns than lay teachers, five priests assigned to the parish. No one ever mentioned public school as an option for me. I cried all the way into the classroom my first day. The Presentation Sisters looked scary in their long black habits. Sister Athanasius prowled the halls, a big, hulking nun who sported a mustache. She carried a wooden bat she called "Athanasius Junior." Even the youngest male students were required to wear neckties. But once I settled in, I grew to like the place. Miss Velasquez, my first-grade teacher, was really nice. The other kids were friendly to me. We didn't have a school yard, but we played games at recess in front of the building, kick the can and Johnny-ride-a-pony and salugi and punch ball. We studied art and music, which you don't normally think of as Catholic school staples, especially back then. I loved playing drums—on a desk, a table, a couple of water glasses, or even the little practice pads they had at school. At St. Gregory's, the teachers believed in educating the whole child. When she put down that bat of hers, even Sister Athanasius turned out to be funny and kind.

I was Ray-Ray to the other kids, studious but athletic—not too quiet, not too talkative, friendly with just about everyone. I was an altar boy, which meant memorizing Latin. In first and second grades, I had leading roles in the school's May Crowning, an elaborate pageant honoring the Blessed Virgin Mary. Alice O'Rourke put the crown on the statue. My friend Billy Carney and I were page boys. Our mothers made suits for us out of white satin and blue fringe, and I swear Billy and I looked like little

James Browns. The only hitch was that I had measles the first year and my mother had to cover the spots with makeup. I hated the makeup, but you can't call in sick for a May Crowning. The second time I was the picture of good health as Alice, Billy, and I and the rest of the school sang together, "O Mary, we crown thee with blossoms today."

That's how it was being a Catholic kid in 1940s New York. They really were mostly carefree times.

When we weren't in school, we had stickball on West Ninetieth Street—dodging the cars when we had to—fastball against the wall on West Ninety-First Street, and football in Riverside Park. There were endless numbers of kids to play with in the neighborhood and endless varieties of minor mischief—snowball fights, prank phone calls, dropping things off the roof—never malicious or destructive, just forbidden enough to be fun. The building rooftops were our hidden playgrounds. We could spend hours up there with our friends almost entirely beyond adult supervision.

We were Irish and Catholic and proud to be both. My mother's family name was O'Brien, a close runner-up to Kelly in the who's-more-Irish sweepstakes. Or was it the other way around? Regardless, all four of my grandparents were born in Ireland, in the counties of Roscommon and Longford. All came to New York in the decade before the Civil War. Ellis Island wasn't open yet. They landed in a mostly Protestant city that was openly hostile to the Catholic Irish, who were thought to be intellectually suited for only the most menial jobs—and untrustworthy at those. Both my parents were born in New York, my father on September 21, 1896, and my mother on February 13, 1899. Though only one generation removed from the old country, my parents hardly talked about Ireland at all. They weren't "professional Irish," as my father liked to call those immigrants who behaved like they'd never left the Emerald Isle. My parents didn't listen to Irish music or read Irish literature. They never once traveled to Ireland. I don't remember my father ever ordering a Guinness—or, come to think of it, alcohol of any kind. I'm not saying he never did, but he never did around me. The Kellys were Americans, and that was that. Years later, long after I became police commissioner, I was asked to be grand marshal of the New York City St. Patrick's Day Parade. I proudly accepted. It was a great honor and a lot of fun. But I didn't grow up in what could truly be considered "an Irish home."

In a similar way, I wouldn't call my family's Catholicism especially devout. I'd describe the Kellys as punch-your-ticket Catholics. We did what was expected of us in the religious department. My parents went to Sunday Mass together, accompanied by the children in the younger years. But my older brothers—soon to be joined by me and my friends—often showed up just in time, stood in the back of the crowded church, and slipped out right after Communion.

*   *   *

Both my parents loved us tremendously. I never doubted that. But those were different times. Parents were more hands-off back then. My parents were older by the time I came along. They'd been through all this before. Their approach, my father's especially, was essentially, "Let us know if you need anything." Sports was the one thing he and I bonded over at all.

My father bought our first television set just in time for the 1951 World Series, the New York Giants versus the New York Yankees, the first World Series broadcast live on NBC coast-to-coast. My father was home after a hernia operation, and we watched most of the games together. He was a huge Giants fan, and so was I. This was Willie Mays's rookie season in the majors, but he was already my favorite player. We thought of the Giants, who played up at the Polo Grounds on Eighth Avenue at West 159th Street, as Manhattan's team. They'd won the National League pennant in a thrilling three-game playoff against the hated Brooklyn Dodgers with Bobby Thomson's legendary "shot heard 'round the world." We were heartbroken when the overpowering Yanks with Mickey Mantle, Joe DiMaggio, Phil Rizzuto, and Yogi Berra won the World Series four games to two.

My father was very much a man of his era. He was a small guy but physically strong. He was especially proud of his grip, which he got from being a milkman. I looked up to him tremendously. I thought he was the smartest person in the world. He did everything he possibly could to provide for us, but emotionally, he could be a bit distant. He'd bring home the *New York World-Telegram.* We'd read the batting averages and the box scores. But I don't think my father ever said, "You want to go out to the park and throw a ball around?" We never went to a Giants game together, even though the ballpark was a quick subway ride from our apartment.

My mom was a totally different story. She was brimming with personality. She was tough—in a good sense—and naturally fun. She was warm and gregarious and could talk with absolutely anybody. She and my sister, Mary, were the ones who played the living room piano. She just had this cheerful confidence about her that seemed to say, "I know what's right, I'll do what I have to do, and everything will turn out fine." She encouraged all of us to be ourselves.

Once I was safely in school, she got a job at Macy's, working 11:00 a.m. to 4:00 p.m. as a dressing room checker, counting the garments people brought in and out. She always looked terrific, probably ten years younger than her age. She took pride in her appearance and dressed impeccably. I'm sure the Macy's discount helped.

With my mother and father working and my older brothers and sister off doing their own things, my mother enlisted our neighbor Mrs. Waters to keep an eye on me after school. Every afternoon I'd go down to her apartment. She was a large person, in every sense of the word. She had a cat named Sligo and a thick

Irish brogue, and her own kids were constantly getting into trouble. It wasn't unusual for Mrs. Waters to grab my hand as we went rushing off to rescue one of her children from some fresh pile of trouble. She had opinions about everything and nicknames for almost everyone. "Here comes Piano Legs," she'd say about a lady clomping up the sidewalks. Or "Oh, look," she'd remark, "another baby carriage in front of the bar."

When I outgrew the need for Mrs. Waters's supervision, I went out on my own. I met my friends for pickup games out on the street and slowly began to toughen up. Sports played a major role in this. Like my dad, I was a small guy, but I was always a strong athlete. And I was pretty fearless. I got into skirmishes on the street, sometimes with boys older than I. It was mostly silly stuff—disputes over ball games, kids at school calling each other names. I found I could usually hold my own, a confidence that would serve me well later in life. But sometimes my friends and I were just idiots. We liked to climb on the backs of city buses, grabbing free rides and hanging on for dear life. Some other kids were even bigger idiots, riding on top of subway cars. Subway surfing, which I never did, was truly life threatening. A boy I knew got killed that way. Another kid fell off a roof and died. Today, deaths like these would garner breathless media coverage, complete with I-team reports, legislative hearings, and lawsuits. Back then, people were just sad. A certain amount of tragedy was taken in stride as part of big-city life.

*   *   *

As I grew older, the streets around me began to change.

I got my earliest taste of that change one Saturday afternoon as I walked in Central Park with one of my third-grade classmates. Suddenly we were surrounded by four or five older boys.

"*Mira, mira,*" I heard one of them say.

I had no idea what "*mira*" meant. But the boy was holding a baseball bat in a distinctly threatening manner, and I understood immediately what was happening to us. We were being robbed. Damned if I can remember my friend's name, but we were two white kids in the park. The other boys were Puerto Rican. Our patch of the city was still teeming with thousands of white ethnic families like the Kellys—Irish, Jews, Italians, assorted eastern and northern Europeans, all living on top of each other. But the neighborhood was just getting its first wave of Puerto Ricans. Even an eight-year-old could sense fresh tension on the sidewalks and in the parks.

No one flashed a knife or a gun that day. The baseball bat was more than enough to grab my attention. One of the older boys reached his hands around my neck and started squeezing.

I could feel other hands reaching into my pockets. I had no money. No one had cell phones or other electronic devices back then. As I gasped for oxygen and my eyes began to bulge, I stole a glance at my friend, who looked just as terrified as I was. The boys were rifling through his pockets too.

The next thing I heard was someone saying "*zapatos.*" A couple of boys shoved us down on the path, while others yanked at our shoes. Barely pausing to untie the laces, they pulled the shoes right from our feet, then ran off into the park.

Neither of us was hurt in the robbery, except for our sense of security and our city-kid pride. But it was a genuinely rattling experience, one that stuck with me and made me empathetic to crime victims for the rest of my life: New York's future police commissioner and his third-grade classmate walking forlornly home across West Ninety-First Street with nothing but dirty white socks on their feet.

*   *   *

The new families were moving to New York for the same old reasons our parents and grandparents had—for opportunity, for jobs, for the great American dream that the next generations might do better than the current one. These rolling waves of newcomers are part of what gives the city its energy, its diversity, its life. But such transitions rarely go entirely smoothly.

I got to know a few of the new kids playing ball in the neighborhood, especially a boy named Porfirio. One day, I didn't come home in time for dinner. My mother decided I was missing and launched a frantic search. She finally found me in Porfirio's apartment, eating Cheerios for dinner. We were having so much fun, I'd lost all track of the time. But as more Puerto Rican families moved in, it didn't take long for attitudes on both sides to harden. My older brothers' friends were trading hostile stares with Puerto Ricans. Fights were breaking out constantly. Inevitably, the younger kids like me were drawn in. There was no real way of avoiding it. I wasn't looking for trouble, but all of a sudden, I was getting into fights on West Ninetieth Street. The new people spoke a different language and listened to different music. They sat outside their buildings for hours, while we came and went. They didn't fold quietly into the life of the Upper West Side. They were trying to find a foothold in a newly adopted city. But the way we looked at it was that we had to defend the neighborhood. That was our job.

Our building superintendent was stabbed to death in front of our building—an unsolved murder. One day a kid put a knife to my neck. That fight, like most of them, was quickly broken up by adults nearby, but the knife was scary. There weren't many guns on the street, but stickball bats were everywhere, as was the gravity knife, which had a blade hidden in the handle. A few people had homemade zip guns. Those shot bullets, though not with much velocity. I looked out our front window one evening and saw my brother Donald walking up Columbus Avenue with at least a dozen of his friends and something in his hand. I couldn't make out what it was, but I'm pretty sure it wasn't a bouquet of flowers.

Walking directly toward them were a dozen Puerto Ricans. It was a Sharks-and-Jets scenario straight out of *West Side Story*—minus the singing, dancing, and Maria—years before the show ever reached Broadway or became a movie hit. Right then, a police radio car turned the corner, and a real-life Officer Krupke dispersed everyone. Just the sight of a police car had that power back then. I can still hear my mother's voice calling for my brother to come upstairs. He kept walking, pretending he was deaf.

It was fascinating how the grown-ups reacted to all this. They weren't sure if we should run or fight. I had a disagreement with a Puerto Rican boy one day, and Mrs. Dougherty, one of our neighbors, set up a makeshift boxing ring so José and Ray-Ray could duke it out. I guess you'd say she was the early-1950s New York version of the modern soccer mom. This was what passed for parental involvement back then. She even gathered a crowd to cheer us on. As I recall, I was creaming José before other neighbors stepped in and pulled us apart.

*   *   *

Some people blamed all the neighborhood's problems on the arriving Puerto Ricans. That wouldn't be fair. Among the old-timers, the Irish, especially, had their own rough crews. I'm not sure who would have won an all-out rumble, but our side was fortified with street-brawling dockworkers and some genuine hoodlums too. The Irish gang known as the Westies was farther downtown. But we had our local Irish gangsters, and they could find plenty of trouble on their own, often in a bar called McGlade's, directly across from us on Columbus Avenue. You could see the sign from our living room window. McGlade's was famous for being the place where Edward "Poochy" Walsh tended bar and was also killed.

Poochy was a midlevel local gangster. Once, a police officer named Mario Biaggi fired three shots at Poochy, narrowly missing him. Poochy, who was driving a stolen car that day, ducked just in time and got lucky. (Biaggi, a legendary cop, later went to Washington as a congressman from the Bronx.) But one night, when Poochy was pouring at McGlade's, Elmer Burke came in.

Elmer hated being called Elmer. He much preferred his nickname, Trigger, which came from his wartime service as a U.S. Army Ranger in Italy and was even more befitting his postwar career as an extortionist, armed robber, and hit man. There wasn't much he wouldn't try—or at least claim he'd tried. "I don't hold up the police station only because they get paid by check," he supposedly once said.

How did we know all this? That's hard to say. But it was common knowledge in the neighborhood, and no one doubted a word of it.

On July 23, 1952, Trigger got into a fistfight with a local hoodlum called Squeeky, who ended up in a puddle of pain on the floor in McGlade's. When Trigger kept beating him while he was down, Poochy raised his voice in mild protest. Trigger finally stopped and left the bar. But once outside, he thought about the uncalled-for interference, turned around, and strolled casually back in. He shot Poochy in the face and left him on the floor, where he bled to death. Then, just as casually, Trigger walked back out to Columbus Avenue. Among those who took Poochy's death especially hard was his sister, who was dating Trigger at the time.

This was the crime that finally put an end to Trigger Burke's one-man crime spree. He was convicted of killing Poochy and sent to Sing Sing prison, where he was ultimately executed for the crime in 1958.

*　　*　　*

I was doing well in school. Very well, actually. For two years, I was named Smartest Boy in Class. Today, that honor wouldn't be politically correct for at least two reasons: first, it might make the other kids feel less intelligent, and second, one of the girls would almost certainly be smarter than any of the boys. But I got two little statues for winning. Around that time, my father's career also took an upward turn. His oldest brother, my uncle Walter, had connections with the Tammany Hall Democratic machine. Walter was the politically wired member of the family. He seemed to know everybody. Some people even said Walter Kelly could be New York's mayor one day. But he was also a big drinker, so I'm not sure how far that would have gone. Still, my uncle used his political connections to take care of my dad. In 1952, he got my father a federal job as a cashier at the Internal Revenue Service. This was totally different from anything my father had ever done before. I was playing on West Ninety-First Street one afternoon with my friends when I looked up to see my father walking home from the subway in a suit and tie with a newspaper folded under his arm. I could hardly believe my eyes. My blue-collar father looked like a businessman. I couldn't remember ever seeing him dressed that way, except maybe for Christmas Mass.

Finally, in the summer between seventh and eighth grades, my father moved us to the suburbs. Well, not quite the suburbs. The 1950s Upper West Side version of the suburbs: Queens. My father didn't want to move, but, as he put it, "With everything that's going on around here, it's time." We said good riddance to Mr. Averett and found a new apartment in Long Island City.

My father was concerned about me and my mother. The older children were mostly gone by then—or half in and half out. My sister, Mary, had just gotten married. My oldest brother, Leonard, was about to. My youngest brother, Donald, had just joined the Marine Corps, following the two oldest. I'm sure my father could see me making some poor decisions and running with a rougher crowd. I think he wanted to get me out of that environment before something more serious occurred. He was worried about the path I was going down.

So we moved.

When I showed up for eighth grade at St. Teresa's in Woodside, Queens, I felt the discomfort familiar to anyone who's ever been the new kid in class. I didn't know anybody. But as I had eight years earlier, I adjusted fairly quickly. In many ways, western Queens was like the Upper West Side a decade earlier. It was mostly white but ethnically mixed—Irish, Italian, Jewish, French, and others. I quickly met another kid named Kelly, though his family was Jewish and their name had originally been Klein. We weren't in Manhattan anymore, and that took some getting used to. But Queens did have one other benefit: it was that much closer to Island Park.

A few years earlier, my father had bought a small bungalow near the beach on Long Island's South Shore. We were a long way from the ritzy Hamptons, in miles and in lifestyle. Island Park was a summer community of unheated bungalows. The Kelly cottage on Kildare Road had three tiny bedrooms, open beams, no drop ceiling. I believe my father paid about a thousand dollars for the place. We went every summer. Everyone relaxed. People whiled away full days in their bathing suits without stepping into a pair of shoes. I spent all day at Casino Beach, which was small but nice and packed with growing families and preening teenagers. There were kids everywhere. At night, there were movies projected against a concrete wall at the handball courts. I met new friends in Island Park, two guys in particular—Tommy Reichel and Gerry Schraeder. We did everything together.

My father loved that house, the only real estate he ever owned. He and my two oldest brothers, Leonard and Kenneth, worked on the house constantly. They were all very handy. They did plumbing and electrical work and added extra rooms. The place wasn't constructed as a year-rounder, but my dad and brothers kept it in excellent shape.

I built my first career in Island Park, if you can call it that, climbing my way up the village's teenage-employment ladder.

When I was fifteen, I got a job parking beachgoers' cars. People left their cars with us despite the fact that most of us were underage and unlicensed. We drove around the parking lot and, occasionally, outside it. After a summer of car parking, my friend Tommy Reichel and I passed the lifeguard test. Lifeguard was a big step up from parking attendant. Among the lifeguards were two new friends, Sammy Latini and Frank Ruddy, who provided endless laughter and fun times. Lifeguarding, I guess you could say, was my first experience in law enforcement, stopping kids from diving off the pier into shallow water and rescuing people from drowning. That happened far more often than you might imagine. The water looked calm but was deceptively dangerous. Those rescues produced an adrenaline rush and a glow of lingering satisfaction, feelings I'd be chasing for many years to come.

Island Park boasted plenty of good-looking girls, but one stood out from the rest. Veronica Clarke was her name. She was smart and tough, funny and beautiful. What I liked most about her, aside from her blonde hair and good looks, was her independent streak. She had a confidence far beyond her years. She came from a family a lot like mine—Irish American but not "professional Irish." She was one of five children, like I was, though she fell in the middle. Her mother's maiden name was Kelly. Her family was even more beach oriented than mine was. She had a brother and sister who were Casino Beach lifeguards. Veronica was the strongest distance swimmer—male or female—I'd ever seen.

When the Clarkes weren't at the beach, they lived in Flatbush, Brooklyn. Her father was a New York police officer who chauffeured a high-ranking police executive. That was a big deal to everyone. But like me, Veronica envisioned a larger future for herself. In each other, I believe, we both saw something we admired in ourselves. We dated. Then we dated some more. I knew right away she was someone special.

CHAPTER TWO

Battlefields

B etween summers in Island Park, I was back in Queens. For the first two years of high school I attended the old St. Ann's Academy at Lexington Avenue and East Seventy-Seventh Street, commuting by subway every morning to Manhattan's Upper East Side. The school, with a long, proud history dating back to 1892, was run by the Marist Brothers. But by the time I got there, the building was kind of dumpy and the brothers were already in discussion with the Roman Catholic Diocese of Brooklyn to pack up and move to Briarwood, Queens. In the summer of 1957, between my sophomore and junior years, that's exactly what happened, and the name was changed to Archbishop Molloy High School.

The athletic teams kept their old nickname, the Stanners, and the school offered a busy schedule of extracurriculars. But except for playing intramural football and drawing some illustrations for the school newspaper, I wasn't involved in many out-of-class activities. I had to work to pay my tuition and help with household expenses. I had a job as a messenger at *Maclean's* magazine. Then, senior year, my mom got me hired as a part-time Macy's stock boy. One of the best things about that job was that I got to work the Thanksgiving Day Parade. I was part of the team that held the turkey balloon. Back in those days, it wasn't as easy as it sounds. You hold on to a cord and fight the wind while the inflated turkey bangs against the light posts down Broadway. By the end of the parade, I was totally exhausted, but it was great fun.

The summer I graduated from high school, I skipped the beach entirely. It wasn't my choice. I had to take a job as an elevator operator at the *Herald Tribune* newspaper building at 230 West Forty-First Street. My oldest brother, Leonard, had gotten married, and his new father-in-law managed the building. My family didn't want to insult the bride's father when he offered me the job. It paid better than Macy's and way better than lifeguarding in Island Park. But hour after hour, as I stood in my brown polyester uniform, all I could think of was my friends and family enjoying another sparkling day at the beach. I couldn't wait to start college, which meant Catholic college, of course. I chose Manhattan College in the Bronx because that's where my brother Leonard went after he'd gotten out of the Marine Corps as an enlisted man and before he went back in as an officer. He'd majored in business, so I majored in business. That included accounting, statistics, and all the basic tools you would need getting started in the business world. I filled out my program with classes in history, Spanish, psychology, and, of course, theology. I didn't have a scholarship, so I took out a loan and went back to Macy's.

Manhattan College boasted top-notch professors, a crowded calendar of student activities, and a beautiful, hilly campus in Riverdale. To graduate I needed 144 credits, 18 per semester. I was always squeezed for time. Joining a fraternity, playing sports, working on the school newspaper—there was no way I could do any of that. I went to class, went to work, and went back home to Queens at night. I received a great education, but because of my situation, I never got the full college experience. Amazingly, in 2014, Manhattan College named the new student commons building in my honor, thanks to the generosity of my classmate Thomas O'Malley and his wife, Mary Alice. Executive chairman of PBF Energy Company, Tom is a titan of the oil-refining industry and a former chairman of the Manhattan College Board of Trustees. Today, the Raymond W. Kelly '63 Student Commons is the hub of campus life. Governor Andrew Cuomo attended the ribbon cutting on October 15, 2014, and gave a memorable speech. "His life is a testament to the virtue of service taught by the Christian brothers and a commitment to excellence," the governor generously said about me. "Manhattan College could not have chosen a better name than Raymond Kelly." It was extremely kind of the O'Malleys and all the others who contributed to the effort. I will always be grateful.

The one activity I did sign up for when I was on campus was Air Force ROTC. It was that or take some course on hygiene. I wore a blue uniform to class one day a week. But I never intended to join the air force. I always knew I'd follow my three older brothers into the Marine Corps. Leonard, Kenneth, and Donald used to tell me stories about their Marine Corps experiences and the tough-as-nails drill instructors who were yelling all the time. They let me read the *Guidebook for Marines*. It really spoke to me. Lying in bed at night, I could easily imagine myself as a Marine Corps officer, leading men into battle, finding adventures on far-off shores. There was a chapter in that book called "Marine Corps Leadership Traits." There were fourteen traits: Justice. Judgment. Dependability. Initiative. Decisiveness. Tact. Integrity. Enthusiasm. Bearing. Unselfishness. Courage. Knowledge. Loyalty. And endurance. I could give a class on those leadership traits today.

*   *   *

Adam Walinsky was a big-ideas guy with a special interest in the criminal-justice system. A young New York lawyer and Marine Corps reservist who worked as an aide to Robert F. Kennedy, he'd grown convinced that America's police departments needed to be dragged into the modern age. A big part of the problem, he decided, was that the undereducated civil servants were too suspicious of new ideas. Early on, it was Irish immigrants who gravitated toward police work because they could already speak English. The ethnic makeup had broadened over the years, but the closed-minded attitudes hadn't. Or so Walinsky believed. He wanted to convince bright young college students to consider police work as a professional career. From the work of Walinsky and others grew something called the Police Cadet Corps, a program like ROTC for policing.

The concept drew skepticism from police unions, which imagined a bunch of clueless know-it-alls getting in the way at the station house and, even worse, working for subunion wages. But Police Commissioner Stephen Kennedy embraced an early version of the program that gave local college students an inside view of police work and some hands-on experience. In my junior year at Manhattan College, I saw an ad for the program in the *Quadrangle*, the student newspaper, and joined the inaugural class. I had no particular interest in modernizing American policing. I was just happy to be out of the children's department at Macy's— size 6, size 6X, and all that. There was also some talk of student loan repayment, which sounded all right to me.

The group consisted of 107 students from public and private colleges around New York. We were summoned to Hubert Street on the Lower West Side and the dilapidated police academy, which was probably the worst possible venue for convincing college students to look at policing as a promising, modern profession. The building looked like it might fall down by lunchtime. We weren't cops, the instructors explained to us. We wouldn't be carrying firearms. We wouldn't even wear uniforms, just button-down shirts and neckties. But for $1.60 an hour, we would move around to different parts of the department, learning how things operated on the inside. Our two-week orientation included a mind-numbing attempt to familiarize us with the NYPD's seemingly endless supply of preprinted, numerically identified, sometimes triplicate forms. No one could possibly learn them all, but we got a fine sample. A UF-61—Uniform Force 61—was a complaint form. A UF-6 was an aided card. A UF-49 was a piece of paper with a letterhead on top. A UF-49A was half a piece of paper with a letterhead. A UF-50 was a plain piece of paper. A UF-50A was half of that. They had forms for everything, including forms for ordering new forms.

That mind-numbing experience prepared me well for my first stop, the lost-property division, hidden away in a decrepit building at 400 Broome Street. The place was every bit as stuck in the past as Adam Walinsky had warned. Many of the full-time officers had been injured or were on what people called "the rubber-gun squad," having gotten in trouble somehow and had their real weapons taken away. The duties involved filing reports from pawnbrokers, which could then be cross-checked against reports of items taken in burglaries. The concept behind the work was solid, and it might have actually functioned if the file cabinets hadn't been such a disaster zone. It may have counted as police work, but all that filing was painfully boring. No one wanted to be there. One day, a cop took a fat handful of missing-property reports and tossed them into a gaping hole in one of the dilapidated building's plaster walls. "Got those filed," he announced to no one in particular.

Fortunately, I soon moved over to the communications unit on the top floor of police headquarters, one of the most fascinating places I had ever stepped inside. The turn-of-the-century building at 240 Centre Street, just north of Chinatown, was imposing and grand, with a pediment and columns at the entrance and a giant dome on top. You just knew important things were happening there, even if you weren't sure what they were. In those days, the department didn't have a single citywide phone number. This was years before 440-1234, the first five-borough number, and the 911 system. Each borough command had its own emergency exchange. SPring 7-3100 was the number for Manhattan. CAnal 6-2000 was the administrative switchboard. The CAnal board must have had a thousand exchanges—lights blinking, wires going in and out, all kinds of connections being made. There was always a lieutenant yelling. You had to keep your cool. Each call could be a life-or-death situation—or some cop's question about procedures, or a cat up a tree. About 25 officers at a time were assigned to the fast-paced, high-pressure work. The pulse of the city ran through that room, and I loved being in the middle of it.

The cadets were there to augment the cops by manning the phones, patching people together, fielding incoming calls. If there was a real emergency, we were supposed to hand the call over to one of the experienced officers. But the place was wild, and I couldn't get enough. I felt an adrenaline rush just being there, in the constant whirl of activity. One guy kept running through the room in his underwear with a number on the back. What did that mean? No one seemed to know. But he ran around where the terminals were and everybody laughed. The atmosphere was frenzied but organized. There was no room for confusion. You couldn't be in there and not feel like you were part of something, right in the center of bustling New York.

A burglary report might come in on one line. Over at another desk, an officer would be dispatching patrol wagons. Then someone would run into the room with a report of a shooting. Every call was hand logged on a card and quickly slapped on a conveyor belt that went to the dispatcher in the radio room. The phone calls weren't recorded, which was definitely a good thing. Even in a city as huge as New York, with all its crimes and associated problems, we still made time for sophomoric fun. When the lines slowed down, some of the cadets, to entertain themselves, would call eight or ten random city phone numbers, connecting the calls together like a party line. We'd listen in silence while

unsuspecting people answered their phones at home and agitat-
edly talked back and forth. "I didn't call you. You called me." "No,
I didn't." "Yes, you did." There was no such thing as caller ID,
but amazingly some of the people recognized each other's voices
because they lived in the same general areas. Sometimes the puz-
zled people would stay on the line for fifteen minutes, trying to
figure out why they were there. It was just the kind of pressure
release all of us needed. We found it hilarious.

Then, as quickly as the juvenile pranks had started, we all
snapped back to the latest emergency on the line. Robberies, run-
aways, knife fights, and then someone called with a report that
their house had been egged.

"What kind of egg? Scrambled? Hard boiled?"

We were college students with a front-row seat to the complex
human drama of life in the city. How could we not like that?

In order to stay in the program, you had to take the tests for
police officer. There was a written test and a physical test, which
involved lifting some weights and scaling an eight-foot wall. I
went ahead and took those tests, not because of any clear commitment to a future in police work but because I couldn't imagine a
better part-time college job.

I passed.

*   *   *

In the summer of 1962, between my junior and senior years at
Manhattan College, I headed down to Marine Corps Base Quantico in Virginia for the Platoon Leaders Course, twelve weeks of
intense training for college students. Most people did it over two
summers, but I did both six-week sessions back-to-back. If you
made it through, which a lot of people didn't, you qualified for
commissioning as a Marine Corps officer. I'd heard plenty of talk
about the Marine Corps from my three older brothers, but it was
still a culture shock when I arrived in Quantico.

We spent the first six weeks living in steel Quonset huts at remote Camp Upshur. I thought I was in excellent shape, but the physical demands of the course were enormous. We'd get up early and go for long runs along the steep Hill Trail. We would return feeling just about ready to collapse, only to have the drill instructors send us right back out on the Hill Trail Extension, which was even more difficult.

The drill instructors were straight from central casting. Zero body fat. At five o'clock in the morning, their creases were perfect. They screamed and shouted endlessly, just as my brothers had promised they would. I don't believe the DIs had any traditional training as psychologists, but they had their own motivational methods. All of them definitely believed in the character-building power of constant harassment, and that included physical contact.

Some of the drill instructors at Quantico that summer had been at the Marine Corps Recruit Depot, Parris Island, on April 8, 1956, for the so-called Ribbon Creek incident. That terrible day, Staff Sergeant Matthew McKeon, pushing with typical DI toughness, marched seventy-four men of Platoon 71 into the water. Six recruits drowned. Since then, the drill instructors had supposedly lightened up, but in my twelve weeks I didn't see much evidence of that. One sergeant didn't like the way one of my squad mates was saluting. He bit the kid's thumb so hard, he broke a bone.

One of my DIs had arms like pencils, yet he could bang out twenty chin-ups hardly taking a breath. The same sergeant would take us out for ten-mile hikes with all our gear on. He did all kinds of things just to harass us. After he barked at you to get to the showers, if he got there first, you had to quickly put your dirty uniform back on and go back downstairs. Once, during a junk-on-the-bunk inspection, a bunk mate of mine was found with a "dirty" belt. The belt looked clean to me and everyone else—everyone but our DI. The sergeant grabbed the offending belt and wrapped it around the kid's neck until he passed out. I heard later that the sergeant was killed in Vietnam.

The name of the game in the Platoon Leaders Course was to scare the hell out of the college boys so they'd drop out and be bounced down to enlisted rank. I understood that even at the time and vowed they wouldn't do it to me.

Thanks to the advice I'd gotten from my brothers, I wasn't surprised by much that happened those three months, and I was already in good physical shape. I'd been running and lifting weights and had upper-body strength. I was a demon on the rope climbs. But they pushed us so hard, those twelve weeks of intense training had a debilitating effect on me. As the days went on, I didn't get stronger. I got weaker, a cumulative wearing-down. A lot of people DORed, dropped out on request. The number of people who finished was considerably smaller than the number that had started. But I told myself that no matter how tough it got, I was going to do this, and I did. I was even voted squad leader by the other members of my squad. I knew I'd finish and that I'd be getting my commission as a second lieutenant in the U.S. Marines Corps.

*   *   *

By the age of twenty, I had been inside two of America's most vaunted institutions, the New York City Police Department and the U.S. Marine Corps. So while most of my fellow Manhattan College business majors were casting their eyes on Wall Street or banking or the large accounting firms, I was mapping out something a little more daring.

I wore marine dress whites for my college graduation on June 11, 1963, which was the second-most important event that day. The first was getting engaged to Veronica. She was eighteen. I was twenty-one.

Our families didn't necessarily approve of our getting married. They were sure we were both too young. We were just as sure we knew what we were doing. Veronica and I had been going out for three years already, an eternity for people our age. I think she liked my drive and my enthusiasm for trying new things. I was sure she was the one for me. We weren't the first in our group to make this choice; people around us were getting married. My lifeguard friend Sammy Latini had. I was in his wedding. My brothers Leonard and Donald and my sister, Mary, were all married by then. Veronica was a popular girl. I certainly didn't want to let her slip away while I was off in the Marine Corps. I wasn't 100 percent sure she'd wait around. So I asked her and she said yes, and we set a wedding date, December 14, 1963.

I didn't have much time to relax after graduation. Veronica started planning our wedding, and I was due to report at the Marine Corps' Basic School in early July. But that wasn't all. I'd also gotten word that the police department was expecting me— on June 26. Obviously I couldn't be a brand-new New York City police officer *and* an active-duty Marine, not at the same time. So I decided I would get sworn in to the police department in June and begin my classes at the police academy, then five days later I'd take a three-year military leave. It certainly wasn't the typical way to begin a police career. I wasn't sure how the department would react. But would they really squawk too loudly at a recruit's military obligation? I hoped not.

June 26 was a steamy early-summer morning. The city was just coming out of a long cold snap, sixteen consecutive days of unseasonably cool temperatures. The ceremony hardly seemed real to me as I sat with my police academy classmates in front of city hall. I didn't have any relatives or friends in the audience, not even Veronica. I knew I'd be leaving for the Marine Corps in five days. And frankly, I wasn't entirely certain I'd be returning to the police department. Three years is a long time in the mind of a twenty-one-year-old. A lot could happen.

We all stood at our folding chairs on the plaza in front of

city hall. We raised our right hands and declared in unison, "I do hereby pledge and declare to uphold the Constitution of the United States and the Constitution of the State of New York and faithfully discharge my duties as a New York City police officer to the best of my ability, so help me God."

And I was officially a member of the New York City Police Department. There was a round of applause and a couple of speeches, and that was pretty much it. Our first official act was to march together as a class to the police academy on Hubert Street. My supervisors didn't seem thrilled when I explained that I'd be leaving almost immediately for the Marine Corps. But they didn't try to fight it or say anything that would make me feel bad. I was given some clerical duties to keep me busy for the next few days and told not to bother with classes. I could join a new class of police recruits upon my return. They promised to hold my place for me and gave me thirty days of paid military leave for my first year on the job. What more could I ask? Things were moving quickly. In less than a month, I'd gone from college graduation to getting engaged to joining the NYPD to putting the NYPD on hold. A few short days later, I would kiss Veronica good-bye and head back to Quantico, Virginia, for Marine Corps Basic School.

*   *   *

I was one of two hundred freshly minted second lieutenants who'd earned a place in this finishing school for Marine Corps officers. The instructors drilled us on discipline, leadership, Corps tradition, and how to behave like officers. They taught us the tactics of infantry warfare—what kinds of weapons and ammunition to use and which formations and principles to apply. The platoon commanders were all captains or majors. To us, the captains were like Jesus Christ. They had unquestioned authority, and they could do no wrong. We all took turns leading the squad and the platoon.

Some of the leadership concepts seemed obvious once you heard them, but the superior officers assured us that if we followed them, we would all be strong leaders. No lightning bolt comes down and makes you a leader, they told us. You behave like a leader and so you become one. I remain a huge believer in the Marine Corps way. I have said this many times, and it's no exaggeration: virtually everything I know about being a leader, I learned in the Marine Corps. How to deliver clear messages. How to set standards and stick to them. How to treat other people and how to treat yourself. Those are lessons every leader needs to learn and to live by. Like how the officer always eats last. That may sound small, but it isn't. Even today, I still can't go through a buffet line until everyone else has been fed.

The Marine Corps has a tradition for almost everything. Beyond our daily khakis and greens, our $300 uniform allowance had to cover two dress uniforms—blues and whites. You also needed a Mameluke sword to drill with, a jewelry box with studs and cuff links, and dress black shoes, impeccably shined at all times. Whatever the occasion called for, we were proud to put that uniform on.

I slipped back to New York a couple of times during Basic School to see Veronica. We attended an express-lane version of the pre-Cana classes her priest wanted us to take. But I had almost nothing to do with planning my own wedding. Veronica and her family took care of everything. My job was to get to the church on time. I bought a new two-door Volkswagen Beetle, the first car I ever owned, and drove the 270 miles from Virginia to New York on the Friday of our wedding weekend. The very next day we had a large ceremony with lots of family and friends at St. Therese of Lisieux on Avenue D and Troy Avenue in Flatbush, Veronica's family's parish. I wore my marine dress blues. My brother Donald was my best man. We had a reception in the officers' club at the Brooklyn Navy Yard. The next day, Sunday, Lt. and Mrs. Raymond

Kelly got into our new Volkswagen for the trip back to Quantico, though we didn't get far. After we pulled into the Holland Tunnel, we were slammed from behind by a Cadillac with four men inside. As I veered into the next lane, the car followed us there and hit us a couple more times, slamming us into the car in front of us, just about destroying the VW. I couldn't believe what had just happened—or that neither one of us was badly hurt. I did have to restrain myself from jumping out and pounding on the men. But that didn't seem like such a good idea. I was technically a New York City police officer on military leave.

In those days, there were Port Authority police officers in the tunnel. An officer arrived in less than a minute. It was obvious that all four of the men were drunk. The driver was arrested for drunk driving. Veronica and I spent our second night as husband and wife at Manhattan night court as criminal complainants. It was not exactly the beginning we imagined for married life, but it might have been a sign that we shouldn't expect to be bored in the years to come.

*   *   *

The Marine Corps was a life-altering experience for me. Up until I joined, I had been a student, worked menial jobs, or been some kind of trainee. Suddenly, at twenty-one, I was a leader of men. I was gaining command experience. I was going to the officers' club with fellow marines who had rank and experience far beyond mine. People were saluting me.

I attended advanced artillery training at Fort Sill in Oklahoma and then was assigned to H-Battery, Third Battalion, Eleventh Marines at Camp Pendleton, California. At that time, Vietnam was becoming a topic of debate on college campuses. Inside the Marine Corps, however, especially among the officers, getting sent to the Southeast Asian nation was still seen as a perfectly fine posting; Vietnam seemed to be an exotic place where you could go and be an adviser, play at some guerrilla warfare, obtain command experience, learn about a different culture, and get your ticket punched. I don't remember hearing about anyone who had died there. The media wasn't even calling it a war. It was the "conflict" in Vietnam. But by 1965, the South Vietnamese guerrillas were proving themselves as fierce, dogged fighters, and President Lyndon Johnson responded by ordering more and more U.S. troops in. I was right in the middle of that. That July, I was ordered to deploy out of San Diego on the USS *Gunston Hall*, part of a Special Landing Force of the Second Battalion, First Marines, bound for the Republic of Vietnam.

We had just learned that Veronica was pregnant with our first child. Obviously that was a concern for both of us. She had a job in a savings bank in Oceanside, California, and the repaired Volkswagen Beetle. She wasn't one to complain. But at twenty-one, she was still very young, living on her own for the first time. And now her husband was going off to what everyone had started calling the Vietnam War.

"See you in a year," I promised Veronica as we said good-bye at the dock. We held a long hug, both of us fighting back tears.

We had a long ride across the Pacific Ocean and into the South China Sea. The Gunston Hall, a World War II–era Ashland-class dock-landing ship named in honor of the estate of founding father George Mason, wasn't much on creature comforts. I mainly remember that the ship wasn't air-conditioned and the cool Pacific breezes weren't nearly what they were cracked up to be.

As an artillery forward observer and fire-support coordinator assigned to a Special Landing Force, I led my team on amphibious-assault landings along the coast of Vietnam. We loaded into *amphtracks*, large tanklike vehicles launched from the back of the ship. Those things were as claustrophobic as metal coffins, twenty-five marines packed in together with rifles, helmets, and not much else. We couldn't see where we were going.

Water poured in the entire time we were moving. Breathing wasn't easy. People hardly spoke. Everyone was wet. It was hard not to wonder, *How do these things even stay afloat?* Then, all of a sudden, we'd feel a sharp thump as the amphtrack pulled up on the beach. Once ashore, we'd take modest sniper fire.

I had two main duties. As a forward observer, I led a team of marines whose job was to scope out potential targets and radio that information back to the marines manning the towed 105 mm and 155 mm howitzers. As a fire-support coordinator, I advised the commander on the appropriate choice of supporting arms. This was all before computer guidance. We were still using slide rules and fire-control tables printed in manuals. After Quantico and my additional training, leading others felt somewhat natural to me, and my urban upbringing helped define my leadership style. I took the direct *I'm from New York* approach. The men I led hailed from all different backgrounds. Catholics from the northeast and Baptists from the southeast. There were a fair number of African Americans. One thing these young marines all seemed to have in common was an excellent, sometimes subversive sense of humor, which is always helpful in a stressful situation.

I also discovered they liked a certain amount of order and regimentation, even when they grumbled about it. They needed it, actually. We were asking them to operate cohesively in a hostile and dangerous environment. Just winging it was a recipe for disaster. There had to be a system in place—rules, chain of command, a commitment to follow directives—that everyone recognized. They all understood that. It was precisely the culture of the Marine Corps.

Now, if only someone had told us what the mission was. This was an uncertain time in Vietnam. The information was all a little murky. No one knew exactly what we were doing there. America had made a commitment and that commitment was growing, but it hadn't yet fully formed. So we approached each day with a list of assignments but never with a full understanding of the endgame.

I spent most of my tour in the valleys near Hue and Phu Bai, a mostly rural area dotted with small villages in the northern part of South Vietnam. We shared the jungle with leeches, rats, and fat, round mosquitoes. There were constant chirping sounds interrupted by frequent bursts of artillery fire. The nights were darker than anything I'd ever seen back home, except when the sky was lit by flares or tracer bullets. The famous marine battle for Hue City hadn't happened yet, but that's near where we were. I'd never heard any of those names before. Now I lived and breathed them.

In December 1965, we were pulled into Operation Harvest Moon, one of the first major campaigns of the war. We were in the rice-filled Phuoc Ha Valley, south of Da Nang, a longstanding stronghold for the Vietcong. Fresh intelligence said the enemy was amassing to attack a government outpost in Que Son. A company of marines had gotten hemmed in at the end of that valley. Their commander had been killed. We had been helicoptered into the middle of the operation. Because of our haste reaching the area, we were not especially well supplied. We ran out of C rations and, at one point, dug casabas out of the dirt to eat. Back in camp, we slept in strong-back tents, but in the field, it was only poncho liners on the dirt. The vegetation was so dense there, tunnels had been cut through it. We could tell the enemy was present and active from the sniper fire and the punji sticks. Fifty-caliber rounds kept flying overhead, ripping branches off the trees. You could feel their breeze. We took cover in rice paddies and returned fire.

We stuck together, marching in narrow columns, constantly picking our way through the thick foliage. The local culture was almost impenetrable to us. On the edge of a firefight, a Vietnamese family came walking by in a funeral procession, carrying a tiny casket. They seemed not to hear the war going on around them, though clearly it had shattered their lives. We took more sniper fire as we went, suffering several casualties of our own. We had no idea where those shots were coming from or where to shoot back. One night, the enemy tried to penetrate our lines. In a hasty response to that, a marine was shot and killed by friendly fire from another unit.

There is something that comes over a group of marines in an environment like that. I saw it vividly on that march. No one was complaining about the difficult conditions, even as some suffered from immersion foot and had to be evacuated. No one was asking questions about the mission, even though its larger purpose was notably vague. Everyone was laser focused on moving ahead. It was an impressive thing to behold.

The fight was even more challenging in the adjacent valley, where my friend First Lieutenant Harvey "Barney" Barnum Jr. was leading the cut-off marines. The commanding officer had died in his arms. His 110 men were surrounded and outnumbered by the enemy, perhaps twelve to one. It fell to Barney to salvage what he could.

Knowing it would be impossible to hold on through the night, Barney ordered his remaining marines to burst out in four-man fire teams. Taking the Vietcong fighters by surprise, the marines managed to cross several hundred yards of fire-swept terrain and break through Vietcong lines. They rejoined their battalion before nightfall. Barney earned the Medal of Honor for his heroism that day. Operation Harvest Moon was written up in the history books as an early American success in the Vietnam War, thanks in part to Barnum's heroism.

While the big picture remained murky in Vietnam, the realities of life and death were vividly clear. No one could lead marines in those years and not feel that. As Operation Harvest Moon came to a close, I stood beside a marine colonel named Oscar Peatross and a large pile of body bags, a dead marine in every one. The colonel was smoking, which almost everybody did. Calm, cool, and collected, just puffing away with an attitude I knew he'd earned the hard way. *I'm a pro*, it seemed to say. *This is my business. This is what I do. Could that be me?*

There were fresh reminders every day of the stakes in Vietnam.

The marines I led were focused and dedicated. I witnessed them being amazingly kind to the locals and to each other. They fought under dire conditions. Sometimes we had no food. Sometimes we had to drink rainwater. It's hard to imagine, but because of ground fire, helicopters couldn't get in to resupply us. If you'd asked these young marines why they fought so valiantly, they wouldn't speak about patriotism or American values or apple pie. They probably wouldn't even mention the goals of the mission they were on. They'd tell you they were fighting for each other, doing all they could to make sure everyone came home alive.

That was life early in the Vietnam War. So was this: I got a message from battalion headquarters one day that there were two envelopes waiting for me in my unit. That usually meant bad news from home. One letter would tell you what had happened. The other letter authorized your leave. I didn't know what to expect, but I walked very slowly back to the battalion. I was expecting the worst. I wanted to steel myself for whatever the tragedy was.

It turned out the second envelope was for someone else. I opened the one addressed to me, and it announced the birth of our son James at Brookdale Hospital in Brooklyn. What an amazing relief that was. Veronica had moved back to New York to be closer to family. Mother and baby were fine. I knew I still had another five months of my deployment. But I did notice that time ticked more slowly after that.

In late February, in a night helicopter operation, we joined Operation New York, a sweep across the Phu Thu Peninsula east of Phu Bai. As we pursued the Vietcong down a sandy peninsula, the tree line suddenly erupted with machine-gun and mortar fire. From fifty yards behind, we watched in awe as marine Second Lieutenant Robert Fellers and his men refused to retreat. Instead, they went rushing toward the fire, doubling back and keeping their wits about them long enough to cut off any Vietcong retreat. Fellers didn't send his men in alone. Though wounded in the hip, he stayed right with them, crossing the fire-raked paddies toward the enemy.

It defied logic almost, young marines running in front of live fire like that, putting their own lives at such dire and obvious risk. In conjunction with an aerial observer in an OV-10 aircraft, I called in artillery fire. But a captain called it off when a 90-millimeter round from a recoilless rifle landed just a few feet from us. The captain thought it was a short round of ours. It wasn't. Our round never fired. It was from the Vietcong. Confusion was a constant part of the Vietnam experience. We were often running around in a state the brilliant Prussian military analyst Carl von Clausewitz and U.S. defense secretary Robert McNamara both warned about—"the fog of war."

I know it's strange to say this, but as June grew near and my days in-country grew short, I really didn't want to leave. The excitement, the adrenaline, the young marines I was leading, even with a mission as confusing as this one—it wasn't easy to walk away from. But I had a baby, now five months old. I couldn't wait to see him. And I knew if I stayed any longer, I might be tempting fate—risking my own survival and Veronica's continued understanding.

In late June, I flew to Marine Corps Air Station El Toro, near Irvine, California. I borrowed a car and got to Los Angeles International Airport just in time to meet Veronica, who flew in from New York with our new son.

She was wearing a blue knit suit. She looked amazing. The baby was all bundled up in a blanket.

"Here is your son, James," she said, handing the baby to me. I couldn't see much, just his little eyes poking out above the very top of the blanket.

I was speechless.

We went to Laguna Beach for the weekend. We took pictures of each other with the baby, sitting at the window of our motel with the beach in the distance.

I'd just spent months in combat with young marines whose lives were in my hands. I wasn't much older than they were. In service to their country and in service to each other, some of them had been killed. I hated to leave them. Like the colonel with the body bags, I hadn't allowed myself to think too deeply about it, though I understood somewhere inside me: any one of those men could have been me.

Now I had this new little baby and this amazing and supportive wife. We were going back to New York City with a whole new life ahead of us.

CHAPTER THREE

On the Job

Were scarecrows in blue uniforms.

After a grand total of five days of blackboard instruction and fifty rounds at the NYPD firing range, my new police academy classmates and I were standing out on the sidewalks of central Brooklyn pretending to be police officers. They gave us badges. They gave us handcuffs. They gave us guns—standard police-issue Smith & Wesson .38 Specials. They told us, "Good luck." In early July 1966, riots had broken out in East New York, Bedford-Stuyvesant, and Brownsville, Brooklyn. Hundreds of angry young men were roaming the streets and throwing bottles and rocks. Already they had injured police officers and attempted to flip over a radio car. On one corner, police found eighteen Molotov cocktails. The borough commander was calling for reinforcements—and fast.

"Send the recruits," someone suggested.

This was a truly dumb idea, busing untrained police recruits into an urban riot. It's hard to list all the things that could easily go wrong. Someone clearly panicked at police headquarters on Centre Street. Nevertheless, we took our orders and traded our gray trainee shirts for police officer blue and hit the smoldering streets of Brooklyn as rocks and bottles flew over our heads. I was finally home from the Marine Corps but suddenly back on a battlefield.

Each recruit was paired with a more experienced officer. I

drew a cop from the Tactical Patrol Force. I had the advantage of three years as a Marine Corps officer and almost a year of combat in Vietnam, but many of my classmates had never patrolled anywhere with a loaded gun. They just looked overwhelmed.

The rioters' two main weapons of choice seemed to be height and gravity. Young men and a few teenage boys pumped with adrenaline and who knows what else hurled heavy objects off the rooftops—paint cans, bricks, cinder blocks, random pieces of construction debris. Every time an object hit the sidewalk, there'd be a loud crash, and everyone would scatter—police, shop owners, neighbors, whoever was standing nearby. It was low-tech but highly effective, and it kept everyone on edge.

"Incoming!" someone would shout, and everyone would jump back. It was almost impossible to identify the suspects. By the time you looked up at the rooftop, you'd be lucky if you saw the back of someone's head.

I followed my new partner up the stairs of a six-story tenement on Pitkin Avenue to a roof where bricks were being tossed. The kids ran as soon as we got up there, leaping from roof to roof along the block. We found rocks stockpiled on the roofs.

*   *   *

The policy was clear: every New York police officer must complete a six-month training course at New York City Police Academy, which had moved from Hubert Street in lower Manhattan to East Twentieth Street in the Gramercy Park neighborhood. During my time there, however, everything was a little disorganized. The recruits took some of their police academy classes in local armories. When they could, the instructors took us out to the shooting range at Rodman's Neck in the Bronx. Our training was conducted in little spurts. We kept being sent out to the streets to pump up the force numbers.

I knew the police academy wasn't supposed to be like that,

but none of it really fazed me. I was back in New York with my wife and baby son. I stayed connected to the Marine Corps by joining the reserves and serving with the Sixth Communication Battalion at Fort Schuyler in the Bronx. After three years of active duty, I didn't want to just walk away, plus I knew the extra pay would come in handy. I felt like I was off and running, getting on with my life.

I made a couple of good arrests while I was still in the academy. The first one was on an 8:00 p.m. to 4:00 a.m. tour in Manhattan's Greenwich Village. Around three o'clock, I was on West Third Street behind the NYU School of Law—a school I would graduate from with a master of laws degree—when I heard a sharp bang across the street. Gunfire. I recognized it right away. I looked up in time to see a woman fall to the sidewalk, two men standing near her, and a gun between them on the ground. The woman was screaming in pain. One man kicked the gun to the other. I ran toward the three of them, jumped over the woman, grabbed one man, and pulled out my own gun. The second man didn't even try to run. Only then did I see that the weapon on the ground was a sawed-off shotgun.

The woman was still screaming. She'd been hit in the leg with birdshot. I warned the men not to move while another rookie, Bruce Drake, helped me put a tourniquet around her leg, which seemed to stop the bleeding. Pretty soon, the corner was crawling with police, and then an ambulance arrived.

The two men and the woman had all come out of a bar and got into some kind of argument. She said the shooting was intentional. The men said it was an accident. A kind lieutenant at the Sixth Precinct, Al LaPerch, helped me process the arrest. The doctors said the tourniquet saved the woman's leg. I felt good about that, and the night's adventure was written up in the *Daily News*.

A couple of months later, I made another arrest, this time in the middle of the day in the Garment District. I was working alone at Sixth Avenue and West Thirty-Sixth Street when I witnessed a large man punch a much smaller man for no reason I could see. I moved in to separate them. As soon as I approached, the big guy spun around and punched me in the chest, knocking my hat off.

The giant was breathing hard, wheezing, almost. He seemed nearly hysterical. He had a frantic look in his eyes. He had a hundred pounds on me and a good ten inches. He'd put all of it into that punch, but I didn't give him time to throw another. I grabbed him and dragged all 260 pounds of him around the corner onto West Thirty-Sixth Street, off the busy avenue. There was a subway entrance there. I held the man against the railing long enough to handcuff him. He was relatively docile by then. A radio car showed up a minute or two later to drive him to the Fourteenth Precinct on West Thirtieth Street.

He got into the car without a struggle, but the moment the door was closed, he exploded a second time, kicking the seat and the doors, yelling words I couldn't make sense of through the closed windows.

It was the first time I'd ever seen anyone go totally berserk, like a child having the worst tantrum ever, only he was a very large man. Back then, people were just starting to use the term *EDP* for "emotionally disturbed person." He was charged with assault and sent off for a psychiatric evaluation.

I didn't use any special tactics to subdue the man—no verbal judo, no martial arts holds. It was all fairly instinctive: *just grab the guy harder than he grabs you*, a skill I learned on Columbus Avenue and West Ninety-First Street long before the police academy.

Someone on the sidewalk had remarked, "Boy, that was a brave little cop." Bravery didn't have much to do with it, I knew. My reaction was mostly adrenaline and a willingness—more like an eagerness—to jump in and be involved. I'm not sure that's something that can ever be taught in the police academy, even in a year when classes aren't constantly interrupted by street duties.

I finished the academy as number one in my class. I took the sergeant's exam even before I graduated. My Marine Corps service meant I had three years of seniority. I passed the test, although I'd have to wait another three years before my name came up on the sergeants list and I got the actual promotion.

At the academy graduation in March 1967, Police Commissioner Howard Leary gave me the Hiram C. Bloomingdale Trophy, an engraved revolver, which went to the student with the highest overall score in academics, physical fitness, and shooting. I think I probably deserved the prize for best arrest, too, but they didn't give me that one.

I was officially a New York City police officer. I earned $173 per week, a bump up from the usual $144 because of my three years of on-the-books "experience."

*   *   *

Before graduation, I'd been told I would be going to the Tactical Patrol Force. But assignments in the police department, as I learned from the very beginning, aren't real until they've happened—and sometimes not even then. I was sent instead to the Twentieth Precinct on West Sixty-Eighth Street. Things hadn't gotten much safer on the Upper West Side since my family left the neighborhood. If anything, street crime was worse. But it wasn't rising crime that got me assigned there. It was bad publicity. The *Daily News* had just run a story saying the Twentieth Precinct had too many unmanned radio cars. The department had pleaded with city hall for extra vehicles. Mayor John Lindsay had found money in the budget to purchase 425 fully loaded Chevrolet police specials at $3,200 each. The total sticker price approached $1.4 million. And now, the *News* had photos of rows and rows of brand-new, idle cars. West Sixty-Eighth Street looked a bit too much like a Northern Boulevard Chevy dealership, and that meant a fast infusion of rookie officers—including me—to drive them.

I was learning something about how decisions often got made. But the work was interesting. You never knew what you would find when responding to calls in a radio car. I worked in a squad of eight or nine officers and a sergeant. The supervisors tried to pair the rookies with more experienced officers. We responded to whatever came in over the radio but also whatever we saw on the street.

"Needle Park" was a small triangle bounded by West Seventy-Second Street, Broadway, and Amsterdam Avenue, later made famous by the Al Pacino movie *The Panic in Needle Park*. The park's official name was Verdi Square, but no one in the neighborhood called it that. The bench-flanked green space came down to a point like a needle, and the cops were constantly shooing the street addicts out of there. *Just keep the junkies moving. Don't let 'em stop.* That was the thinking in those days.

Compared to the crack addicts of later years, the heroin users of the 1960s were a fairly benign group, as long as they had their drugs. They'd nod off on the benches and sit for hours by themselves. The real problems were the street muggings and apartment burglaries that often paid for their habits. We arrested the junkies for the crimes they committed, but they rarely stayed in jail for long. These people needed treatment and motivation, and that wasn't the business we were in. The police, I soon discovered, were often asked to solve social problems far beyond their training or expertise.

*   *   *

Veronica, Jim, and I settled into our new home in Baldwin, Long Island. About thirty miles east of Manhattan, it had three bedrooms, a small backyard, and a one-car garage, the kind of house even a young cop could afford back then, thanks to the GI Bill. Our second son, Gregory, was born in December of 1968, after I'd already enrolled in the night program at the St. John's University School of Law in downtown Brooklyn. The professors pushed us hard and taught us to reason like lawyers. Dean Harold McNeese was a master at the Socratic method of step-by-step interrogation. I still have *Palsgraf v. Long Island Railroad Co.* seared into my brain. I had the brilliant Mario Cuomo, New York's future governor, as my legal research and writing professor and moot-court judge. The days were long but the weeks were short. Because of my college degree, I had gotten reassigned to the Youth Aid Division, a new unit that allowed me to work steady days and attend my law-school classes at night. Mostly, I picked up kids at local precincts and drove them to the Spofford Juvenile Detention Center, the large juvenile lockup in the Hunts Point section of the Bronx. I liked talking to the kids, who were too young to go in a regular police wagon. I got to see the inside of every precinct in the city. The first year, our classes met five nights a week.

A college degree was unusual for cops in those days. Even more unusual was a law degree. When I decided to go to law school, it wasn't because I had a burning desire to be a lawyer. I thought law school might be interesting, and I'd heard I could probably get an NYPD scholarship. That last part didn't happen. Since I was eligible for the GI Bill, the department let Veterans Affairs subsidize my tuition. Their attitude and mine was: Why let the military benefits go to waste? Because I was so busy, I didn't get to enjoy law school fully. I endured it, more like. But I had a terrific study group: Scott Smith, John Burke, and the off-the-charts-brilliant Fritz Behr, who finished first in our law school class. Though raised Jewish, Fritz became an Ethical Culturist, then a Jesuit seminarian, and finally an NYPD lieutenant.

*   *   *

I was still in law school when the promotion to sergeant finally came through. There was something called Sergeants Prepara-

tory School, but no one seemed to think it was especially important. The police department didn't train its leaders anything like
the way the Marine Corps did. I wouldn't get to sergeants school
until I'd already been doing the job for three or four months. After
approximately zero minutes of police supervisory training, I was
sent to the Twenty-Third Precinct on East 104th Street between
Lexington and Third Avenues.

"Here are these guys," the administrative lieutenant told me.
"Supervise them." Several of the officers I would be leading were
older than me and had far more time on the street. As always, I
was grateful for my Marine Corps training. One thing I knew for
certain was that the leader wasn't one of the boys. I didn't hang
out with the people I supervised. I also believed it was important
to look like a leader. My pants always had creases. I shined my
shoes and Brassoed my belt buckle every day. I had sharp creases
in my light-blue wool shirts. When I became a sergeant, the shield
I inherited, number 627, had been handed down through generations of sergeants. It was made of real brass, unlike today's shields.
By the time it got to me, it was a dull shade of brown. I shined it
up until it positively glimmered.

The blocks we patrolled in the Twenty-Third Precinct—86th
Street to 110th Street, where the Upper East Side gave way to
East Harlem—were strikingly diverse. The northern two-thirds
of the precinct was heavily Puerto Rican and saw a lot of drug
activity. The southern third, which included Gracie Mansion, the
mayor's official residence, was affluent and almost entirely white.
The precinct commanders when I was there—Solomon Gross,
John McCabe, and John Rogan—had genuine respect inside the
precinct and knew the community well.

That didn't mean there weren't problems. On my second night
in the precinct, a plainclothes tactical patrol officer shot and killed
a man who was robbing him on Fifth Avenue and 109th Street.
When I reached the scene, bricks were coming off the rooftops

again. Dozens of people were throwing things and shouting at the police.

The body was still on the sidewalk. That didn't look good. I didn't need sergeant school to know its presence was inflaming the crowd. "Get that body out of here," I ordered.

I had two officers lift the body into a radio car and drive to Metropolitan Hospital. Then officers from Housing Police showed up. Like the Transit Police, they were a separate agency back then. Together, we led a brief charge against the crowd, pushing people back from the scene, urging everyone to go back home. Most of them listened.

Sometimes the drama originated from within the ranks, rather than on the streets. In January 1971, the Patrolmen's Benevolent Association was up in arms over the Knapp Commission, which had been formed the previous April by Mayor Lindsay to investigate corruption up and down the New York City Police Department. By now, chairman Whitman Knapp and his four commissioners were highlighting plenty of it, and some of the cops were starting to feel picked on. Officers were mostly upset about their pay. It wasn't bad money for the time. At about $11,000 a year, the average New York patrolman earned more than police in most cities. But the cost of living in New York was higher than almost anywhere else. A back-pay dispute erupted in a Brooklyn precinct on January 14, and the union called for a work stoppage. Within a day, the job action spread across the city as twenty thousand patrolmen stayed home. Suddenly detectives and supervisors were about the only people patrolling the streets. Calls simply went unanswered. As a sergeant, I found myself working the gate at Gracie Mansion one night during the strike. But with so much area to cover, I was constantly being called away, in and out of the precinct. Another night, a detective and I responded in a radio car to a disturbance at Julia Richman High School Annex. Students were fighting and throwing things in a giant melee. I was in uniform. The detective was not. I was the one who looked like a cop. It really was me against twenty high school kids. It took a minute, but I managed to calm everyone down. I had often found in tense situations that if I kept my cool, those around me would calm down, too. Calm, like anxiety and uproar, is almost always contagious.

The job action lasted six stressful days. Thankfully, the weather was on our side. Temperatures stayed frigid all that week, and the city survived with no early-January crime wave. Still, 1971 turned out to be a very dangerous year in New York, especially for the police. Fifteen officers were killed in the line of duty in those twelve months. Two of the deaths were accidents. One was a heart attack. But twelve were intentional killings—eleven by gunfire, one by knife. Joseph Piagentini and Waverly Jones were ambushed outside their radio car at 159th Street and Harlem River Drive by members of the Black Liberation Army. Arthur Pelo was gunned down as he tried to question a robbery suspect on Rockaway Avenue in Brownsville. Kenneth Nugent was shot to death when he interrupted an armed robbery at a luncheonette on Hollis Avenue in Queens on his way in to work.

Every one of these cases was different, but those officers' combined sacrifice created immense anxiety on the force, and it manifested in unsettling ways. An officer who drove me turned up one day with an M2 carbine. "Get that back in your locker," I told him. "That's not how we win this war." There was just a lot of wild stuff on the street.

As I completed law school that June and began studying for the New York State bar exam, stories about the rising disorder and crime in the city seemed to make the front page of the newspapers every day. Mayor Lindsay and Police Commissioner Patrick Murphy were facing growing demands to do something—*anything*. People began to openly wonder if this seething metropolis of competing constituencies was simply impossible to govern. Lots of New Yorkers were moving to the suburbs, the tax base suffered, and observers dubbed the trend "white flight."

Murphy and his chiefs launched a new program of proactive policing. They installed an anticrime unit in each of the seventy-six precincts. The idea was to send plainclothes officers onto the streets and urge them not to wait around for radio calls. Instead, they were expected to seek out the crime and arrest the criminals. That sounded tailor-made for me.

John Rogan put me in charge of the Twenty-Third Precinct's anticrime unit and let me choose my own people. I knew what I wanted—officers who had initiative, were street-smart, and could easily blend into the community.

The concept worked beautifully in our precinct. We blended in by using our own cars, including my Volkswagen Beetle, and borrowing taxicabs from a local garage. We got out on the streets and hid our radios like whiskey bottles in paper bags. Early on, it was relatively easy.

We lurked in empty doorways and waited until we spotted someone acting suspiciously—someone who appeared to be waiting for a mugging victim, casing a local business, or checking the door handles on parked cars on Fifth Avenue. We'd follow. One officer would watch from the sidewalk a block behind. The rest of us would parallel the suspect from a fake cab across the avenue until he committed a crime and we had a reason to swoop in. In one month, our anticrime unit made an astounding twenty-seven robbery arrests, an incredible number for a single precinct and a good indication of the magnitude of the problem. None of these were calls that came over the radio.

The street crimes we witnessed occurred primarily in the blocks just south of East Ninety-Sixth Street, the racially integrated part of the precinct. That's where the easy victims were. Young men and teenagers were coming down from the blocks to the north. It was very common for us to find guns on the people we locked up.

One afternoon, we were patiently shadowing two young men when they walked into a Western Union office and brandished guns, demanding money from the clerk. We grabbed the men just as soon as they walked back out the door. They were carrying newspaper clippings in their back pockets about previous robberies they had committed. Some arrests were dumb luck. One day, we stopped our fake cab in front of the 92nd Street Y and I went in to use the bathroom. When I came out, a man lugging a television set was trying to get into the cab. He'd just stolen the TV from an apartment across the street.

"You picked the wrong cab," I told him.

We cuffed him and found the apartment he had just burglarized.

*   *   *

As the years rolled on, more and more of the story of New York was becoming the story of race. On April 14, 1972, officers responded to a false 10-13 call—assist police officer—at the Nation of Islam Mosque No. 7 on 116th Street. Phillip and his partner were the first to respond. Once inside, they were attacked by fifteen to twenty people, beaten, and stripped of their weapons. During the melee, Officer Cardillo was shot at point-blank range with his own gun.

The mosque was in the neighboring Twenty-Eighth Precinct. No call for assistance ever came over our radio frequency. When I eventually heard what was happening, I went straight to the scene, arriving about an hour after the initial shooting. An angry mob had formed around the police barricades and were calling the officers pigs.

The people in the mosque refused to leave at first. Then Minister Louis Farrakhan and Harlem congressman Charles Rangel turned up to negotiate. In order to quell the crowd outside, Chief of Detectives Albert Seedman—with the consent, I am sure, of Commissioner Murphy—allowed the witnesses to walk away, giving them appointments to be questioned later at the precinct. Hardly any of them ever showed up. The standoff was grossly mishandled by the executive corps of the police department, and the officers at the scene all knew it.

Phillip Cardillo died six days later.

*   *   *

I loved my life in the police department. But I also had the law degree, and my older brothers were settling into professional careers, Donald at Emigrant Savings Bank, Kenneth in the press office at the United Nations, Leonard at the Phipps Foundation. Once I passed the bar exam, I started practicing part-time in Garden City and, with a couple of law school friends, enrolled in the master of laws program at New York University, an advanced course of study that focused on criminal law from a global perspective. I wasn't interested in being an international criminal lawyer. I had no interest in leaving the police department. But I believed in education. There was money from the federal Law Enforcement Assistance Administration to help pay the tuition, and I figured, why not? With all that going on, though, I hardly had time to breathe. Besides the law practice, the master's program, and my day job at the police department—which was often a night shift or a four-to-twelve tour—I also had the Marine Corps Reserves. What got badly squeezed was the time I spent with my wife and two young sons. They were at home in Baldwin, and I was almost always everywhere else. I treasured the time we had together, but there was much too little of it. My family sacrificed tremendously in those years.

I kept coming back to the realization that police work was what inspired me. I'd never get rich doing it. I understood that. But it was far too rewarding to even consider abandoning—important, exhilarating, satisfying, almost addictive. Once, I was drafted to work in the NYPD Internal Management Consulting Section. My superiors kept seeing my college diploma and my law degree and assuming I craved a desk job. They were wrong. Two months in, I asked to be transferred back to the Twenty-Third Precinct. Then John Rogan went to the NYPD Crime Prevention Section and asked me to go with him as a sergeant. Part of his charge was to launch something called the Block Security Program. The department had never done anything like this before. Mayor Lindsay was planning to highlight the program in his upcoming presidential campaign as a fresh way of fighting crime. It made some sense, actually.

The idea was for local community groups to raise small amounts of money to pay for door locks, window guards, burglar alarms, security lighting, and other anticrime measures in their neighborhoods. The city would then match—or double or triple—those funds. The concept was promising, but no one had thought about any of the practical details. That was my job. I wrote the regulations, determined who was eligible, and established what the money could be used for. I received no guidance from anyone. I just did what seemed to make sense. I even called on my artistic talents to create a logo and draw the pictures that were used in the brochure. No one else seemed able or interested or available to make the Block Security Program a reality. I *was* the program, and city hall couldn't get enough of it—or me. The experience gave me my first inside look at the upper levels of city government. And here was the best part: the program actually seemed to be working.

On September 13, 1973, Mayor Lindsay traveled to Washington to testify in front of the House Judiciary Committee about this wonderful new program of his, and I went along. I didn't get to say anything, but I sat behind the mayor in the hearing room as

he testified, knowing that much of what he was touting had originated with me. Over time, I got to know Chief of Staff Jay Kriegel, mayoral assistant Steve Brill, and several of Mayor Lindsay's
other "whiz kids." I saw Kriegel as the de facto mayor. He was
amazing, making top-level decisions at city hall, and he wasn't
much older than I was. The crew around Mayor Lindsay emphasized to me how bright, young, energetic people really could have
an impact working in government. That insight was genuinely
inspiring.

After a brief stop at SOD, the Special Operations Division,
I was promoted to lieutenant in 1974 and, of course, wasn't sent
promptly to Lieutenants Preparatory School. They'd get around
to sending me eventually. In the meantime, my job was to address
the turmoil inside the Tenth Precinct on West Twentieth Street.

Things at the NYPD always moved slowly until they didn't.
The Tenth Precinct cops were spending time at Off Track Bet-
ting when they were supposed to be on the job. In addition, one
of the lieutenants had allegedly been using the captain's office for
trysts with his policewoman girlfriend. Clearly the place needed
closer supervision. All the old lieutenants were transferred out.
I was the new administrative lieutenant, sent to help the commander, Frank Lynch, gain control of the place. He was an eru-
dite man, a rising star in the department.

The territory was a little bit of a sleeper—a narrow patch of
Manhattan's West Side that ran from West Fourteenth Street
to West Forty-Third Street. The neighborhood, though mostly
quiet, had its flashes of colorful action, as all neighborhoods do.
A lot of this was concentrated around the entrance to the Lincoln Tunnel, a hotbed of street and vehicle prostitution. We had
the "nobbers," the "he-shes," the "chicken hawks"—the cops had
special terms for all the different actors in New York's many-
splendored underground sex drama. It kept the police in my new
precinct busy.

It was during my time at the Tenth Precinct, where I was operations officer, administrative lieutenant, and integrity-control officer, that we had the first mass layoffs in NYPD history. I used to tell people with utter confidence, "There will never be layoffs in the police department." I was certain of it—until the layoffs came.

In 1975 the city budget was awash in red ink. Regular people started to use the phrase *fiscal crisis*. President Ford refused to approve a federal bailout. FORD TO CITY: DROP DEAD, the front-page *Daily News* headline bluntly summarized. The city came so close to bankruptcy that aides to Mayor Abraham Beame even drafted a statement announcing the city's default. The solution to the fiscal crisis, when it came, was deep and painful. The municipal unions agreed to use their retirement funds to back city securities. City finances were put in the hands of the state Emergency Financial Control Board. City services were cut drastically. Salaries were frozen. Subway fares went up. Some hospitals, libraries, and firehouses were closed. Welfare spending was slashed. Tens of thousands of municipal workers, including three thousand police officers, were laid off and sent home.

It was a troubled time. The department was undermanned and hurting. One night in the Tenth Precinct, I found myself covering the desk alone on a late tour. Apart from me, there was one cop in the back with the prisoners and a civilian manning the switchboard. We had a single radio car on the street.

A man rushed into the station house. "There's a guy stabbing a woman down the block," he managed to blurt out.

There was no one else. "Let's go," I said.

I ran across Eighth Avenue, where I came upon a woman lying in a vestibule. There was blood on the walls. Still standing over her was a man with a broken umbrella. He had used the pointy end to stab her in the face. The woman was unconscious, and the man was obviously intoxicated. I grabbed him and waited twenty

minutes for the ambulance and the radio car to come. The cop
I'd left guarding the prisoners also showed up eventually. Thankfully, the woman survived. Later she sent me a nice thank-you
note at the precinct. The man who attacked her was a second-
felony offender. I testified at his trial.

It was years before the force was back to full strength. The
city was almost unguarded at times in that era. We are lucky it
wasn't far worse than it was.

*   *   *

In every long police career, some assignments will be far more
enjoyable than others. I bided my time in the Legal Bureau and
the License Division before landing a truly wild, crazy, gritty,
and constantly surprising post: Manhattan South Public Morals.
I arrived in 1978, at the height of an era mythologized by Robert
De Niro in *Taxi Driver* and Al Pacino in *Cruising*. Times Square
in those days attracted every imaginable variety of hustler, per-
vert, and lowlife, and we had special squads for most of them. We
had the pimp squad, run by Sergeant George Trapp. We had the
pedophile squad. The gambling squad. The streetwalker squad.
Once a week or so we'd round up the male cruisers too. That duty
wasn't too popular. We had officers from other commands who
wouldn't be recognized come in and pretend to be johns.

We covered everything south of Sixtieth Street and even did
cases in Brooklyn and Queens, but the busiest territory was still
Times Square. We kept an eye on Peep-O-Rama, Girls-Girls-
Girls, and the grandest of the Times Square porn palaces, Show
World, which featured "private viewing rooms" and stage shows
by big-name adult stars like Vanessa del Rio. Certain things were
allowed by law, and certain things were not. I spent one evening
undercover at the Mineshaft, the gay leather club on Washington Street that inspired *Cruising*. I was in good shape and breezed

right past the notoriously fickle bouncers. Once inside, I witnessed acts the nuns at St. Gregory's had never warned me about.

Mixed up in all of this were some genuine organized-crime cases. There was money to be made in vice, gambling, and loan-sharking, and New York's biggest mob families had always profiteered there. Sergeant James Malvey conducted a sophisticated racketeering case against Lucchese family figure Ray Argentina. One night in a dimly lit social club, we arrested Alphonse Persico, the Colombo mobster known as Allie Boy. On the chair where he'd been sitting, I found a loaded handgun. We arrested priests for pedophilia. We sent teenage girls back home to Iowa. In late-night raids, we'd tear apart a gambling parlor or an after-hours club, dismantling the bar with saws and crowbars, confiscating the liquor and cash, all the while knowing they'd be rebuilding the place by noon. We tried to keep up with the ever-changing fronts and euphemisms for prostitution—massage parlors, negligee modeling studios, body-scrub salons, escort services, intimate photography workshops, surrogate therapy sessions, and something else the next day. Say what you will about the sleaziness of the sex-for-money industry, but the proprietors had imaginative marketing skills.

Manhattan South Public Morals consisted of about fifty officers. John Ridge was the captain, a smart and colorful man. We had two undercovers working with us, Joe Mazzilli and Sal Montano, who could play dead-on mafiosi. They would get in with the wiseguys by going to bars and selling untaxed cigarettes. The mobsters were always looking for an easy scam. Joe and Sal played their parts perfectly.

We had Karen Clark, an attractive young police officer with some genuine acting skills. She could stand on any West Side corner. Eager johns kept soliciting her. We also had our own phony pimp, and we procured a Cadillac for him. He hung out at a pimp club called the Pork Pie Hat. The pimps arrived in fur coats and flashy jewelry. They squabbled over territory. They boasted about the girls who were making them rich, trading them back and forth to settle drug and gambling debts. In one of his reports, our undercover pimp wrote, "I'm in the back of the Pork Pie Hat, just bullshitting."

"No!" I laughed when I read that. "This is an official police report. You can't write that."

We constantly heard stories about pimps at the Port Authority Bus Terminal on Eighth Avenue and West Forty-Second Street picking up runaway girls fresh off the Greyhound from Minnesota and Iowa and Montana. Media reports frequently quoted Father Bruce Ritter, the charismatic Catholic priest who founded Covenant House, a well-respected shelter and social service agency for homeless youth. I sat one day in Father Ritter's office as he told me chilling stories of pimps by the gates in the bus station, trolling for fresh recruits.

"Hundreds of them," he said alarmingly. "It's happening every day."

"When? Where?" I asked. We staked out the bus station, and we never seemed to see any pimps. "We'll go over and arrest them right now."

He looked at me like I was clueless. "Everyone knows about that," he assured me. Father Ritter promised to get back to me with more details. He never did, of course. No doubt the pimps were active and plentiful. We rarely had trouble finding them. And teens from small-town America did end up in the strip clubs, apartment house brothels, and porn sets of New York. I just didn't believe the recruiting process was quite as out in the open as Father Ritter's fund-raising letters portrayed. But who knows? In those wild days, it was often hard to tell the scary urban legends from the honest-to-God truth. Almost anything was possible in that murky world. Among the secrets that came to light eventually: the once-beloved Father Ritter was accused of sexual abuse by more than a dozen young men and boys, some of the same youngsters he'd been praised so lavishly for "rescuing." Covenant House did a lot of good work, though. I hated to see its reputation trashed.

We had no illusions that what we were doing was permanent. One night, we'd sweep the hookers off Ninth Avenue. They'd come back the next night. The strip joint with "extra services" we closed on Wednesday would be open on Friday under another name. When we busted a pimp who'd been especially greedy or surly or brutal, the women who worked for him thanked us and smiled, then often went right back to work for one of his buddies. It would take a far larger revival of New York City to clean up the public morals of Times Square, and I hoped one day to be a part of that. In the meantime, our squad did what we could to keep a lid on things, nudging the city's underworld in a more law-abiding direction.

The assignment certainly gave me an appreciation for the variety of the crime in the city. One night in Public Morals, we went to raid a high-end Asian gambling operation on East Sixty-First Street. The pai gow tables and roulette wheels shared the building with a restaurant, which had outdoor tables in an open patio. We had an undercover inside, but he couldn't just unlock the place and invite the rest of us in. The entrance to the gambling parlor was blocked by two locked doors—an outer door of fortified steel and an inner door that wasn't fortified.

With the two biggest men on the squad, I climbed over the wall and onto the restaurant patio. People eating dinner looked up with a typical New York nonchalance. No one said anything. My two large cohorts then lifted a metal grate that led to a narrow tunnel. I was the lieutenant, but I was also the smallest guy on the team. So I was the one who was going in. It was tight, but I crawled through the dark, claustrophobic tunnel. I felt my way to the end. Just as I'd been promised, the tunnel came up in the entryway between the two locked doors. I shimmied up cautiously and opened the heavy steel door to the outside. The others quickly slipped inside.

We easily forced our way through the second door. With a burst of shouts and waving badges, we announced the raid.

"Police! Don't anybody move!"

We truly caught everyone by surprise, except for the diners on the patio, who'd thankfully just kept eating their dinners.

Most of our work never made the papers or got many thank-yous from city hall. But it was the little accomplishments that kept us going, even if the wheels were back to spinning the very next night.

CHAPTER FOUR

Taking Command

Each police precinct, I kept discovering, had its unique culture and quirks. When you walked in the door the first day, you never knew who was really in charge. It might have been the previous commander—or maybe not. Sometimes the lead clerical person ran the place. Nothing got done without her blessing. Sometimes the union guys—the Patrolmen's Benevolent Association delegates—ran things. Or the administrative lieutenant. Or someone who used to work there and didn't anymore, but still had a shadowy grip on everything. You couldn't find any of this written anywhere, certainly not in the Patrol Guide or on some organizational chart. But many precincts and police commands had their own unofficial, permanent governments in place. These people stayed. The commanders came and went.

As I continued climbing the commanding officer's ladder of the New York City Police Department—from cadet to recruit to patrolman to sergeant to lieutenant to captain to deputy inspector and beyond—I tried to stay alert to the real power dynamics, the ways things actually got done. Human organizations are run by human beings, and the NYPD was human to its core, in both the good and the bad senses of that term. By the time I was promoted to captain, in 1980, I had really come to appreciate that. After a year in the Emergency Service Unit, where the cops did an amazing job dealing with the deinstitutionalized mentally ill, among other things, I took over the Eighty-Eighth Precinct in central

Brooklyn, which covered the Bedford-Stuyvesant and Clinton Hill neighborhoods. The Classon Avenue station house, built in 1890, was a creaky mess. It had serious roof leaks and a dank, musty smell. But as I soon learned, the precinct's deterioration was more than physical. The Eighty-Eighth had become a destination for problem cops. I counted 25 administrative transfers, as disciplinary cases were called. That's a huge number in a precinct of 120 officers or so. Some previous commander must have done something that really annoyed someone at headquarters.

Just before I arrived, there'd been a retirement party in the station house basement. When the partying cops got upstairs to the main room where the desk was, someone fired a shot at the clock. The bullet missed. When I got there, the bullet hole was still in the wall a couple of feet from the clock. After a long night of drinking, no one's aim was very good. There might have been some shots fired on the street, as well. Nobody could prove it either way.

There was a back door that led into an alley next to the station. The cops had held barbecues out there. You could see the area from DeKalb Avenue. "We won't be holding any more backyard barbecues," I said as I put a padlock on the door.

In the months to come, we transferred out many of the twenty-five disciplinary cases. A lot of them, I knew, could and did become good cops with a change of scenery. They had to put in a UF-57 form, a transfer request. They didn't want to be in that mess of a precinct either. With the help of the personnel bureau, we just expedited the transfers.

I instituted a lot of other changes. Charlie DiRienzo, a lieutenant who worked closely with me, was a valuable ally in making the place run like a professional precinct. This wasn't brain surgery. It was basic police practice and leadership psychology: elevated expectations, clear responsibilities, an orderly work environment, objective performance measurements, praise for those who succeeded, and closer supervision for those who did not. I'm sure some officers grumbled about my moves. But I was the commander, so I was in charge.

After two years, the changes we'd made earned the Eighty-Eighth Precinct a unit citation, recognizing it as being one of the best precincts in the city.

*   *   *

As I moved from precinct to precinct, I discovered, you could make things better by being collaborative. Other times you had to take a firmer approach. Almost without fail, there was the challenge of dealing with the unions—that's right, unions, plural. Every rank had its own union. The Patrolmen's Benevolent Association. The Sergeants Benevolent Association. The Lieutenants Benevolent Association. The Detectives' Endowment Association. Even the captains had a union. I had been a member of four of the five unions and realized that if it wasn't for the unions, cops—myself included—would probably all be earning minimum wage. Unions did lots of good things. But relationships among all these ranks weren't like in the military, where officers and enlisted personnel spend their entire careers on separate tracks. In the police department, everyone started together at the bottom, and some worked their way up. This meant that supervisors were overseeing their buddies from all the way back in the police academy. This structure tended to keep the department somewhat inward-looking and resistant to change.

My next post was the Seventy-First Precinct, which covered Crown Heights, one of Brooklyn's most interesting and challenging neighborhoods—perhaps a hundred thousand Caribbean and African Americans and fifteen thousand Eastern European Lubavitch Hasidic Jews. The relationship between the two groups was tense, and some of that tension spilled into the precinct. There were strong feelings—in the community and inside the Empire

Boulevard station house—mostly around the belief that city hall was pressuring the police to do special favors for the Hasidic community. Long before I got there, a radio car was stationed twenty-four hours a day at 770 Eastern Parkway, the Lubavitcher headquarters and the office of Grand Rebbe Menachem Mendel Schneerson, and at the *mikvah*, where Hasidic women went to ritually cleanse themselves. There was a term for these assignments. It was a house-of-worship car. I had a lot of interaction with the Hasidim and also the black community. That's where I first got to know a charismatic young minister named Al Sharpton, who was beginning to gain a following in the neighborhood.

In those days Crown Heights had a serious violent crime problem. Hasidim were being attacked on the street. They formed their own vigilante groups for self-defense. One day, someone poured five gallons of gasoline against the side of the Lubavitcher headquarters and tried to ignite it. For some reason, it didn't catch. Officers from the Seventy-Seventh Precinct who happened to be passing by grabbed the arsonist. The growing drug epidemic was a big problem, too. It produced vicious gun battles for street-sale turf. I could hear the gunfire from my office. There were almost one hundred murders that year in our precinct alone. The crime numbers were rising fast. We were out on the streets protecting all segments of the diverse community. If a police officer was involved in a shooting, it meant my tour would be extended another twelve hours because of the extra investigation involved. I remember some very long nights in the office.

* * *

I left Crown Heights temporarily for Harvard University, where I spent the 1983–84 academic year earning a master's degree in public administration in the Mid-Career MPA Program at the John F. Kennedy School of Government. As I had moved up in the police department, I had learned a lot about the NYPD and about law enforcement in general. But I thought a broader view might be helpful, too. I figured that top people from other disciplines might have some fresh ideas worth considering. How to structure large organizations. How to use data to guide good decisions. How to select the right people for the right jobs. We had our ways of doing all these things, but police departments, I knew, could be insular places. I really wanted to hear what other smart people thought. Harvard was hugely impressive. There were senators, authors, CEOs, and heads of state just walking down the hall. In the course work, there was a great emphasis on collaborative problem solving, an approach that runs counter to the sometimes hierarchical business of policing. I worked with some brilliant professors and fellow students from around the world. At Harvard I got a chance to step out of the cauldron of daily policing and into an environment that encouraged deeper thought. I was especially impressed with Dean Graham Allison, who also taught classes. I found him to be thoughtful and deep but very approachable. The same could be said of Professor Mark Moore, who had great insights on how to lead public agencies into the modern age. With the guidance of those two and others, I came to understand how police departments were first and foremost organizations composed of human beings who could be developed, encouraged, and motivated in ways that few police executives had ever thought of before.

After earning my master's degree, I returned to New York and, for a short time, to the Seventy-First Precinct and to the streets of Crown Heights, where not much had changed. Then I got a call from Commissioner Benjamin Ward.

"I want you to go to the 106th," he told me.

I knew immediately what that meant: another troubled command. This time I was being assigned to the notorious stun gun precinct. I had never met Commissioner Ward, who'd been sworn in by Mayor Ed Koch sixteen months earlier as the city's first African American police commissioner. Apparently he'd heard about a captain in Brooklyn who was a marine, a lawyer, and a recent Harvard graduate. "I think you'd be right for this," he said on the phone. "We need your help."

On April 17, 1985, an eighteen-year-old high school senior named Mark Davidson was arrested for selling a ten-dollar bag of marijuana to an undercover officer on a quiet street in Ozone Park, Queens, not far from John F. Kennedy International Airport. What happened after that minor arrest was something more than minor corruption or major sloppiness. It was torture.

Davidson was the first of four suspects to step forward and charge that, during interrogation at the 106th Precinct, he had been tortured with electric shocks from a handheld stun gun. Davidson allegedly gave a confession after one of the officers threatened to use the stun gun on his genitals. The story was all over the papers. Outside investigations were soon under way. An angry Mayor Koch asked U.S. Attorney General Edwin Meese to open a civil rights inquiry.

By week's end, four officers had been arrested on assault charges. Commissioner Ward ordered the transfer of all nineteen of the precinct's top command. More than fifty uniformed officers were questioned by the Queens district attorney's office. Declaring a "crisis of confidence," Commissioner Ward also removed the borough commander in Queens.

The assumption was that the command was out of control. In reality, what I found was a few cops guilty of horrendous acts. Sergeant Richard Pike and Officer Jeffrey Gilbert, and Officer Loren MacCary, the officers accused of stun-gunning Davidson and the others, were ultimately convicted of assault and sent off to prison.

The vast majority of police officers had no idea what was going on, nor did they countenance it when they found out. My message to them was, "The whole world is watching. You guys have to perform to the highest standards." We had to repair relations with the community, which had been badly strained. We tried to show that the police were there for them. And we did.

Commissioner Ward seemed pleased with the precinct's turnaround. He pulled me into headquarters several months later to run the police cadet program. In the time since I'd left the program nearly a quarter century earlier, it had veered away from its innovative purpose, becoming a "trainee" program with no college requirement. Ward wanted to get the program back to Adam Walinsky's original intent. Jeremy Travis, who was counsel to Commissioner Ward and would later become president of John Jay College of Criminal Justice, oversaw the process. It was my job to design the new program—the training, the assignments, the uniforms, the logos, everything. The cadet program, we decided, should be the start of a professional career path in policing. We recruited students from top private and public universities. I felt like we really were recruiting the department's next generation of top leaders.

After I finished rebooting the cadet program, Ward asked me to take over the Office of Management Analysis and Planning, which meant reporting directly to him. He and I began working closely together. Ben Ward was a terrific role model for me. He was an excellent police official—period. He had the self-confidence to make tough decisions. He didn't need to please everyone all the time—a quick road to mediocrity. He really didn't care whether you liked him or not. Like other commissioners before him, however, he had his quirks. Even before the New York police officially traded their old six-shot revolvers for semiautomatics, Ward kept a Glock on the credenza behind his desk in the commissioner's office. "Kelly, don't walk behind me," he'd say when I came in the door. "Don't walk behind me." He always thought he was going to be attacked somehow. Before he retired, he sent me back as commanding officer of the Special Operations Division, which encompassed the Harbor Unit, the Aviation Unit, and some of the department's other shiniest assets. I'm not sure if he did this purposely, but the commissioner was broadening my experience in ways that would prove highly useful. I was an assistant chief by then.

When David Dinkins took office in January 1990 as New York's first African American mayor, he appointed Lee Brown as police commissioner. Brown wasn't a New Yorker, but he had run police departments in Atlanta and Houston. He had what I would call a professorial demeanor and was known as a big booster of community policing: the concept that police officers shouldn't see themselves merely as crime fighters, but as social problem solvers as well. The new mayor certainly believed in that. Ben Ward urged Lee Brown to appoint me as first deputy commissioner, the department's number two job, and Brown did. Robert Johnston Jr., Ward's chief of department, the top uniformed position, stayed on in that job.

I knew Bob Johnston well. He'd been an assistant chief when I was a captain in Brooklyn and Queens. He could be a bit tart, but he had great knowledge of the department and the city. He and I actually got along fairly well. Lee Brown was cautioned that he shouldn't have Johnston reporting to me, a former subordinate. So the new commissioner made clear to both of us that we had very different areas of responsibility—Johnston handling day-to-day police operations, I overseeing longer-term and strategic issues. We both reported directly to Brown. That sounds like bureaucratic trivia. But this internal structure remained in place even after Johnston retired, and its limitations ultimately hurt the department when Crown Heights blew up.

CHAPTER FIVE

Crime Waves

C rime numbers can be slippery.

Prior to 1928, the New York City Police Department did not keep citywide crime statistics. No one even bothered to try. Then Mayor Jimmy Walker ordered his police commissioner, Grover Aloysius Whalen, to start keeping records on the frequency of murders, robberies, and other kinds of crime. Commissioner Whalen, a ruthless enforcer of Prohibition laws, was rigid in other ways as well. He was famous for saying, "There is plenty of law at the end of a nightstick." Whalen also said, "The fundamental weakness of police service is lack of scientific knowledge and training." He went on to create the New York Police College, a precursor to today's Police Academy, promising that "in the course of time, virtually every member of the New York department—and there are upward of 19,000—will have taken courses in the College." But perhaps one of his most lasting contributions to modern policing was his role as the city's first number-crunching police commissioner.

For the next four decades, New York usually recorded four hundred to six hundred murders a year.

The numbers jumped around a little, and their trustworthiness was at times a subject of hot debate. But by crime-stat standards, homicide numbers were generally considered the most reliable. That was for one simple reason: it was a whole lot easier to recast a robbery as a larceny—or to slip a simple-assault report into the circular file—than it was to hide the bodies at the city morgue.

Like many other things, the homicide figures started to change in the 1960s. Racial tensions were rising. Guns were easier to find. Violent crime was getting more violent everywhere, not just in New York City, and more people were being killed. In 1967, John Lindsay's second year as mayor, the city logged 746 murders. By 1970, Lindsay's fifth year, the total hit 1,117. It was 1,680 in 1973, his last. Lindsay's one-term successor, Mayor Abraham Beame, managed to stabilize the numbers. They went from 1,554 murders in 1974 to 1,557 in 1977, even with the pressures of the city's fiscal crisis and police layoffs.

The numbers remained fairly stable through the first seven years of the Koch administration. Then came crack cocaine.

The drug arrived from the West Coast in 1985. I'd never heard of crack before. But one day that summer, I was out with the narcotics unit of the 106th Precinct in Ozone Park, Queens, when I felt something crunching between the sidewalk and my shoes.

"What's that?" I asked.

The cops explained that those were crack vials. Suddenly they seemed to be everywhere. Crack, I learned, was created by heating small pinches of cut, powdered cocaine until it formed into tiny rocks, which could then be smoked in a glass pipe. The drug was cheap, fast acting, and highly addictive. In a matter of months, the city had an enormous crack problem.

New York had been through many drug waves over the decades. The city had absorbed opium addicts, pot smokers, acid trippers, heroin junkies, and pill heads. But we'd never experienced the fast and brutal ravages of a drug like crack cocaine.

Nineteen eighty-five saw 1,384 homicides. Two years later, the city had 1,672 murders. Then 1,896. Followed by 1,905 in Koch's final year in office.

Oddly, Mayor Koch didn't suffer much politically. No one

really seemed to blame him. He had been a reliable booster of the police department. The police unions generally supported him. The city's tabloids—*New York Newsday* had recently joined the *Daily News* and the *New York Post*—gave extensive coverage to the crack wars and all the resulting violence. But responsibility was rarely placed at Mayor Koch's feet.

The Koch-era crime momentum was so tenacious, it spilled into the first year of the Dinkins administration, 1990, when New York City murders would hit an all-time high of 2,245. But David Dinkins didn't get off nearly as easily as Ed Koch had. Even before the first-year totals were in, when Dinkins had been on the job less than nine months, the *New York Post* came at the city's new African American mayor with a pounding front-page headline.

DAVE, DO SOMETHING!, the headline demanded.

Just in case anyone missed the point, *Post* editor-in-chief Jerry Nachman penned his own personal slam titled "Do-Nothing Dave Dinkins," which followed up on the previous day's editorial, "Where Are the Voices of Outrage?"

Koch, who'd been in office for twelve years, had gotten a pass. Now, after eight months, Mayor Dinkins was being pilloried as the crime wave crashed in on him. And the new mayor didn't like it one bit. He decided to do something.

Dinkins summoned Commissioner Brown to city hall and demanded, with obvious frustration in his voice, "Tell us how many people you need."

It was a remarkable request. Many of the people around Mayor Dinkins in city hall, including former city budget director Paul Dickstein, had argued for years that the precise number of police officers really didn't have much of a correlation with the level of crime. Crime, they were convinced, was a product of large socioeconomic forces like poverty, unemployment, family disintegration, and substance abuse—not the number of cops on the beat. The police couldn't possibly be everywhere. All they could hope to do was respond after crimes were committed. Police staffing was just a political number, fine for pacifying community leaders and police union bosses but largely meaningless in the battle to reduce urban violence and crime. But Dinkins felt cornered, I believe. He thought the attacks were unfair, but he also felt like he couldn't just ignore them. Dave had to "do something"—now.

Commissioner Brown, who'd been in New York for only the same eight and a half months Dinkins had been mayor, had no independent view of how many police officers the city of New York might need. At his previous job in Houston, he had overseen approximately five thousand officers, a force barely one-fifth the size of the NYPD. I, on the other hand, had now been in the NYPD for more than a quarter century. So he turned to me, his first deputy commissioner, and asked me to come up with a number and a plan.

I knew we had to move quickly, and we couldn't afford to miss anything. I assembled a task force of eighty people. I brought in experts from the department's Office of Management Analysis and Planning, where I had once worked, who knew the police bureaucracy better than anyone.

In forty days—lightning speed for a city bureaucracy—we assembled a report that advocated an aggressive staffing plan coupled with dozens of practical ways to make the department more efficient. For instance, we used to send a squad car to every fire. The fire department didn't want us there and, in most cases, didn't need us there. They already had large red trucks to block the traffic. We discovered we could save 250,000 radio runs a year if we quit responding to fires except when the FDNY asked us to come. Load shedding, we called that. It freed up police resources for actually fighting crime.

We devised formulas (based on caseload and types of cases) for determining how many detectives should be assigned to each precinct.

We estimated that the average radio call should take thirty minutes. With that average and a count of how many calls went to each precinct, we came up with more efficient ways of managing the radio-car assignments. Our goal was to free up patrol officers so they could be engaged in community-policing tasks for 30 percent of their tours.

We reviewed practical strategies for community policing, a concept to which the mayor and the police commissioner were both committed.

In the end, we settled on a number, the data point everyone was waiting to hear. The NYPD needed five thousand more cops, we declared. Along with the many new efficiencies, it would be enough to make a difference and still seemed doable in a city the size of New York. In addition, we proposed adding a few hundred new officers each to the city's housing and transit forces, which were still separate agencies back then. On October 2, 1990, Mayor Dinkins announced a plan we called Safe Streets, Safe City.

We still had to pay for this somehow, which would mean a new city surtax and an increase of some city property taxes. But even though most of the money would come from city residents and businesses, under New York law, the state legislature would have to approve the tax hikes. Some of the money, city hall suggested, could be raised with a new two-dollar scratch-off lottery ticket. It took almost a year of tough negotiations in Albany and sometimes with the city's own representatives in the state legislature. But city council speaker Peter Vallone helped us rally support in important Democratic and Republican circles, and both the state assembly and the state senate ultimately supported the plan.

I likened Safe Streets, Safe City to the Spruce Goose, Howard Hughes's oversize prototype for a military transport plane. It was large. It was impressive. Many thought it would never fly. But it finally got off the ground—and what a difference it made.

There was turbulence to come. The great diversity—economic,

racial, ethnic, religious—that made the city vibrant also delivered fresh challenges every day. But Safe Streets, Safe City gave us a map into the future, which turned out to be vitally important in pulling the city back from one of its most frustrating and damaging challenges, the scourge of violent crime.

*　　*　　*

It was always something in New York, where a tragic traffic accident could assume huge symbolic potency and burst overnight into major social conflict. At 8:20 p.m. on Monday, August 19, 1991, Yosef Lifsh, age twenty-two, was driving a station wagon west on President Street in the Crown Heights section of Brooklyn. His car was the last of three in the motorcade of Menachem Mendel Schneerson, grand rebbe of the Chabad-Lubavitch Hasidic sect. The rabbi was returning from his weekly visit to the grave of his late wife. The procession was led by an unmarked police car with its lights flashing.

Crossing Utica Avenue, where the light was yellow or red, depending on whom you believe, Lifsh's station wagon struck another car and careened onto the sidewalk, toppling a six-hundred-pound stone pillar and pinning two children against an iron grate. One of the children was seven-year-old Gavin Cato. The son of Guyanese immigrants, he was on the sidewalk near his apartment on President Street, repairing his bicycle chain. The other child, Gavin's seven-year-old cousin, Angela Cato, was also hurt.

By the time an EMS ambulance crew arrived at 8:23, Lifsh was being pulled out of the station wagon and beaten by three or four men. A crew from the Hatzolah ambulance corps, a volunteer service that operates in Jewish communities around the world, also arrived on the scene, as did a police car. The Hatzolah crew drove Lifsh from the scene while the EMS crew worked to pull Gavin and his cousin from the wreckage. Once EMS freed Gavin, they drove him to Kings County Hospital, arriving at

8:32. Gavin was pronounced dead soon after that. Volunteers from a second Hatzolah ambulance treated Angela Cato until a second city ambulance arrived and took her to the same hospital.

Rumors, most of which turned out not to be true, spread quickly through the neighborhood. That Lifsh was intoxicated. That Gavin Cato died because the Hatzolah ambulance crew refused to help non-Jews. That Lifsh was on a cell phone. That Lifsh lacked a valid driver's license. That police prevented people, including Gavin's father, from assisting with the rescue. Regardless of the truth, the rumors spread. Over the next couple of hours, the crowds grew. Soon several hundred young people were on the streets. Some rocks and bottles were thrown. Around 11:00 p.m., someone reportedly shouted, "Let's go to Kingston Avenue and get a Jew!" A group of black teenagers set off toward Kingston Avenue, a predominantly Jewish street several blocks west, vandalizing cars and tossing rocks and bottles as they went.

Shortly before midnight, a few blocks away on President Street, about twenty black teenagers surrounded Yankel Rosenbaum, a twenty-nine-year-old doctoral student from the University of Melbourne in Australia conducting research in the United States. The teens stabbed him several times in the back and beat him severely enough to fracture his skull. Before being taken to the hospital, Rosenbaum was able to identify one of his assailants, sixteen-year-old Lemrick Nelson Jr.

Mayor Dinkins and Commissioner Brown went to Crown Heights seeking to dispel some of the tension on the street. Their presence had no noticeable effect on the rioters, who rampaged late into the night. Rosenbaum died before dawn at Kings County Hospital. The New York State Health Department later decided that his death was a result of inadequate treatment by doctors in the hospital's emergency department, though the stab wounds, including one the doctors missed entirely, certainly didn't help his prognosis.

*   *   *

As the violence was erupting on the streets, I was at the home of Jeremy Travis, the police department's general counsel. The New York media were surprisingly slow to jump on the story, but we got a couple of reports from headquarters about what was going on.

The timing was especially unfortunate—and not just because of the steamy August heat. Friday, August 16, three days before Gavin Cato and Yankel Rosenbaum were killed, the NYPD's highly experienced, well-respected chief of department, Robert Johnston, had retired. His successor, David Scott, had gone on vacation, leaving Chief of Detectives Joseph Borelli as the acting chief of department.

I was available to help. I'd been precinct commander in Crown Heights. I knew the neighborhood. I had relationships with people on both sides of the uproar. But I had my orders: Commissioner Brown had told me directly that my responsibility as his first deputy commissioner did not include dealing with operational matters like this. That was the chief of department's job. Lee Brown made clear to me that those orders still applied even after Johnston handed over the position to Scott.

The first night of rioting led to a second night of rioting, which seemed to be hurtling toward a third. By Wednesday afternoon, the media were all over the story, emphasizing the senseless violence of it all. The Crown Heights riot was news around the world. People in the Jewish community were outraged. They called it a pogrom. People in the black community were outraged. The police, who had turned out in large numbers by then, seemed to lack a plan.

Joe Borelli did his best. David Scott was still vacationing. But Crown Heights was still teeming with gangs of young people running around, grabbing random victims, setting cars on fire, throwing rocks and bottles at police, and ripping open the occasional storefront and grabbing armloads of merchandise. Much of this was caught on camera and ended up on TV. Most of the rioters looked very young, thirteen- and fourteen-year-olds, with a few hardened adults in the mix. People on the street were shouting vile things: "Kill the Jews.... Hitler didn't do his job.... Get the cops."

The police appeared to be holding back. They were not moving aggressively into the crowds. When the police did act, their response seemed haphazard and poorly organized. They just looked lumpy out there. You had thirty-five-year-old uniformed officers carrying ten pounds of gear chasing teenagers in Nikes who knew the neighborhood better than the cops did. That's a losing footrace every time. If there was a clear strategy for crowd control, no one could seem to articulate it. The people running the operation seemed like captives of political paralysis. Timidity, I knew from my own experience with street disorder going back to the scarecrow days, was never a good way to regain control of out-of-control streets.

I think the police officials were all trying to second-guess the city's racial politics. This was a new time in New York. There was a black chief of department, David Scott. There was a black police commissioner, Lee Brown. There was a black mayor, David Dinkins. Some people said the police commanders were trying to read the political risks to their own careers. The biggest danger, police commanders may have calculated, was overreacting on the street. So they hardly reacted at all. No reality on the ground seemed to cut through this fog. *Newsday* columnist Murray Kempton summed it up like this: "Higher public office in New York is a bastion of ignorance that no fact can penetrate except as a rock thrown through your windshield."

At 4:45 p.m. on Wednesday, as the media was setting up for a third night of violence, Commissioner Brown was announcing that the streets of Crown Heights were finally under control. This turned out to be wishful thinking. After the press conference he was driven to P.S. 167, an elementary school on Eastern Parkway in the heart of Crown Heights, for a meeting with Mayor Dinkins. As the commissioner's car arrived at the elementary school, a group of young people broke away from the crowd, surrounded the vehicle, and began pelting it with rocks.

A 10-13, assist police officer, call for "Car One" was broadcast over the radio, and police came rushing to the scene. At least nine officers were injured in the melee. I heard that call come over, and I could hardly believe my ears. The police commissioner's car was under attack on the streets of Brooklyn? Regardless of my instructions, I thought I really had to act. I got in my car, and I drove out to Crown Heights.

I went to the school on Eastern Parkway where the mayor and the police commissioner were. I heard the commissioner exasperatedly telling someone in uniform, "These are kids! These are kids! Why can't we handle them?"

A good question, I thought.

After the meeting at P.S. 167, Mayor Dinkins visited the home of Gavin Cato, the young boy who had died. Outside the house, Dinkins used a bullhorn, trying unsuccessfully to calm the gathered crowd. Later that evening, the mayor visited eight of the injured officers at Kings County Hospital. At the hospital, the mayor and Milton Mollen, the deputy mayor for public safety, had a tense conversation with Lee Brown, questioning the effectiveness of his tactics and directing him to "take all steps necessary to end the violence."

"Do you want me to get involved in this?" I asked Commissioner Brown when we finally had a chance to speak privately.

"Yes," he said. "Yes."

I called a meeting of chiefs and commanders for the next

morning at seven o'clock in the first deputy commissioner's office at 1 Police Plaza.

"What the hell is going on here?" I asked quite pointedly. The vagueness and equivocation that I got in response were more than a little disturbing—though hardly surprising, given what had just occurred.

As far as I could tell, the mayor had made the previous day's visit to the Cato home with thoroughly inadequate security. I didn't want the mayor's detail to be the next one calling a 10-13. "Why didn't you put any cops on the roofs?" I asked the supervisors in the meeting.

"It's very dangerous," one of the chiefs answered.

"Too dangerous to protect the mayor?" I asked. "That's what we get paid for."

We quickly drew up a plan and put it into action that day. This was a basic take-back-the-streets operation. We brought fifty horses to the streets of Crown Heights. These are impressive animals, and the police mounted unit knew how to handle them. They generally do not get spooked.

We had two rows of patrol wagons as well. We moved the wagons and horses to wherever the disturbances were brewing. We would seal off one end of the street. By the time the kids ran in the opposite direction, we would have that end sealed off, too. At that point, we could pick them up one by one.

The streets were calm again in a matter of hours—and they stayed that way.

*   *   *

For years, people would debate what happened in Crown Heights and why. The good news was that we learned something there. And we didn't have to wait around for the two years it took Richard Girgenti, the state's criminal justice director, to complete his six-hundred-page report. Girgenti had some perfectly good insights about the senselessness of the violence and inadequacy of the police response, though his report did read like a bit of a political hit on the Dinkins administration. His biggest complaint about my performance was that I showed up too late to the riot. That was certainly true. But my hands were tied.

"Mayor Dinkins later acknowledged that the police had been using techniques for a peaceful demonstration, but not for violent civil unrest," the report concluded. "First Deputy Commissioner Raymond Kelly, not previously involved, assumed responsibility for devising more appropriate tactics."

Waiting for Girgenti to draw his conclusions would have been a waste of valuable time. After the riots, I asked Deputy Chief Louis Anemone to help put together an NYPD disorder-control guide so every officer on the scene of a disturbance would know exactly what to do. The plan included specific street formations and manpower charts and other nuts and bolts of urban riot control. The message was a practical one: instead of just swarming a neighborhood with cops, think strategically. Going forward, we would emphasize teamwork and mobility. The department acquired a new fleet of police vans that could carry one sergeant and eight officers to the scene of a disturbance and move them around as a team once they got there.

That technique and our mobile-team approach got its first serious test less than a year after Crown Heights and one full year before the Girgenti report. It happened on Monday, July 6, 1992, a week before the Democratic National Convention was set to open in New York. Three days earlier, in Manhattan's Washington Heights neighborhood, police officer Michael O'Keefe and two plainclothes partners surrounded and attempted to disarm a suspected drug dealer named Jose "Kiko" Garcia, who was carrying a fully loaded .38-caliber Smith & Wesson revolver. After a struggle in the lobby of an apartment building at 505 West 162nd Street, Officer O'Keefe shot Garcia twice, killing him.

The shooting appeared to be justified, but some people in Washington Heights were clearly upset. Dinkins went to the neighborhood to calm the rising tensions. He paid for Garcia's funeral. None of that seemed to have much effect. That Monday, a large part of the neighborhood erupted in violence around 7:30 p.m., when an angry crowd of about two hundred people was blocked from approaching the Thirty-Fourth Precinct station house, where O'Keefe was assigned. It was a scary night.

Lee Brown was out of town. I was acting commissioner. I went up there immediately. I could see fires burning on Broadway all the way from 135th Street to 160th Street. People shot out the streetlights. Others rushed into a sneaker store and came out with as many pairs as they could carry. Many other stores were looted as well. Teenagers on the streets were throwing bottles. Someone fired on a radio car. A police helicopter was hit by gunfire and had to return to base. An NYPD Emergency Service truck came along, spraying water on the burning cars. The whole neighborhood was in chaos.

The lessons of Crown Heights proved invaluable. Officers dispersed into vans and moved around the neighborhood, jumping out at the scene of any disturbances. The violence didn't stop instantly. It took several hours for things to calm down. One man died when he fell five stories from a rooftop at Audubon Avenue and 172nd Street while officers were chasing him. By dawn, dozens of people were in custody on charges ranging from disorderly conduct to arson. But our new methods proved themselves unmistakably on the streets of Washington Heights that night and became standard NYPD procedure from then on.

The rioting lasted one night—not three. I stayed in the area until dawn. What was surprising to me was how clean the streets were by 8:00 a.m. The Sanitation Department did a terrific job. Only in New York could you have a seventy-block riot at night and still have clean streets the next morning. I met with Mayor Dinkins at 8:00 a.m. at city hall and gave him a report.

Kiko Garcia wasn't the only police controversy that summer. The papers were also filled with reports of disgraced officer Michael Dowd, who'd spent the past six years robbing drug dealers in East New York with a crew of corrupt cops in Brooklyn's Seventy-Fifth Precinct. He then dealt some of the stolen cocaine in middle-class neighborhoods on Long Island.

It was a major embarrassment, and Mayor Dinkins felt he had to do something, which I understood. Lee Brown also asked me to do an investigation of the Dowd case. I produced a comprehensive report on the subject that we would later use as a guide for reforming our internal investigative processes. Dinkins created a group called the City of New York Commission to Investigate Allegations of Police Corruption and the Anticorruption Procedures of the Police Department. Chaired by deputy mayor and close Dinkins friend Milton Mollen, the group became known as the Mollen Commission. The panel was being described as the most extensive outside review of the police since the Knapp Commission of the 1970s. I later ended up testifying before the Mollen Commission as police commissioner. Dinkins also asked the city council to establish the Civilian Complaint Review Board, which I opposed. I testified against its creation, which to his credit Dinkins permitted me to do. I wasn't against oversight. I just didn't believe this model would work because the panel didn't have police department personnel involved in the investigations. I knew that such a structure would set up an adversarial relationship that would become more a political platform than any search for objective truth.

On August 3, 1992, Lee Brown announced he was stepping down as New York police commissioner. This wasn't because of rising crime or growing disorder. The crime numbers still weren't good, but they weren't quite as bad as they had been. Murders, which had peaked at 2,245 in 1990, dipped to 2,154 in 1991 and were on pace toward another decline for 1992.And for the first four months of the year, overall crime reports fell by 6.7 percent compared to the same period the previous year. People were crediting Safe Streets, Safe City for boosting the number of officers on foot patrol to 3,000 from 750, even though the program's big wave of new hiring wouldn't happen for another two years.

At a news conference at city hall, Brown announced he would be returning to Houston on September 1 to care for his wife, Yvonne, who was ill. "My family comes first," the outgoing commissioner said. That day, Dinkins announced that David Scott, the chief of department who'd stayed on vacation during the week of the Crown Heights riots, was retiring as well. He cited health reasons.

The mayor named me acting police commissioner. Scott, whose relationship with Brown apparently was not great, suddenly changed his mind and decided to stay.

*   *   *

I got the job for real on October 16, 1992, two years and nine months into the Dinkins administration, making me the thirty-seventh police commissioner of New York. I was fifty-one years old.

By any measure, the job was historic and enormous. I oversaw twenty-five thousand police officers in the largest department serving the largest city in the United States. My predecessors included such towering figures as Theodore Roosevelt—though, technically, the job title back then was "president of the police commission." Like many commissioners before me, I sat at what I was told was Roosevelt's desk, although I have to say I have never seen a picture of him sitting at it.

In his two years running the department, 1895 and 1896, the man who would become governor, acting secretary of the navy, vice president, and finally president made radical changes on the job. He appointed recruits based on their physical and mental qualifications—not their ethnic backgrounds, political affiliations, or social connections. He reorganized the Detective Bureau. He started a bicycle squad to ease traffic congestion. He opened a pistol-training school. He adopted the Bertillon system, a precursor of fingerprint identification. He instituted annual physical exams and regular inspections of firearms. He hired the first woman to work in police headquarters, Minnie Gertrude Kelly. He had telephones installed in the station houses. He invited big-time newspaper writers like Jacob Riis and Lincoln Steffens to tag along with him. Roosevelt even popped up on officers' late-night beats to make sure they were on duty, a stunt that produced glowing write-ups for him in the press.

Not bad for a two-year term.

But I didn't have much time for dwelling on history. We had some pressing issues staring us right in the face. One of them was making the NYPD more diverse. When I took over, the department was 11.5 percent black in a city with a black population of 25 percent. I knew we had to do better than that. My first full day as commissioner I went on WLIB radio, popular in the African American community, and spent forty minutes on *The Breakfast Club* with Art Whaley, taking calls from listeners and talking up police recruitment.

Fighting crime would always be our top priority, I said. But I was also committed to having a department as diverse as the city it served. "This is the first day, the first official day that I am police commissioner," I said. "It's nine o'clock in the morning. I think it shows my level of commitment and my level of concern.... My goal is to see if for once we can break the back of this 11.5 percent African American representation that has been our maximum representation level for nine years."

New York wasn't alone in facing this challenge. Police departments across the country were having trouble diversifying, either because the departments weren't welcoming to minority candidates, because the candidates weren't interested in the job, or because of lingering historical legacies of prejudice and discrimination. Clearly the effort would require real leadership from the top.

The applications started coming in.

At the same time, we were doing better with the crime numbers. The murder rate continued to dip, going down to 1,995 in 1992. We targeted subway beggars and squeegee men, homing in on quality-of-life offenses.

Back-loaded as it was, Safe Streets, Safe City still hadn't delivered the truly big burst of hiring it promised, but we put more and more of the cops we had out on the street, engaging with the community in a wider variety of ways. Crack never fully went away, but the epidemic did show its first signs of easing, which was fortunate and sad at the same time. Part of the explanation was that so many addicts were dead or in prison, but I also think the drug had lost some of its allure on the street. Crackheads had become a subject of ridicule and derision. They were seen as the lowest people on the block—physically violent, mentally deranged, and so desperate they would do anything to get high. "I may be a whore," you'd hear someone say on an especially ragged street. "But I'm no crack whore."

By comparison, "a bong and a forty" were suddenly gaining popularity again.

*   *   *

On Friday, February 26, 1993, when I'd been police commissioner a little more than four months, something happened that no one was remotely prepared for—not the city, not the police department, not the FBI or the CIA.

The modern age of Islamic jihadist terrorism came to New York.

An explosion occurred in the parking garage below the World Trade Center at 12:18 p.m. I was in my office at 1 Police Plaza when the call came in. I jumped in my car and reached the Trade

Center by 12:25. The initial reports said, "Likely transformer explosion."

That must be a mighty big transformer, I thought when I saw how much smoke was already in the air on West Street. I was impressed by how quickly the first responders were on the scene. This was less than ten minutes after the explosion, and scores of police, firefighters, and paramedics were already out of their vehicles and rushing toward the center's twin towers, the underground concourse, and the parking garage. Five minutes later, that number was well into the hundreds. The whole neighborhood was filled with sirens and flashing red lights.

We set up a temporary command center in a ballroom at the Vista International Hotel, which was connected to the twin towers in 3 World Trade Center. I was standing on a chair directing people when someone said sharply, "We have to evacuate now. The engineers say the building could collapse."

I wasn't waiting to hear that twice. We left the ballroom immediately. It was cold outside. There was a light snow falling. But we walked out to the sidewalk, where I led a multiagency meeting to assemble an initial strategy. The city's Office of Emergency Management was within the NYPD at the time. As we spoke, the tenants were streaming down from the towers on their own. We had reports of stairways filled with thick, dark smoke. Other people were stuck in elevators. Our Aviation Unit plucked some people off the roof. As the people were escaping the buildings, firefighters and police officers were heading up the north and south towers, aiding with the evacuation, directing people down, trying to pry open some of the stuck elevator doors.

In all, six people were killed in the attack. Bob Kirkpatrick, Steven Knapp, Bill Macko, and Monica Rodriguez Smith, who was pregnant, were having lunch in their basement Port Authority office. John DiGiovanni was a salesman who happened to be in the parking garage when the bomb exploded. Wilfredo Mercado was at his desk checking in food deliveries for Windows on the World restaurant. His body was found by police seventeen days later in the rubble. He was still in his chair. One thousand and forty-two people were injured that day, including eighty-eight firefighters, thirty-five police officers, and one EMS worker. Most of the injuries to first responders were from smoke inhalation and falling broken glass, but others were more serious. The terrain was difficult, causing broken kneecaps, ankles, and facial bones. One firefighter, Kevin Shea, was attempting to reach trapped victims when he fell into a massive crater, badly injuring himself.

Fairly quickly, the investigators discounted the whole transformer idea, mostly because of the size of the explosion and the fact that there was no electrical machinery nearby that seemed capable of producing such a blast. I went down and looked at the hole on level B-2 of the parking garage myself. The crater measured nearly one hundred feet wide and went three levels up. A far more disturbing narrative gradually took shape. No credible group claimed immediate responsibility, but as the investigators began combing through the wreckage and debris that afternoon, the explosion looked more and more intentional. No perpetrators waited around. The scene bore some similarities to recent terror attacks in the Middle East, where zealots would enter a bus or a marketplace and blow themselves up. We didn't yet know exactly what we were facing, but I immediately called for tighter security around the region's airports, hotels, business centers, and major tourist attractions, putting the city on a level of alert higher than at any time since the Persian Gulf War. We put extra people on the bridges and tunnels and in the subway.

That evening, I had a conversation with a building engineer who'd been trapped in an elevator and had managed after several hours to cut himself out with a key. By then people were asking whether someone might have intended to knock one building into the other, toppling both of them. The engineer was adamant. "It can't happen," he told me without an ounce of doubt in his voice. "The way those buildings are constructed, there is just no way. Those buildings could never come down."

Later that night, Veronica and I walked outside our apartment in Battery Park City, a few hundred yards from the towers, and stared at the darkened World Trade Center from several different angles. It was eerie. Those towers were never dark. We were still looking when the lights came back on.

I knew not to read too much into that, but it was encouraging nonetheless.

We held a press conference the following afternoon, Saturday, with Governor Mario Cuomo, New York FBI chief James Fox, and other officials from the fire department, police department, and FBI, whose agents took immediate charge of the investigation. Mayor Dinkins was on a trade mission in Japan, but the first deputy mayor, Norman Steisel, was there. It was Cuomo who first shook off the investigators' natural hedging and caveats. "There is an immense crater," the governor said. The damage, he continued, "looks like a bomb. It smells like a bomb. It's probably a bomb."

We were already working on the theory that the bomb had been brought into the garage in a vehicle that then exploded. The first big break in the investigation came on Sunday. I was standing outside the Trade Center in my leather jacket when I saw a group of city police detectives and FBI agents walking out of the garage with what looked like a piece of scrap metal.

"A differential from a truck engine," someone explained to me. I'm not an expert on truck engines. I learned that the differential is the part of the transmission that allows the outer drive wheel to rotate faster than the inner drive wheel during a turn. Whatever. What made this differential so important was what was imprinted on it.

NYPD bomb squad detective Donald Sadowy, who had graduated from Brooklyn's Automotive High School, was sifting through the debris when he found this engine part and knew it might contain a vehicle identification number. With that number, investigators were able to trace a yellow Ryder truck back to a rental agency in Jersey City. The renter, a young man named Mohammed Salameh, had reported the truck stolen and returned for his $400 deposit. He was taken into custody at the rental agency. Finding and identifying the blown-up truck part, then tracking down the driver—that was the key step in cracking the case.

At the center of the plot, investigators determined, were a militant Islamic organization called al-Qaeda and a young man named Ramzi Yousef. Born in Kuwait, he had spent time in an al-Qaeda terror training camp in Pakistan, where in 1991 he began planning an attack in the United States. This seemed like an utterly unique story when we first heard it. At that time we were completely unaware of how other, similar stories of Islamic fundamentalism and violent radicalism would come to affect the future of New York.

Ramzi Yousef recruited his uncle, senior al-Qaeda member Khalid Sheikh Mohammed, to help finance and organize the plot. Yousef arrived illegally at John F. Kennedy International Airport on September 1, 1992. He carried a false Iraqi passport and claimed political asylum. He was allowed into the country and given a hearing date. He rented an apartment in Jersey City and began scoping out locations to attack, settling on the World Trade Center as an iconic symbol of capitalism and the West. He phoned Sheikh Omar Abdel Rahman, a fiery blind cleric who preached at the Al-Farooq mosque in Brooklyn. With the blind sheikh's blessing, Yousef began gathering the ingredients for a 1,500-pound urea-nitrate, hydrogen-gas-enhanced explosive device. A bomb that large, placed just right, he believed, could topple the north tower into the south tower, bringing both towers crashing to the ground.

On the morning of the bombing, a Friday, Yousef and a Jordanian friend, Eyad Ismail, drove the rented Ryder truck into the World Trade Center parking garage. They arrived around noon and parked on the B-2 level. They got out of the truck. Yousef ignited a twenty-foot fuse. He and Ismail fled. Later that day, Yousef got a ride to Kennedy Airport, where he used falsified travel documents and escaped on a flight to Pakistan.

One by one, suspects were captured, mostly from abroad. In October 1993, Salameh, Nidal Ayyad, Mahmud Abouhalima, and Ahmad Ajaj went on trial at U.S. District Court in Manhattan on charges of conspiracy, explosive destruction of property, and interstate transportation of explosives. All four were convicted in March 1994 and sentenced to life in prison.

Back in Pakistan, Ramzi Yousef continued planning terror attacks, including the bombing of Philippine Airlines Flight 434 and, with his uncle Khalid, the so-called Bojinka plot. This was an elaborate three-phase plan that included assassinating Pope John Paul II, bombing eleven airliners flying from Asia to the United States, and crashing a plane into CIA headquarters in Fairfax County, Virginia. In 1995, a tip from a South African Muslim man named Ishtiaq Parker led agents from the Pakistani intelligence service and the U.S. Bureau of Diplomatic Security to Yousef. They went to the Su-Casa Guest House in Islamabad, which was owned by Osama bin Laden, where Yousef was arrested while trying to set a bomb inside a child's doll.

Yousef was extradited to the United States. In two separate trials at U.S. District Court in Manhattan, he was convicted of being involved in the Flight 434, Bojinka, and World Trade Center plots.

"Yes," he declared in court, "I am a terrorist, and I am proud of it. And I support terrorism as long as it was against the U.S. government and against Israel, because you are more than terrorists. You are the one who invented terrorism." He was sentenced to three life sentences, one for each plot.

His uncle Khalid wasn't captured until 2003. In the intervening years, Khalid would remain an active plotter and funder of international terrorist attacks, including 9/11.

* * *

I learned some larger lessons from the 1993 World Trade Center bombing. Everyone did.

We learned how dangerous the threat of radical Islamic terrorism could be. We learned that these weren't random individuals in solo acts of violence. This was a network. It might be loosely organized. It might have many tentacles. But it did have some kind of organizational structure and an impressive ability to plan. We had no idea yet how well funded the organization was or how extensive it might become or how grand its aspirations were. But it was capable of training operatives in far-off countries like Pakistan and Afghanistan and slipping the attackers into America and other countries of the West. I also learned how little information the New York City Police Department had about these and similar threats. With the FBI running the investigation, we knew only what they told us, and they didn't tell us much. There was a Joint Terrorism Task Force at the center of the investigation, and a handful of NYPD detectives were part of that. But the FBI was very much in charge. They held the information closely, and they seemed to like it that way. That grated on me more than a little. I was the police commissioner of New York City. New York City was the site of the attack. I wanted daily reports, hourly reports— I wanted to know everything that was happening in this important investigation. I wanted a strong voice when major decisions were being made. I'm not sure anyone was purposely trying to hide things from us, but they certainly weren't too forthcoming. I didn't like the arrangement, but that was how cases like this one were handled in that era, and I wasn't quite sure what to do about it yet.

*   *   *

In the spring of 1993, I got a call from the White House. It was Bernard Nussbaum, counsel to President Clinton. He had a question for me. "You have any interest in being FBI director?"

It was not a call I had expected or a question I had a ready answer to. I knew the Clinton administration was trying to replace FBI director William Sessions, who'd been appointed by President Ronald Reagan and had been criticized in a scathing internal ethics report that was prepared in the final days of George H. W. Bush's administration. The report questioned Sessions's use of perks like FBI aircraft and armored limousines.

Though I'd never worked in the FBI—or anywhere else in the federal government outside of the Marine Corps—I was certainly flattered by the call. I was also floored by it.

"Let me think about it," I told Nussbaum.

I'd had regular contact with Jim Fox in the FBI's New York office and with the Joint Terrorism Task Force, which the FBI controlled, about the World Trade Center attack. I'm not sure whether that's what sparked the call. Nussbaum left me with the impression that people in the Clinton administration had been impressed by how I responded to the bombing.

But I felt like I was just getting started as New York police commissioner. I had a heaping pile of issues on my plate—the terror aftermath, the Mollen Commission, a big debate over what kind of firearms police should carry, the need to keep pushing the crime numbers down. David Dinkins was running for reelection. He'd put a lot of faith in me.

I retuned Nussbaum's call. I told him how much I appreciated the inquiry—but no, thanks. I had too much to do in New York. I had to follow through on my commitment. I wasn't ready to leave yet. Louis Freeh, who was a federal judge in Manhattan and a friend of mine, became FBI director.

*   *   *

For years, New York police officers had been complaining that they were outgunned in the urban arms race. With drug gangs carrying Uzis and terrorists packing who knew what, the cops sometimes felt like they were showing up with peashooters and cap guns. Many were eager to trade their standard-issue six-shot .38-caliber service revolvers for 9-millimeter semiautomatic handguns.

At the same time, New York state assemblyman Joseph Lentol of Brooklyn was pushing a bill in Albany that would essentially have allowed police officers to carry whatever weapons they liked. Such a law would have been disastrous. A police department is not a mob of self-armed vigilantes. It should be a professional law enforcement agency with standards, balance, and rules. By 1993, I was ready to take a comprehensive look at the issue.

There was some resistance to the idea of changing to semi-automatics from the old-timers. They argued that revolvers were more reliable, easier to keep clean, and less likely to jam. They weren't entirely wrong about that. Critics in other cities had also found that some officers had a tendency to overshoot when they were given faster-acting weapons that held at least twice as many rounds.

We conducted extensive testing at the Rodman's Neck shooting range. We tried a 9-millimeter pilot program in the Organized Crime Control Bureau and the Emergency Service Unit and found there was no overshooting. I became convinced. We had to bring our weaponry into the modern era. With proper training, the police could deal with the jamming issue and learn to shoot only as many times as needed. In August 1993, three 9-millimeter automatics were approved—the Glock 19, the SIG Sauer P226, and the Smith & Wesson 5946. We also limited the ammunition to ten-round magazines.

When we made the announcement about the new firearm regulations, I explained that the reasoning behind the change was both ballistic and psychological. "Officers feel more secure, and that's something that can't be discounted."

I wouldn't say the new guns arrived with no negative repercussions. But on balance, making the switch was the right thing to do.

*   *   *

Mayor Dinkins faced a very tough reelection campaign in 1993. Republican Rudolph Giuliani, the former United States attorney who'd been beaten by Dinkins four years earlier, was running again. With a strong assist from New York's tabloid newspapers, the *Daily News* and the *Post*, Giuliani succeeded in portraying Dinkins as passive, unfocused, and vain. I didn't agree with Mayor Dinkins on everything. His core constituents were not always the police department's strongest supporters—nor were some of the mayor's closest aides, for that matter. But on the important issues related to policing, Mayor Dinkins supported the department. I believe he got a bum rap. As commissioner, I felt supported by him.

He started Safe Streets, Safe City, ultimately putting thousands of new police officers on the streets of New York. In the final thirty-six months of his term, he ushered in a crime decline that ended a violent thirty-year spiral and lasted for decades to come. During that period, crime dropped more swiftly, in actual numbers and by percentage, than at any point in modern New York history up until then.

Throughout the reelection campaign and even later, Mayor

Dinkins never got proper credit for this. Most of the benefits of Safe Streets, Safe City, his signature law enforcement achievement, didn't happen during that term. The new police hiring wasn't scheduled to take root until the latter part of 1993 and 1994. Some of the mayor's advisers thought he might even back away from hiring extra police after he won a second term.

When the *New York Times* endorsed Dinkins for reelection, the paper's editorial board made a positive comment about his selection of me as police commissioner. But Dinkins never got the chance to reap the rewards of the policies he helped create. On Tuesday, November 2, 1993, Giuliani beat him by two percentage points, becoming the city's first Republican mayor in a generation.

It was a hard-fought race, and Giuliani ran an impressive, disciplined campaign. However, much of what happened next was set in motion by David Dinkins. Murders were down again in 1993, dropping to 1,946. When 2,800 new police officers hit the streets in January 1994, he wasn't mayor anymore. Giuliani was. Others, many others, took the credit.

The new mayor appointed his own police commissioner, William Bratton.

CHAPTER SIX

Haitian Heat

I had come to see the villain in charge.

On a bright Tuesday morning, October 4, 1994, I walked into a mustard-yellow building in the center of Port-au-Prince, headquarters of the famously violent and corrupt national police. These thugs with badges had been terrorizing the Haitian people for the past three years, as their predecessors had on and off for centuries. I was there to meet Lieutenant Colonel Michel-Joseph Francois, the department's dreaded chief and, it was widely believed, a valuable friend to drug traffickers across the Caribbean. I was eager to look Francois in the eye and explain to him with perfect clarity that a new day had dawned at last.

Haiti was occupied by twenty thousand American troops, some on ships off the island but most already on land. Operation Uphold Democracy, the effort was called. After three years of slow diplomacy following a 1991 military coup, the U.S. forces had come to remove the murderous military regime of Lieutenant General Raoul Cédras, who'd grabbed power from the democratically elected president Jean-Bertrand Aristide. Two weeks before I helicoptered in from Camp Santiago in Puerto Rico, the American forces had been on the verge of invading. Planes were literally in the air when former president Jimmy Carter, who'd been dispatched by President Bill Clinton, persuaded General Cédras to step aside. Colin Powell, the former chairman of the Joint Chiefs of Staff, was involved as well. Now the Haitian people nervously awaited the October 15 return of Aristide, a forty-one-year-old Catholic priest turned politician.

I was in the country as director of the International Police Monitors, part of the U.S.-led Multinational Interim Force in Haiti: eight hundred police officers from twenty countries around the world with a couple of hundred interpreters and a company from the U.S. Army's Tenth Mountain Division. We were a truly international monitoring force, with police officers on loan from Poland, Israel, Jordan, Belgium, Argentina, the Philippines, and the CARICOM nations of the Caribbean. There was an American component, though not a large one, since the United States has no national police force. In addition to the Tenth Mountain Division, we had a handful of Marine Corps reservists and some former U.S. police officers who were recruited, somewhat haphazardly, by DynCorp International, a private military contractor. We all carried weapons, but we made clear to everyone that we were not in Haiti to perform actual police duties.

Instead, we had the daunting responsibility of reforming and reconstituting what was left of the Haitian police, turning these bitter and dispirited *ofisye polis* into a democratic force. In a place so out of control, though, it was often impossible to avoid some policing—of the citizens and of the police. Truly, there was no one else to do it.

As I walked into the police headquarters that morning, I had Mario LaPaix, a major in the U.S. Marine Corps Reserves and a New York City employee, as my guide and translator. He was born in Haiti and spoke some French and Creole. I knew him from the marine reserves. Mario was the one who'd first called me about coming to Haiti.

After I'd left the police department at the end of the Dinkins administration, I'd had a brief stint at New York University teaching leadership—thanks to Jay Oliva, the university's president and a fellow Manhattan College alum—before taking a position as president of the corporate intelligence firm IGI, Investigative Group International. The firm was chaired by Terry Lenzner, a former federal prosecutor and Senate Watergate counsel. I enjoyed the private sector. The firm was staffed by smart, sophisticated people. But when Mario reached me at IGI in late September of 1994, nine months after I'd left the police department, I was definitely open to the idea of a new adventure. The State Department, he said, was looking for someone to be in charge of an entity they were putting together called the International Police Monitors. No one in Washington wanted the U.S. military to be the police for an all-black population in Haiti. "It wouldn't look good," Mario said. The notion instead was to bring in a cadre of professional police officers from around the world and have them monitor the Haitian police.

That sounded like a fascinating challenge to me. It sounded so fascinating, in fact, that I barely even considered what it might mean to spend six months in Haiti, away from my family, away from my other work, away from anything approaching normalcy. When the State Department agreed to hire me through IGI, I said yes immediately, and things moved quickly from there.

I wanted the multitalented Paul Browne to come as my right-hand man. A former news reporter in Albany and aide to New York senator Daniel Patrick Moynihan, Paul had gone to the NYPD, where he wrote speeches for Commissioner Lee Brown and then became my spokesman and close aide when I became commissioner. Paul had left the NYPD when I did at the end of the Dinkins administration and was working at the *Daily News*. I couldn't imagine going to Haiti without him. I called Mort Zuckerman, the paper's owner, to see if Paul could take a leave of absence. Mort said no. Paul resigned the next day. I reached Port-au-Prince just ten days after I had gotten Mario's call, and Paul quickly followed.

*   *   *

When Mario and I got upstairs, the feared Lieutenant Colonel Francois was nowhere to be found. At that very moment, he was fleeing the country, crossing the border into the neighboring Dominican Republic. The Haitian people were so angry with him, a huge mob had descended on his ridgetop home and torn it apart with their bare hands, one floorboard and roof tile at a time. *Dépeçage*, that ritual destruction is called in Haiti. It's made easier by the country's lax building codes. Things are often halfway falling down to start with.

The colonel's replacement, a Haitian police major, did not seem thrilled by our arrival. The words "international" and "monitors" sounded like nothing but trouble to him. He immediately rejected the joint patrols I was proposing. He fumed that the U.S. military had just detained seven of his men. Did I understand, he wanted to know, that angry mobs with machetes were gathering outside right now, intent on revenge against the police?

Our meeting lasted more than three hours. As I listened to the major's numerous complaints, grumbling officers wandered in and out of the room, seething with a variety of American-directed insults. Outside, I could hear people chanting in Creole.

I did what I could to lower the temperature. I told the major that the handcuffing of his men had been a mistake. It had happened during a chaotic American military raid at the headquarters of a violent Haitian paramilitary group. But I refused to back down from the joint patrols. Small steps, steady steps, all in the same direction. It's always impressive how much can be accomplished simply by refusing to stop. In the face of opposition, I have often found that effective. "We must do this," I told him.

Finally, the major relented, on the condition that I would join the first patrol with one of his lieutenants. The lieutenant and I, dressed in bulletproof vests, walked a twelve-block loop along some of Port-au-Prince's rougher streets. We did not know what to expect, but I was convinced this was the best approach. If police are going to have an impact, they have to be present and visible and reliably there. Otherwise it's too easy for crime and disorder—even anarchy, in a place like Haiti—to take hold.

We got plenty of glares on the sidewalks but also some cheers and handshakes—and, thankfully, no flying bullets or machete blades. The international monitoring of the Haitian police had officially begun.

*   *   *

The six months I spent in Haiti were some of the most demanding and exhilarating of my life. Just being on the island was a constant challenge. The poorest nation in the Western Hemisphere, it had suffered from every imaginable social ill—severe overpopulation in the cities, a chaotic economy, terrible housing, constant power outages, dirty water, frequent earthquakes and landslides, and a sour aroma that constantly hung in the air. Raw sewage? Garbage in the street? Mold and mildew? Dead bodies left for the pigs? Any and all of the above, depending on the day of the week and the corner you chose.

I loved the place, despite all its problems, and I especially loved the people, who were open and warm and decent, even as they sometimes did inexplicable things. I had never been in any place—not Vietnam, certainly not New York—quite so anarchic and raw. In New York, we'd spoken often of the importance of social order. This was disorder to the tenth power. The electricity was on maybe half the time. There were no sewers. There didn't appear to be traffic laws. Breathing was a constant struggle because of the low-hanging clouds of dust and who knows what else. You didn't want to drink even the bottled water in Haiti. One day, there were twenty-one murders in Port-au-Prince. The next day, there were zero. No one could seem to explain either number. The poverty was so grinding, the oppression was so thick, even the most fundamental principles of modern policing seemed like foreign concepts here. Without a doubt, the Haitian police needed a top-to-bottom culture change. There would be no torturing prisoners, no taking bribes, no behaving like the street-level auxiliary of the Haitian Army, doing the daily dirty work of the brutal military regime. One of our first orders of business: disbanding the armed civilian *attachés*, quasi-official vigilantes who seemed to operate with no rules at all.

Before we could get started, we had to pick out a location for our headquarters. We needed somewhere that could serve as both a command center and a place to sleep. We drove out to an old Club Med. The trip was like a sightseeing tour of everything that was wrong with Haiti. Tires were burning on the side of the road. Bandits were stopping cars and shaking people down. The potholes were just as unforgiving. The Club Med, when we finally got there, was too isolated and too far from the city. We settled into the abandoned and dilapidated Hotel Villa St. Louis on Avenida John Brown in the heart of the capital instead.

I began meeting with William Swing, the smart and supportive U.S. ambassador to Haiti. In his career in the diplomatic corps, he'd been in the People's Republic of the Congo, Liberia, and some other challenging corners of sub-Saharan Africa. He knew what we were up against. Haiti, he said, was as tough as anywhere he'd been. The local police were terribly equipped. They had no working radios. Their wrecked patrol cars were often sitting up on concrete blocks, the perfect mechanical embodiment of the cops' own work ethic. To be fair, the issue wasn't only laziness. Many of the officers had nowhere to live. In the past, they'd gotten by on whatever they could collect in bribes, but those had dried up. Now many were too scared to go out on patrol. I'd never seen that before, cops too frightened to go outside. The whole broken department needed to be rebuilt and rebranded, right down to the mustard-yellow color scheme. That was the color of army facilities, a connection we had to break any way we could. We ordered the police buildings painted light blue.

As the foreign police contingents gradually reported for duty on the island, we kept the national groups together, sending each one to a different part of Haiti to patrol with local police. Having contact with these outside professionals would gradually acclimate the Haitians to modern law enforcement techniques. That was my strategy, anyway. The head of each foreign contingent stayed back at the St. Louis, so I had immediate access to each group in the field. I kept moving around the country by helicopter and truck to the various local outposts.

Trouble could pop up anywhere. One morning, I got word that two hundred people had surrounded a police station in Cité Soleil, Port-au-Prince's most violent slum, frequently described by the United Nations as the most dangerous place in the world. I rushed to the scene. I couldn't say their grievances weren't legitimate, but they quieted as soon as we walked up. "We are here and things are changing," I announced through an interpreter. That was a message at least some of the people were willing to hear. The crowd backed away from the building and some of them began to cheer. Someone was going to police the capital's neighborhoods, and they would need a building to do it from.

Days later, I returned to the Cité Soleil police station. When I got there, another mob had gathered outside. Again I wasn't quite sure why they were angry, and no one could explain it to me with clarity. Again I assumed their grievance was probably legitimate. They were armed with machetes and crowbars, and they were about to take the building apart, another example of

Haitian dépeçage. As I approached the crowd, they lowered their tools and weapons. Quietly, respectfully, they nodded, smiled, and dispersed. No one put up any kind of a fight. They didn't have to. They knew I'd be gone and they'd still be there. And when I came back the next day, the Cité Soleil police station was little more than a giant pile of powdered cement.

Another day, beside a row of tumbledown shacks, we passed a procession of people leading a young boy whose hands were tied behind his back. Someone was carrying a bike. We stopped our truck and got out.

"What's going on?" I asked through an interpreter as unthreateningly as I could.

"He stole the bicycle," said one of the men in the crowd. "We have to hang him."

It was said so matter-of-factly, at first I wasn't sure if the man was being serious. But he was. The kid had stolen a bicycle, so he would be killed. "We have to," the man said when I raised an eyebrow.

"You're not going to kill anyone," I said calmly but firmly. "Not today."

And they didn't. We put the boy in our truck and drove him out of there.

Despite their occasional violent outbursts, Haitians could be extraordinarily warm and friendly. I often played the conga drum with Haitian workers at the St. Louis Hotel. They immediately respected authority. When I said "Don't," they didn't. But there was such a deep tradition of curbstone justice, I don't think they believed they were doing anything wrong. Quite possibly, there'd be another bicycle thief—and a successful hanging—tomorrow.

As we made our way through tense urban ghettos and along muddy country roads, we kept running across scenes like these. On one busy block, there was a large truck piled high with charcoal. A suspected *attaché* was cowering in fear at the top. A crowd had surrounded the truck, and they were yelling "Kill, kill," as people tried to scamper up and pull the man down.

We stopped the Jeep. Paul Browne and I got out. We climbed to the top of the pile and rescued the suspected *attaché*, putting him in the Jeep with us and driving him to at least temporary safety.

Was he a good guy, a bad guy, or something in between? We had no idea. Did the crowd have every right to be angry with him? Perhaps. But I wasn't going to stand by idly while a mob killed someone, even if in their eyes there was understandable cause. Sometimes, it seemed, we were training the Haitian people as much as their police.

The prisons were a special challenge. In general, the conditions were deplorable, especially at the municipal lockup in Port-au-Prince. The jail was more like Attica in 1971. One day during my time in Haiti, five hundred prisoners rioted there. Seven inmates were killed. The others banged tins in their cells and started fires with anything they could burn. They were looking for retribution against the guards. The guards had obviously been very heavy-handed, and now that dynamic had begun to change. It was a very scary place.

I arrived at the prison with an Argentine police officer. We made our way inside and then out onto a catwalk in the cell block. The inmates started going crazy. Was it me or the Argentine? Were they happy to see us, or did our presence make them angrier? The whole scene was just so chaotic, it was impossible to decipher the mood. On balance, I believe they were just desperately grateful that outsiders, foreigners, anyone who might have some authority was finally paying attention.

Intermingled with all parts of life in Haiti were the ancient potions, blessings, and curses of voodoo. African slaves, who were brought to Haiti by the French to work the sugarcane fields, carried many of those rituals with them. Though many Haitians were forced to convert to Catholicism in the 1700s and 1800s, the old ways never really disappeared. "Ninety percent of Haitians are Catholic," someone explained to me. "One hundred percent believe in voodoo."

In mid-November, a Haitian soldier named College Francois, who worked as a bodyguard at the American embassy, robbed an embassy payroll car. He shot all three men in the car—his own embassy coworkers—before escaping with $59,000 in cash and checks. Two of the embassy workers died immediately. We got to the hospital in time to interview the third man through an interpreter before he, too, died. "It was College Francois," he told us in the emergency room.

We launched a manhunt—interviewing witnesses, putting flyers on cars, doing everything we could think of to find Francois. My son Jim, who had come down to see how I was getting on, even joined the search.

Several weeks later, Francois went to see a *houngan*, a male voodoo priest, near Jacmel in southern Haiti. He told the houngan that he wanted a disappearing potion. The houngan offered to be helpful.

"Come back tomorrow," he told College Francois. "Come in your underwear. Bring a dead goat. Bring the money, and we'll do business. No guns."

The next day, Francois returned. Underwear. Dead goat. Twenty-nine thousand dollars. No gun.

The houngan grabbed College Francois, tied him up, took the money, and turned him over to us.

Where else but Haiti could something like this occur? Francois was twenty-five years old. He'd used computers and flown in helicopters. He'd been in the army and worked at the U.S. embassy. And his escape plan still involved a houngan, a dead goat, and disappearing potion.

The only disappearing he did was off to prison.

Once, outside Port-au-Prince, Paul Browne encountered a woman who had narrowly escaped being stoned to death by angry neighbors who accused her of being a witch. They claimed she was responsible for a rash of infant deaths. They believed she would fly at night from house to house, sucking the life out of babies.

As we kept encountering these otherworldly dramas, officials kept coming down from Washington. The visitors included top State Department people like Richard Clarke, Michael Sheehan, Strobe Talbott, and Bob Gelbard, the assistant secretary of state for international narcotics and law enforcement. Drugs and thugs, we called Gelbard's unit. Many visitors—not these four—would go to see Ambassador Swing at the U.S. embassy or at his elegant ambassador's residence and not see the real Haiti. When I received people, I preferred taking them to Cité Soleil, where they would get a far grittier eyeful of Haitian poverty and despair. That was Haiti, people walking miles to get water, sharing the roads with the skinniest pigs in the world. We might see a live dépeçage or maybe a bloodsucking woman flying from rooftop to rooftop. Anything was possible in Haiti.

*   *   *

The national groups represented in the monitoring force were as different from each other as you could imagine, as was the expertise they brought. Different cultures, different attitudes, different levels of training. Our multinational force spoke six different languages. The Belgians were highly efficient. The Jordanians were constantly on edge. We had a contingent of special-forces soldiers from Poland—large, fair-haired fighters in excellent physical shape. Unlike most of the others, they carried assault rifles. At a couple of locations where the local police commanders were being uncooperative, I sent the Polish soldiers in with instructions to just stand there. Say nothing. Do nothing. Just stand there beside the commander and watch. It was highly unnerving. Their mere presence was enough to fundamentally alter the dynamic. Those Poles knew how to make a point. One day, just to show they could, the Polish contingent decided to skip the door and climb up the front wall of their four-story hotel. They did it in near-perfect unison.

Twice a day we tried to have meetings with all the contingent heads. Veronica couldn't believe what those meetings were like when she came down for a weekend visit. Everyone gathered in a room next to my bedroom. The meeting room was its own multicultural experiment. Everything you said had to be translated into five other languages. Every sentence was followed by a strange buzzing echo as the translators repeated what you'd just said. We had no headsets, no microphones, no modern technology. Just everybody whispering in different languages, trying to be heard.

Truly, I'd never been anywhere like Haiti. If you're bored, wait five minutes. Something bizarre will occur. On December 26, some Haitian soldiers had gone to the Port-au-Prince army depot demanding back pay they were owed. A Haitian general heard them shouting to a clerk and panicked. He locked himself in his office and began shooting through the door with a machine gun. He hit several soldiers, including some of his own security guards.

The soldiers who'd come for their money ripped open a gun locker and grabbed a pile of rifles. That's when they ran into a contingent of American troops.

The U.S. soldiers responded with a firefight, shooting several Haitian soldiers and wounding some other people, too. When I got there, it was still an active shooting scene. People were bleeding. I was carrying bodies out. This was far more like what I remembered from Vietnam than anything resembling normal police work.

When the shooting finally ended, the U.S. troops grabbed the soldiers they believed were responsible, tied their hands behind their backs, put blindfolds over their eyes, and transported them to a warehouse. This made a bad situation considerably worse.

When I finally arrived at the warehouse, the Haitian soldiers were still tied and blindfolded, several hours after they had first been grabbed.

"What is this?" I asked the commander from the Tenth Mountain Division.

He had no idea that this wasn't standard police practice. He was used to dealing with prisoners of war. I knew that he and his troops had been in Somalia, and I think they were still traumatized. I emphasized to the soldier that it wasn't a good idea to keep unpaid Haitian soldiers tied up for hours like rodeo calves. "You build a lot of unnecessary resentment that way," I explained.

Then there was Mardi Gras. The pre-Lenten celebration fell that year at the very end of February. We knew Mardi Gras could be an especially wild time in Haiti. Those three nights of dancing, drinking, voodoo, and assorted other dusk-to-dawn debauchery usually left many dead bodies behind. Mardi Gras in Haiti was the perfect time for seeking retribution and settling scores. I was committed to making this year different. I summoned most of our monitoring crew.

Altogether, we had 240 beat-up U.S. Army trucks called CUCVs. They were pieces of junk, but they ran. We took those vehicles and lined them up along the main parade route a block or so apart. We had two or three monitors standing on the back of every truck, in sight of each other, their yellow hats that we all wore plainly visible above the teeming crowds. I wanted the message to be clear: someone was watching. None of our officers had any real problems. No killings were reported at that year's celebration.

* * *

Our mission was set to end on March 31, 1995.

All peacekeeping responsibilities were being transferred from the Multinational Interim Force to the United Nations Mission in Haiti. Going forward, they'd have the job of overseeing the Haitian police and making transition changes permanent. We had made a lot of progress. Everyone had seen it. In those six months, Haitian police officers were learning to be police officers in the modern sense of the term. They had been out on patrol with law enforcement professionals from around the world. Their supervisors had been taught what it means to have standards and live up to them. Many of the officers were eager students and seemed proud of the progress they had made. Others considered the approach too hard, too dangerous, or just not something they wanted to do, and they melted away quickly.

While we were there, we did so much more than monitor the police. We saved lives. We cleared out prisons. We interrupted countless acts of vigilante violence. I don't kid myself; we certainly didn't end those outbursts for good. But we delivered new equipment. We improved local facilities. We spread a lot of light-blue paint. We taught some basic human rights principles to police officers—veterans and recruits—who had never heard of those concepts before. We created Haiti's first police test, establishing an orderly system for finding capable recruits.

All of that was hugely gratifying. We also achieved it with lightning speed. But we didn't stay, and neither did the U.S. troops. Once we were gone, it would be natural for some of the old forces to assert themselves. Six months is a blip in Haitian history, and Haiti is prone to backsliding. No improvements last forever there. Even as we were making some, I was aware that ours might not last either.

President Clinton flew down for the official transfer of power, a day of celebration that felt almost like the Fourth of July. The National Palace was whitewashed for the nine-hour visit. The shabby Port-au-Prince airport was hosed down with a brand-new American fire engine. It was the first time an American president had visited Haiti since 1934, when Franklin Roosevelt came. There was genuine hope in the air. This being Haiti, of course, there were worrisome signs as well. Just as the president was arriving, the local papers said a team of FBI agents suspected Aristide's interior minister, Mondesir Beaubrun, of being involved in the assassination of a political rival. I went to the scene of the killing. But it would take more than that to dampen the mood in Haiti.

I made some real friends there. We had a great team of people from around the world working together on a shared mission under conditions that were often absurd. That was a bonding experience for all of us. I also remained in contact with some of the Haitians I got to know. One was René Préval, a local agronomist who became president after Aristide and visited with me in New York. President Aristide sent me a beautiful Haitian painting and an eloquent letter of thanks. Another friend was a popular singer and keyboardist whose stage name was Sweet Micky. His genre was *compas*, a style of Haitian dance music that relies on synthesizers and is sung in Creole. Using his real name, Michel Martelly, he was elected president in 2011, after Préval's second term. Though it is a nation of nine million people, Haiti can feel like a small town.

At the palace, President Clinton met with Aristide, United Nations secretary-general Boutros Boutros-Ghali, and Madeleine Albright, the U.S. ambassador to the United Nations. With white doves and balloons in the air and Aristide at his side, Clinton declared the mission "a remarkable success" as thousands of students waved tiny U.S. and Haitian flags.

"We celebrate the restoration of democracy to your country," he said. "Never, never again must it be stolen away." For his part, Aristide thanked the Americans "who helped restore democracy to our country" and moved the country "from death to life."

The president asked Paul and me to fly back to the United States with him. We could travel on Air Force One as far as Little Rock, where he was planning to cheer on his Arkansas Razorbacks, whose men's basketball team had made it to the NCAA Final Four. The first game, against North Carolina, was the next day at the King Dome in Seattle.

We were supposed to take off at 2:00 p.m. After telling everyone good-bye, Paul and I got to the Port-au-Prince airport in time. What we didn't know was that the president had finished his meetings early and we'd kept him waiting for almost an hour.

He didn't seem to mind. Once we got on board, he talked about Haiti with his aides Bruce Lindsey and Harold Ickes. He took me to the back of the plane to speak with the reporters about Haiti and banter about basketball. He could recall every player, every coach, all the records and scouting reports, as if he were reciting precinct-by-precinct voting returns on election night. I'd never seen someone who seemed to know so much about so many things.

"How do you know all that?" one of the reporters asked him.

"Every once in a while," he said with a smile, "you gotta do something to keep your mind off government." Bill Clinton had a steel-trap mind—for politics, foreign affairs, and basketball.

Since this was our first time on Air Force One, he gave Paul and me a tour. He took us into the galley, the dining area, even the plane's high-flying presidential bathroom.

"I just took a shower in here, Ray, right here," he said, talking with all the exuberance of a regular Arkansan showing off his new Winnebago. "Pretty neat, huh?"

When we got to the aircraft's conference room, the president put in a videotape. It was a clip from the movie *Forrest Gump*, which had opened in theaters the previous summer. This was the part of the movie where Forrest, wearing number 44, scores a phenomenal ninety-nine-yard touchdown for the University of Alabama. "He might be the stupidest son of a bitch alive, but he sure is fast," a grinning coach Bear Bryant declares.

Only it wasn't Tom Hanks anymore playing the lovable simpleton who was everywhere. Someone had altered the video. Now peeking from beneath that crimson helmet was the grinning face of Bill Clinton.

"Can you believe that?" the president said, shaking his head.

CHAPTER SEVEN

Federal Time

T here's a fire in the Treasury building. Get down to Washington at once."

The voice on the phone was unmistakable, a mad collision between Hell's Kitchen and Harvard Yard. My chief Washington patron, Senator Daniel Patrick Moynihan of New York, was calling me from the capital.

"Don't wait another second," Senator Moynihan said. "Just come."

This was June 25, 1996. President Clinton had nominated me as undersecretary of the Treasury for enforcement, and I was awaiting confirmation by the U.S. Senate. It was a big job that would have me overseeing the Secret Service; the Bureau of Alcohol, Tobacco and Firearms; the Customs Service; the Office of Foreign Assets Control; the Financial Crimes Enforcement Network (FinCEN); and the Federal Law Enforcement Training Center.

Suddenly the Treasury building next door to the White House was in flames. Materials used in a restoration project had ignited. The fire didn't threaten the whole building, but it did extensive damage to the roof. The people above me in the hierarchy happened to be away. Treasury Secretary Robert Rubin was at the G7 Summit in Lyon, France. Larry Summers, his top deputy, was somewhere else. Confirmed or not, I had to respond.

Among Moynihan's many talents was the ability to sniff out a power vacuum. Moynihan, along with fellow New York senator

Alfonse D'Amato, was a member of the Senate Finance Committee, where I'd been questioned during my confirmation hearings a few weeks earlier. The day after the fire, around midnight, the Senate confirmed my appointment. There was no turning back now. Before I knew it, I was standing on the White House lawn, reporting on $46 million in damage to the pre–Civil War Treasury building next door, which is featured on the back of the ten-dollar bill, sounding very much like I belonged there. I had barely unpacked my suitcase, and I was already learning the ways of Washington.

*   *   *

I hadn't gone looking for the Treasury job. I was back from Haiti, back to work as president of IGI in New York, and back at home with Veronica in Battery Park City—and happy about all of that—when I got the call from Robert Rubin, the secretary of the Treasury.

"I need someone with law enforcement experience in here," he said.

I knew the job would mean moving down to Washington without Veronica. She had her life in New York City and her own career selling medical supplies to physicians and hospitals. She couldn't just pick up and leave. We'd need two apartments and the patience for weekends back and forth. But Rubin had recruited a highly impressive management team, and now he wanted me to be part of it. Deputy Secretary Larry Summers, who'd been chief economist at the World Bank, went on to be Treasury secretary and then president of Harvard University. Timothy Geithner, who served in several undersecretary and deputy-secretary roles, later became president of the Federal Reserve Bank of New York and then Treasury secretary himself under President Obama. Rubin's chief of staff, Sylvia Mathews (Burwell), ran global development at the Bill and Melinda Gates Foundation before returning to

Washington as director of the White House Office of Management and Budget and, later, President Obama's secretary of health and human services. Michael Froman, who followed Mathews as Rubin's chief of staff, held several economic and national-security posts in the Obama administration, including U.S. trade representative. Summers's chief of staff, Sheryl Sandberg, went on to become chief operating officer of Facebook and the best-selling author of *Lean In*. These were all top-notch talents on the rise.

People don't normally think of Treasury as a law enforcement hub. But, in fact, when I showed up there, nearly 40 percent of federal law enforcement officers were in the Treasury Department. The Secret Service protected the president and battled counterfeiters. ATF had the mammoth duty of enforcing America's firearms and explosives laws while also regulating tobacco and alcohol, grabbing moonshiners and cigarette-tax cheats. The Customs Service was responsible for controlling just about everything that anyone wanted to bring into the country—keeping illegal contraband out and collecting taxes and duties on legal imports. The Office of Foreign Assets Control and the Financial Crimes Enforcement Network enforced foreign sanctions and took other actions to keep international finance legal and fair. The Federal Law Enforcement Training Center trained all of federal law enforcement except the FBI and DEA. After 9/11, the bureaucracy would get scrambled, and most of those agencies would be pulled into the new Department of Homeland Security. But that was still six years away. In the mid-1990s, all those people reported to the undersecretary of the Treasury for enforcement.

The previous undersecretary, a former law professor named Ronald Noble, also had an impressive résumé. At Treasury, he oversaw the internal review of the ATF's performance at Waco. Along with his other duties at Treasury, Noble had been vice president of the Americas for Interpol, the international police organization. Headquartered in Lyon, France, Interpol helps law enforcement agencies in 190 countries combat cross-border crime. At a 1996 general assembly in New Delhi, India, I was elected to replace Noble as vice president of the Americas. Ironically, three years later, I would cast the deciding vote to elect him Interpol's first American secretary general.

Interpol is a fascinating organization—and increasingly important as crime has grown more global over the years. I worked closely with Toshinori Kanemoto, a senior Japanese law enforcement official who was the organization's president, as well as the other board members. I learned a lot about international crime and formed valuable relationships with international law enforcement that would prove helpful for years to come. As police commissioner I would also assign New York police detectives to Interpol headquarters in France and another to Interpol's central bureau in Washington to act as our liaison. But that was all in the future. Now, Noble was leaving Treasury to return to New York University School of Law and Rubin was looking for a law enforcement type to replace him.

I was excited about learning the federal side and overseeing such a diverse portfolio. There was a world beyond New York City. Haiti had opened my eyes. I was going to be responsible for a fascinating range of agencies. Thankfully, Paul Browne agreed to come along as my chief of staff.

This was a trying time for the enforcement side of the Treasury Department and for federal law enforcement in general. Washington was still reeling from the attack on the Alfred P. Murrah Federal Building in downtown Oklahoma City, a shocking case of domestic terrorism. The federal building had been bombed the previous year, killing 168 people and injuring more than 680 others. The two men who carried out that attack, Timothy McVeigh and Terry Nichols, claimed they'd been seeking revenge against the federal government for deadly standoffs in Waco, Texas, in 1993 and Ruby Ridge, Idaho, in 1992. Waco, especially, had been an issue for Treasury. The fifty-one-day siege on the Branch Davidian compound was sparked by a failed raid involving agents from the department's Bureau of Alcohol, Tobacco and Firearms.

During the first week of July 1996, after months of investigation, federal agents in Arizona arrested twelve members of the Viper Militia. Speaking from the Rose Garden, President Clinton was clearly pleased with the ATF, thanking "the law enforcement officers who made the arrests in Arizona yesterday to avert a terrible terrorist attack. Their dedication and hard work over the last six months may have saved many lives." He even singled me out. "I'd like to offer a special congratulations to the gentleman to my right, Ray Kelly, the undersecretary of the Treasury for enforcement, for his role in that endeavor."

"A lot of evidence has been gathered in this case," I told the White House press corps, "and as the indictment alleges, they conspired to blow up some federal buildings. They possessed automatic weapons. And this is a serious group, no doubt about it."

Janet Napolitano, the U.S. attorney in Phoenix who later was elected governor of Arizona and after that served as secretary of the Department of Homeland Security in Washington, had done a great job managing the investigation. She didn't seem so happy about my being the spokesperson only weeks into my new job. But the Treasury Department press office had asked me to speak.

As I got my bearings at Treasury, the event on everyone's mind was the 1996 Summer Olympics in Atlanta, Georgia. The opening ceremonies were set for July 19, and security was severely disorganized. The eyes of the entire world were on Atlanta, yet no one seemed to be in charge. Coming from the NYPD, I'd had a fair amount of experience overseeing large public events—entry screening, credential control, perimeter access, all the nuts and bolts of keeping people safe at high-profile gatherings. I couldn't believe how haphazard everything in Atlanta seemed. The U.S. Olympic Committee also didn't have the people on the ground to get the job done. Their notion was that security was going to be a cooperative, collective effort with no one in charge. It was asking for trouble.

As the games were set to begin, the Olympic Committee called on Treasury to provide reinforcements in Atlanta. They were desperate to throw together a recognizable and cohesive security force. We did what we could to help, rounding up uniforms for Treasury law enforcement people and sending Customs inspectors, too. I went with President Clinton and much of his cabinet on Air Force One to the opening ceremony on July 19, 1996. Jimmy Carter, who lived in Georgia just a couple of hours away, met us there. As the Treasury Department representative, I had a seat next to Secretary of State Madeleine Albright.

The first week of the Olympics proceeded without a security hitch. Then, on July 27, an explosion went off at Centennial Olympic Park, killing one person and injuring 111, and the weakness of the security plan was plain to everyone. The scene in the park was bedlam. The investigation was a multiagency mess. The initial suspect, a security guard named Richard Jewell who'd discovered the pipe bombs before they detonated and heroically cleared many people out of the area, was falsely implicated by the FBI. The real culprit, Eric Rudolph, was a seething extremist angry about abortion who hoped his pipe bombs would force a cancellation of the Olympic Games. It took three more bombings in 1997 for the FBI to identify Rudolph as a suspect. He wasn't captured until 2003.

*   *   *

Only after I settled in at Treasury did I really come to grasp how huge the territory was. Monitoring all those individual agencies under a single departmental umbrella could be a bureaucratic nightmare. There were so many moving parts, it was hard to see the whole. Each agency had a different mission and different constituencies. The ATF had to balance its crime-fighting duties with the hair-trigger sensitivities of gun-rights advocates. The Customs Service was half trade facilitator and half border defender. FinCEN had to navigate between the investment community and Wall Street. The Secret Service did have duties relating to counterfeiting but essentially had a constituency of one. Keep the president safe and happy; everything else would take care of itself.

I had to wrap my head around all this. The only way I knew how was to bore in deeply, learning the intricate details of the various operations—and start meeting with the personnel. By and large, I discovered, these people were really good at what they did. But sometimes they hadn't gotten the direction and supervision they required. The ATF, I decided, needed more of that. The local agents were involved in investigations that had little to do with alcohol, tobacco, or firearms. They were conducting raids with local police against crack-cocaine traffickers. They liked the excitement of traditional police work, which I understood and shared. But that had very little to do with their core mission of regulating alcohol, tobacco, and firearms. For law enforcement operations I separated the agency into east and west divisions and ordered detailed briefings on all their major operations.

We made a careful study of Secret Service motorcades. Were twenty-five or thirty vehicles really required to escort the president from the White House to Capitol Hill? Despite some grumbling, the agents agreed to trim the vehicle count—at least a little—thereby easing traffic flow in Washington. I knew nothing in Washington was forever. I told Paul that the minute we turned our backs, they'd be lining up the tinted-glass vehicles for another long convoy.

With such a diverse portfolio, it was hard to sit in Treasury headquarters and know exactly what was going on in the field. There was no way to stay abreast just by meeting with agency liaisons. Less than two years after being sworn in as undersecretary of the Treasury for enforcement, I was getting restless in the upper-middle bureaucratic ranks of the nation's capital. I was itching to run an operation closer to the ground. So I did something hardly anyone ever does in status-conscious Washington: I asked for a demotion.

*   *   *

The commissioner of Customs, as the head of the U.S. Customs Service was known, was George Weise, who had come to the agency from Capitol Hill with a strong interest in trade legislation and establishing new user fees for the shipping industry. "Power to the ports" was the slogan of the moment. A Customs commissioner always has to balance the needs of law enforcement and trade promotion. Both are clearly important. The Customs Service generated $20 billion a year in import fees for the U.S. Treasury, a huge sum that was second only to the Internal Revenue Service. But by the summer of 1998, controversy was swirling around Customs on issues such as drug smuggling, racial profiling, and personal-search policies. Weise decided to resign for a private-sector job.

To help find his replacement, I set up a committee of three assistant Treasury secretaries whose judgment I trusted—Elisabeth Bresee, David Medina, and James Johnson. We collected résumés, interviewed fourteen candidates, and settled on three finalists. I passed those names to Secretary Rubin, who didn't like any of them.

I thought about what to do next. Should we start the process over again? Should we round up more candidates? Should we take a second look at some of those who didn't make the round of finalists?

It seemed like an interesting job. The Customs commissioner was responsible for twenty thousand employees, 328 ports of entry, and an agenda of challenging issues such as personal search.

"What about me?" I asked Rubin when I went to his office to discuss the matter.

"Let me think about that," he said.

As he reflected, I proposed this scenario: promote James Johnson from assistant secretary to undersecretary. Johnson was a Harvard College and Harvard Law graduate who'd overseen some complex prosecutions as an assistant U.S. attorney in Manhattan. He and I would swap levels. Instead of him reporting to me, I'd report to him.

Rubin went for the idea, and it worked for me. I had learned I was much better suited for running an operational agency like Customs than being inside a sprawling, multilevel oversight bureaucracy. What I enjoyed most—and what I was best at, I thought—was rolling up my sleeves and running things, not being three or four levels removed. Plus, I liked my report-turned-supervisor, Undersecretary Johnson.

I still had to get my new nomination as Customs commissioner confirmed by the Senate. For a second time, I was asked to appear at the Dirksen Senate Office Building before the Finance Committee. It was almost exactly two years since my last confirmation hearing. Once again I stood before a panel that included my home-state senators, Daniel Patrick Moynihan and Alfonse D'Amato.

The hearing was more a formality than anything else and took on a lighthearted tone when D'Amato gave his lengthy opening statement. The senator decided to tell everyone how we knew each other as teenagers in Island Park. In great detail, he recalled the years we both volunteered for the beach patrol and how I was later promoted to lifeguard, a position he said he never attained. The senator went on like that, recounting various embarrassing moments from the ancient myths of Long Island's South Shore. He ended strong: "Here we are, having, once again, Ray Kelly before us with an opportunity to safeguard our children once again, and this time to safeguard our borders in the fight against the flow of drugs that come across the borders."

I appreciated the fulsome endorsement. Senator D'Amato certainly delivered for New York in Washington.

I'll admit I did bury Sammy Latini's swimsuit and shoes in the sand, as the senator claimed I had. Actually, it was worse than that. I buried a whole set of Sammy's clothes. But, in my defense, it was only after Sammy had hidden our clothes during a skinny-dipping jaunt.

When I moved into my new office at Customs Service head-quarters in the Reagan Building three blocks from the White House, I could tell immediately: this was my kind of challenge. I jumped in and grabbed hold of the place. The agency had a far-flung mission, some hugely dedicated employees, and a bevy of critics, inside and outside government, who were ready to pounce. The IRS had just been decimated in three days of hearings before the Senate Finance Committee. Republicans on the committee showed no mercy. Customs was next in their sights. Despite the warm welcome during my confirmation hearing, I had no doubt they'd be just as tough on us.

The best strategy, I believed, was to highlight the good things the agency was doing, then get ahead of the critics and make improvements on our own.

Customs inspectors, who are now part of Customs and Border Protection in the Department of Homeland Security, were the official federal presence at America's 328 points of entry—international airports, seaports, and major border crossings—recovering money owed to the United States and preventing contraband from coming in. It's a big country and a big job. When you come back into the United States from abroad, these are the people who check your bags. Customs inspectors are everywhere, and this can pay great dividends.

They find cocaine and heroin in the cargo holds of commercial airliners and in the bellies of third-world drug mules. They discover blood diamonds masquerading as costume jewelry and the ivory tusks of endangered elephants. If it's illegal and there's profit to be made importing it, Customs inspectors are the ones who are supposed to find it before it gets here—and arrest the people trying to bring it in. At times, a single find in a single suitcase can lead, one investigative step at a time, to a sprawling international criminal conspiracy.

That's how Customs inspectors and investigators helped to break up a Jamaican-led narcotics ring that bribed FedEx drivers to distribute 121 tons of Mexican marijuana to East Coast markets. Working with the Drug Enforcement Administration and FedEx executives in Memphis, our people seized 2 tons of marijuana, 18 firearms, and $4 million in cash and other assets. The 101 arrests included 22 FedEx employees. The FedEx drivers sold out cheaply, for bribes of less than $2,000 a week. "They thought they had built a foolproof system," I said when the arrests were announced. "They were mistaken."

Customs agents also did huge damage to the Mexico-based drug cartel founded by Amado Carrillo Fuentes. Operation Impunity, we called that probe. Fuentes had died in 1997 from the botched plastic surgery he'd hoped would make him unrecognizable. But his organization was as potent as ever, using a fleet of planes and sophisticated communications technology to bring tons of cocaine, heroin, and marijuana into the United States. We turned informants. We leveraged cooperation from the governments of Mexico and the Dominican Republic. We were able to identify key players up and down the cartel. We ended up with dozens of people in custody in Chicago, Miami, and Texas. "The drug smugglers in this case used an incredible array of sophisticated electronics equipment," I said when we announced the arrests. "It took our best to beat their best."

The Customs Service and Treasury's other enforcement

agencies could be a hugely valuable resource in the war on drugs—and not just because of cocaine, heroin, and other narcotics we confiscated at the airports and borders. On May 18, 1998, Secretary Rubin announced the culmination of "the largest and most comprehensive drug money laundering case in the history of U.S. law enforcement," Operation Casablanca. It was the tireless Brian Ross of ABC News who broke the story. For more than three years, Customs agents targeted banks and other financial institutions that were used by Mexico's Juárez cartel and Colombia's Cali cartel. Indictments were brought against three major Mexican banks and officials from nine other Mexican financial institutions, all of them directly involved in helping the cartels hide their huge profits. Nearly two hundred people were arrested. Drug importers face two major challenges: getting the drugs to the people who consume them, and hiding the money they earn. Over the years, law enforcement had focused mostly on the product side of the equation, but the money part was just as important. The kingpins could usually keep their distance from the street-level smuggling and selling. But they would never separate themselves from the profits of their illegal enterprise. We could have taken the money laundering even further. But the numbers were getting so huge and so many Mexican banks were involved, we worried about destabilizing the nation's entire economic system. We were also concerned that too many people were learning about the operation, and that the details might leak. We made our arrests and brought Operation Casablanca to a close.

It wasn't just narcotics operations we were focused on. In September 1998, Customs agents, coordinating with police in twenty-two states and a dozen countries, busted an Internet child-pornography network called the Wonderland Club. More than one hundred thousand sexual photographs of naked boys and girls—some of them younger than two years old—were seized. Nearly a hundred people were charged, including a University of

Connecticut professor. "The volume is enormous," I said when we announced the operation.

There really was no form of criminality an alert Customs employee couldn't sniff out, and that included terrorism. It was Customs inspectors who captured Ahmed Ressam, an Algerian al-Qaeda member known as the Millennium Bomber. He'd lived in Montreal, received extensive terrorist training in Afghanistan, and had big New Year's Eve plans: he was going to plant powerful explosives at Los Angeles International Airport, ringing out 1999 with a dramatic and deadly blast.

On December 14, Ressam hid the explosives and bomb components in the wheel well of a rented green 1999 Chrysler 300M luxury sedan and drove aboard the MV *Coho* ferry at Victoria, British Columbia, Canada, for the ninety-minute ride to Port Angeles, Washington. He passed through the U.S. Immigration and Naturalization Service checkpoint without a problem. But after the ferry docked in Port Angeles around 6:00 p.m., U.S. Customs inspector Diana Dean thought Ressam was acting "hinky." She asked him to step out of the car as another Customs inspector searched the trunk. In the wheel well, he discovered ten green plastic garbage bags containing a total of 118 pounds of a fine white powder, two lozenge bottles filled with the primary explosives HMTD and RDX, 14 pounds of aluminum sulfate, and two 22-ounce olive jars with 2.6 pounds of a secondary explosive known as EGDN, twice as powerful as TNT. There were also four timing devices, small black boxes containing circuit boards connected to Casio watches and nine-volt batteries. The devices were rigged so that when a watch alarm rang, an electrical charge would pass from the battery to a small lightbulb, which had its glass covering removed, exposing the filament. The bulb would heat, then ignite and detonate the other bomb ingredients in a chain reaction. As one of the Customs inspectors escorted Ressam from the ferry, he broke free, leading the inspectors on a six-block chase. They grabbed him as he tried to force his way into a car stopped at a traffic light. One month later at Customs headquarters we held a major awards ceremony for all the inspectors involved.

Explosives experts said later the material in the wheel well could have produced an explosion the size of forty car bombs. After a nineteen-day trial at U.S. District Court in Los Angeles, Ressam was convicted on eight terrorism-related charges and is now serving a life sentence at the federal prison known as ADX Florence in Colorado, or just "Supermax."

No one in U.S. law enforcement had much experience yet with murderous zealots like Ressam, trained in the ways of terror and dedicated to mass destruction. But looking back, his plans for the new millennium certainly seem like an early precursor to the kinds of plots we would become extremely familiar with in the coming decade in New York.

*   *   *

All along, I was working to bring greater administrative order to the Customs Service. We had many talented people, but when I became commissioner, the agency was disorganized. Nothing was uniform—not the cars, not the guns, not even the uniforms. They were different from posting to posting, from port to port. One hundred and eighty ports had their own websites. We shut those down. We put in the first Customs-wide web strategy.

All this disorganization wasn't just untidy or bureaucratically complex. It was costly and potentially dangerous for the inspectors and the public. Customs was an agency whose mission involved establishing a national system for bringing goods into the country by land, sea, and air. It made no sense for some ports of entry to be governed by strict regulations and others to have hardly any at all. It wouldn't take long for savvy importers—both the legal and illegal kinds—to begin exploiting variances like that. We wrote up standards and enforced them.

We brought in a director of training. Eleven thousand of our twenty thousand employees carried guns. Yet we had no records documenting which, if any, of them had been trained to shoot. We sent them to the shooting range and kept records on how people did. That might sound routine now. At the time, it was anything but.

You couldn't live in Washington and work in federal law enforcement and not notice the awesome political power of the FBI. J. Edgar Hoover may be dead and buried, his name known to young people only from a building sign, but the bureau he left behind still has major influence in the executive branch and Congress. Part of the reason for that, I concluded, was the eighty FBI employees assigned to various committees on Capitol Hill. Customs, I thought, should try to copy that strategy. We didn't get anything close to eighty. But with a little pressure, we got three or four agents on the hill, and those congressional liaisons began developing some fruitful working relationships with senators, congressmen, and their staffs. I knew that would pay dividends over time. I forged a relationship with Senator Robert Byrd and got his support for our funding initiatives. It didn't hurt that Customs would have a training facility in Byrd's home state of West Virginia.

The biggest criticisms Customs faced had to do with who was stopped when coming into the country and why—an early international preview of my own future battles in New York over our so-called stop-and-frisk techniques.

Some of this was fairly routine: watching people through two-way mirrors, picking out the guy wearing the heavy overcoat on the seventy-degree day, going over and saying, "May I speak with you for a moment, sir?" Not surprisingly, the flights carrying the most marijuana and cocaine came from Jamaica, Colombia, and the Dominican Republic. From time to time, someone would complain that we were picking on Jamaicans or Colombians or Dominicans. Then we'd do some extra screening of flights arriving from Norway and find nothing.

Politically, Customs was always being squeezed on the personal-search issue from both the left and the right. The long-serving Democratic congressman from Georgia John Lewis, a former aide to the Reverend Martin Luther King Jr., and other civil rights activists were raising objections of racial profiling, saying Customs agents were singling out their targets according to demographics more than activity. That wasn't official policy, but I wanted to know if it was happening in the field. At the same time, conservative activists complained about intrusive government overreach, asking why federal employees literally had their hands in people's pockets. Meanwhile, drug-war supporters were pushing for more aggressive interdiction. Drug-war opponents thought any interdiction was futile. Caught in the middle was the Customs Service. And we were constantly being dragged into court.

When I arrived there were multiple lawsuits pending on alleged personal-search abuses, mostly at the Mexican border and at airports. With lax standards, the Customs Service was constantly being sued by people who claimed their rights were being violated. Some of the claims seemed crazy. Some probably had merit: agents pumping people's stomachs at the border, singling out attractive women for strip searches—taking intrusive measures without much logic or justification.

I thought we needed some objective outside analysis. Sometimes agencies will listen to credible outsiders more willingly than they'll listen to their own. But the investigation had to be led by someone with deep credibility on both sides of the political aisle. There weren't too many people like that in Washington. I put together a team to take a fresh look at the issue and, hopefully, bring some rationality to Customs' policies.

Thanks to the recommendation of New York attorney John Connorton, I found my point person in Constance Berry Newman, who was undersecretary of the Smithsonian Institution. She was smart, trustworthy, and balanced, a politically savvy African

American Republican. She must have learned something about the halls of power running the Smithsonian Institution.

Her group and my staff came up with a flurry of new initiatives designed to confront the search issue.

We reduced the searches by 75 percent and increased the drug finds by 25 percent. We beefed up supervision and set up specific search criteria. Who to search, how to search, who should make the decision—all of that had been entirely free-form. We finally got some rules spelled out. Under federal law, Customs agents needed only "mere suspicion" to search someone coming into the country. That was a very low standard—far more lax than the "reasonable suspicion" generally required of regular police.

We still conducted aggressive searches when we had cause to. Sometimes that was necessary. But we were guided by rational policies. Supervisory approval became a must. Stomach pumping wasn't used as a fishing expedition anymore. Again, some of this was very basic. But someone had to lead it.

When the government's General Accounting Office issued a detailed report on Customs Service searches, Illinois senator Dick Durbin declared: "I commend Commissioner Ray Kelly for his work to address concerns that have been raised, and I look forward to working with him to ensure no one is stripped of his or her civil rights or dignity by being unfairly selected to be searched by the Customs Service."

He'd been one of our tougher critics. Given where we'd started, I considered that progress, I assured Senator Durbin.

"Customs is searching fewer innocent travelers of all races and genders, and more effectively targeting those carrying contraband," I said proudly. Sitting next to me at the press conference and lending his support: John Lewis, the Georgia congressman and civil rights leader who had raised many of the original concerns.

CHAPTER EIGHT

Fighting Chance

I had hoped to spend a little longer in Washington, even after George W. Bush finally defeated Al Gore in the contested presidential election of 2000. Technically, I was a political appointee. I understood that. President Clinton had named me undersecretary of the Treasury for enforcement and, later, commissioner of Customs. President Bush had every right to put his own people in those jobs. Still, I didn't consider the idea of staying all that far-fetched. I never thought of myself as a creature of politics. I certainly never did my job that way. I didn't even belong to a political party. I was a registered Independent, a professional law enforcement executive doing a professional's job, able to work comfortably with Republicans and Democrats. Plus, I had Al Lerner supporting me.

Al was a former Marine Corps pilot who had flown missions for the CIA. In the years since, he'd become the billionaire owner of the Cleveland Browns and chairman of MBNA, a giant credit card issuer based in Wilmington, Delaware. He was known for writing large checks to causes he believed in. After a $25 million gift from Al, Columbia University, his alma mater, had just named its new student center Alfred Lerner Hall. I sat with Al at the opening celebration. He was also, I'd been told, the largest single donor to the 2001 Bush inauguration. His main contact, as well as I could figure, was Donald Evans, a close oil-business friend of the incoming president and soon-to-be commerce secretary.

I knew Al from the Marine Corps reserves and from several law enforcement groups he was active in. We had lunch in Washington before the 2000 election. "I'd like to stay for at least a few months," I said. "I have some things I want to finish." I told him I'd also heard that if I completed five years of federal service, I might be eligible for a government pension. "That would be nice," I said.

"No problem," Al told me. "I'll take care of it."

His assurance was good enough for me. While most of the other top Clinton administration appointees were interviewing for jobs and saying good-bye to their civil service staffs, I stayed put, running Customs, confident I'd be around awhile.

Al and I spoke a couple of times in late December and early January. Everything appeared to be on track.

On Thursday, January 18, two nights before the Bush inaugural ceremony, I went to a party hosted by Robert Cummins, who owns an elevator company in the Bronx and has some high-placed friends in Washington. I had just had a fascinating conversation that night with another guest, Supreme Court justice Antonin Scalia, about the *Bush v. Gore* case, in which he was intimately involved. Then my cell phone rang. It was Al Lerner.

"Ray," he said, "I can't do it."

He didn't say why, and there didn't seem to be much room for discussion. Just, "Ray, I can't do it"—and my reply, "Thanks for trying, Al."

I never did get a full explanation of what had happened or why Al Lerner couldn't deliver. I learned later that I had a staunch opponent in the Air Transport Association of America. That group was a powerful voice in the airline industry, representing the chief executives of U.S. and foreign-flag corporations and cargo carriers. People there supposedly considered me too much of a "law enforcement type" and insufficiently boosterish toward foreign trade, a lucrative sector of the air-cargo industry. I don't think it was meant as a compliment.

Whatever the full explanation, the appointees of George W. Bush would soon be moving their framed diplomas and cardboard boxes in, and I didn't have a job—with the new administration or with Al. He'd already hired Secret Service director Lewis Merletti as chief of security for the Cleveland football team. When Louis Freeh left the post of FBI director later that year, he too would go to work for Al—at the credit card company. Washington could certainly be perplexing to me, even after I'd been there for more than four years.

I watched the inaugural parade with Daniel Patrick Moynihan, the senator from New York, who happened to live in the same Washington apartment building I did, the Residences at Market Square. For the first time in a long time, I had to go looking for a job. I started networking in the private sector, something I hadn't had to do much of over the years. I spoke with a couple of people in the business world about job possibilities. I also discussed potential jobs with a New York billionaire named Michael Bloomberg. He had a successful financial-media company—you may have heard of it—Bloomberg L.P. Some months earlier, he and his political adviser, Kevin Sheekey, had come down to Washington to have lunch with me, saying they'd heard I might be moving back to New York to run for mayor. That was, to put it mildly, wildly premature, but we did have an interesting lunch, talking politics, terrorism, and international trade, three topics that seemed to captivate Bloomberg.

While I was looking for someplace to land, Andrew Maloney, who had been the U.S. attorney in Brooklyn, reached out to me on behalf of his son, Patrick, a compliance attorney at the investment bank Bear Stearns. They were looking for someone to run their security.

Ultimately, that's what happened. I got hired by Bear Stearns as global head of security. Alan "Ace" Greenberg, the firm's legendary leader, was good to me. I was able to spend some personal time with him, getting my feet wet on Wall Street, learning how to protect a fast-moving financial firm and its highly sensitive data. The salary was nice, too. Bear Stearns paid investment-bank wages that made government employment look almost like volunteer work.

So I moved back to New York full-time and settled into my new life in the corporate world.

*   *   *

I've followed boxing my whole life. As a little kid, I sat in front of the television on Columbus Avenue, watching matches with my father. Later I went with my friends to the old St. Nicholas Arena, an ice rink turned boxing venue on West Sixty-Sixth Street. St. Nick's, as everyone in the neighborhood called it, was built by Cornelius Vanderbilt and John Jacob Astor. It began hosting boxing matches in 1906, five years before prizefighting was first legalized in New York. That ring had hosted some legendary fighters over the years, including Jack Johnson, Jess Willard, Kid Chocolate, Rocky Graziano, and many other early boxing greats. Future heavyweight champion Floyd Patterson fought his first professional match there in 1952.

On June 26, 2001, just as I was settling in at Bear Stearns, a boxing match was held on the USS *Intrepid*, a decommissioned *Essex*-class aircraft carrier that was built during World War II for the U.S. Navy. The *Intrepid* survived five kamikaze attacks and one torpedo strike before seeing service in Vietnam and in anti-Soviet Cold War operations. In 1982, thanks to the efforts of philanthropist Zachary Fisher and others, the ship was docked permanently on the Hudson River off midtown Manhattan as the centerpiece of the Intrepid Sea, Air & Space Museum, one of the real treasures of New York.

I wasn't on the *Intrepid* that June night, as a twenty-six-year-old fighter named Beethavean Scottland and his opponent, George

Khalid Jones, entered the ring, but I would soon come to learn every detail about these men and the match.

Jones, a sturdy left-hander with a powerful right hook, proceeded to pummel Scotland through nine and a half punishing rounds. Scotland went down after a left-right combination with thirty-seven seconds left in the tenth and did not get up again. As the fight was called, Beethavean Scotland lay on the canvas, breathing but unresponsive. Once medical personnel were able to get a full-size stretcher onto the ship, after some difficulty, he was taken by ambulance to Bellevue Hospital Center, where he lingered in a coma. Two operations did not relieve the pressure that had built around his brain. On July 2, six days after the fight, doctors at Bellevue pronounced him dead, citing a subdural hematoma, a rupture of the veins between the skull and the brain.

Scotland, who had a 20-6-2 record including nine knockouts, hadn't fought in eleven months. He'd been itching to get back in the ring. A scheduled match one week earlier had fallen through when his middleweight opponent backed out, blaming a pulled hamstring. Scotland had agreed to fight Jones only two days before the match, filling in for David Telesco, who pulled out after breaking his nose during training.

Scotland usually fought in the super-middleweight division, which had a weight limit of 168 pounds. To fight Jones, who had a record of 15-0 with eleven knockouts, Scotland moved up to the light-heavyweight division, which had a limit of 175 pounds.

The death in the ring was a big story in the New York papers and all across the boxing world. Fighters were often beaten on the canvas, but they were not supposed to get killed. The papers said Scotland was the fourth fighter since 1979 to die from injuries received in the ring in New York State. The previous one was in 1989, when John Gross died from a subdural hematoma at an upstate fight. Like Scotland, he'd been hit many times in the head.

The questions came like gloves against a speed bag. Why didn't the referee stop the fight earlier? Why wasn't a paramedic crew standing by? Was an aircraft carrier off midtown Manhattan really an appropriate venue for professional prizefights? Where was the New York State Athletic Commission, the agency that was supposed to regulate boxing? Who was looking out for the safety of the fighters and the credibility of the sport?

The roar grew loud enough that Governor George Pataki felt compelled to find a Mr. Clean to come in and, hopefully, rescue boxing from itself. That Mr. Clean was going to be me.

In September 2001, less than three months after Beethavean Scottland was killed on the *Intrepid*, Governor Pataki appointed me chairman of the New York State Athletic Commission. This was a part-time position. Jimmy Cayne, the Bear Stearns CEO, gave me his blessing so I wouldn't have to leave the firm. The state salary was $110,000 a year, though I decided I would take the assignment without pay.

When I said I would do the job, I intended to do the job. I wouldn't be a do-nothing political hack, looking the other way while the sport was corrupted, undermined, or ignored—regardless of what I was being paid. I got busy restoring a sense of professionalism to the battered sport of boxing. I was committed to turning things around, but I knew I needed help. My friend Bill Gallo, the beloved sports columnist and cartoonist at the *Daily News*, served as my special adviser. To oversee the staff and run the day-to-day business, I brought in Charles DiRienzo as the commission's executive director. Charlie was affable, meticulous—just perfect for the job. I had worked with him in the 88th Precinct and he had helped reorganize the 106th Precinct after the stun gun scandal. He'd retired as an inspector and was running the fraud division of the New York State Insurance Department. So he already knew something about state government and happened to have a deep knowledge of boxing. With Charlie's help I was eager to dive into the tough issues immediately, starting with an in-depth state police investigation of Beethavean Scottland's death. I wanted to know everything that had happened that night and exactly what had led up to it. I asked the governor's office to assign some state police investigators.

That seemed like a reasonable request—and an obvious place to begin. The Athletic Commission was a state agency. We were part of the New York Department of State. I was appointed by the governor. Our employees were on the state payroll. We were supposed to oversee and regulate boxing. Yet we had no investigators of our own. How could we hope to reform this undeniably troubled sport unless we had a clear idea of what the troubles were—and what the possible solutions might be? Wasn't that Oversight 101?

Unfortunately, our request for state police investigators was denied by the governor's office. The state police, we were told, would not be asked to probe boxing.

That was too bad. We knew a lot of corruption and double-dealing had historically been tolerated in boxing. And there were many questions just begging to be asked: What qualifications should be required for trainers, ringside physicians, and boxing referees? What medical checkups should fighters receive before and after they went into the ring? Why was there no standard way of taping boxers' hands? It sounded so simple and so necessary. But apparently there was not much interest in addressing these questions head-on.

I knew what our job was—to make a dangerous sport as safe and honest as it could possibly be.

We began changing the commission's policies and rules one at a time, finding our own creative ways to reform the boxing industry. The more time I spent around the sport, the clearer I came to see: the best people involved in boxing were the boxers themselves. Almost everyone else, it seemed, was somehow taking advantage of them. I saw the commission as the boxers' friend.

We set up an 800 number so fighters and gym workers could report injuries that happened during training. We attempted to mandate MRIs. We began a program to tape hands consistently. We required doctors to go into the ring between rounds and examine the fighter after a knockdown. A doctor was standing there. Why not use him?

We couldn't hope to change the sport all by ourselves. But clearly, a new day was dawning in the boxing world.

* * *

If anyone had doubts about the need for improvement, they were laid to rest at the Roseland Ballroom in Manhattan on November 23, 2001. "Fighting for America—A Night of Thanksgiving," the nine-bout card was billed. The promoters promised that all box office receipts would be donated to the Twin Towers Fund. Five hundred free tickets were given to firefighters, police officers, and other first responders.

The main event matched two super middleweights, Brooklyn's Richard Grant and James Butler, known as the Harlem Hammer. Butler, who'd been favored to win, ended up losing by the judges' decision.

Minutes later, Butler walked over to Grant as if to congratulate him. But instead of shaking hands, Butler coldcocked Grant in the jaw with a bare right fist, sending the winner to the mat with blood spurting from his mouth.

I was at ringside that night. I couldn't believe what I'd just seen.

"I want this guy arrested," I said to Joe Esposito, NYPD chief of department, who happened to be there. As Joe walked toward the locker room with a couple of uniformed officers, Grant was still lying on the canvas, his dyed-blond hair matted beneath his head, blood still flowing out of his mouth.

Someone yelled to the balcony, "Aren't there any medics up

there? Why isn't a medic down here?" A moment later, a doctor stepped into the ring.

The police officers placed the sucker puncher under arrest. We pressed charges and he was taken off to central booking. He was arraigned the next morning on second-degree assault, a charge that carries up to seven years in state prison.

Grant was taken to the hospital, where he was treated for a split tongue. His jaw was knocked temporarily out of its socket. He had loose teeth and was experiencing headaches. He received twenty-six stitches before being released shortly before dawn.

At the next meeting of the Athletic Commission, the free-swinging Harlem Hammer was stripped of his $10,000 loser's purse and given a temporary suspension from boxing.

I thought the message was a good one—and long overdue. There were some things that wouldn't be tolerated anymore, even in boxing. The Athletic Commission was behaving like an Athletic Commission at last.

CHAPTER NINE

Then Everything Changed

I had never felt further away from the action.

When the first plane, American Airlines Flight 11, struck the north tower at 8:46 a.m., I was in a breakfast meeting at Bear Stearns, at 245 Park Avenue between East Forty-Sixth and East Forty-Seventh Streets.

This was three miles from the World Trade Center. It might as well have been three hundred—or three thousand.

"A small plane crashed into the Trade Center," someone at a nearby table said (wrongly, it turned out). At the start, it sounded like a tragedy, a terrible accident, something bad—but nothing that was going to threaten the very future of New York. That assessment changed seventeen minutes later, when I heard a CNN anchor say that a second commercial airliner—a second *commercial* jetliner, United Airlines Flight 175—had hit the south tower.

There was no getting around it now. This was terrorism on a life-altering scale.

I'd spent thirty-four years in the New York City Police Department, rising from police cadet to police commissioner, and nearly another five in top federal enforcement roles. But on the morning of September 11, 2001, that was all in the past for me. The city was under attack in a way it had never been before, and I wasn't in law enforcement anymore. I liked the job at Bear Stearns, overseeing corporate security. Smart people, good people—but their business was making money, not countering terrorism or fighting crime.

Over the next eighty-five minutes, I watched on TV, like everyone else, while the tenants scrambled to safety from the twin towers and firefighters, police officers, paramedics, and other first responders ran upstairs in full gear to rescue them. The uniformed personnel had no idea they were rushing toward their deaths.

As the shocking details trickled in, people everywhere struggled to understand what this meant. In the Bear Stearns office, no one even tried to work. They stared in silence at their televisions and computers or simply into space. No one seemed to know what to say.

I did my job. I met with the executives about the precautions the firm should undertake. I was told there were people panicking in the building around the corner on Madison Avenue, where the firm's headquarters was moving in a month. A skeleton staff was already there. I walked around the corner to calm the people down. Then I rode to the top floor of that new forty-seven-story building. From there, I could see the tops of the two towers and all the smoke pouring out. That's where I was when the first building fell.

"Look, look!" I heard someone shout as the tower collapsed to the ground. I'm not sure if it was an employee or a vendor or who. It didn't matter. Everyone felt the same way.

"Oh my God," I heard someone mumble.

Less than two hours after the first plane hit, both 110-story office buildings were in a mammoth heap on the ground, killing 343 New York City firefighters, 37 Port Authority police officers, 23 New York City police officers—2,753 people in all. As many times as I repeat those numbers, they never lose their power to shock.

So many thoughts were rushing through my head. The sheer enormity of it, the horror, the otherworldliness, the insanity. The fact that our apartment was a two-minute walk from there. And how could this have happened? Modern skyscrapers aren't supposed to collapse like pancakes, no matter what slams into them. And what might happen next? No one could possibly say.

I thought about the conversation I'd had with the building engineer who'd been stuck in an elevator during the 1993 World Trade Center attack and had cut himself out with a key, the one who'd promised me, "Those buildings could never come down."

It had sounded so rational when he said it to me. I'm sure he believed every syllable. And now my eyes were telling me he'd simply been wrong.

The towers were rubble on the ground, and thousands of New Yorkers were evacuating the city on their own. No one told people to leave, except in the immediate downtown area. People just left. It wasn't through any plan or orderly process. They started walking. Up streets, across bridges, just *away*. Some got in cars or buses or the trains that were still running. Some even got into boats. By any means necessary, they were just gone.

*   *   *

Even a veteran government official will quickly revert to the role of husband and father in a situation like this one, and I felt it happening to me. At the same time I was taking in the basic facts and directing people at the investment bank, I was attempting to make contact with my own family. Veronica was in Paris. So she was out of harm's way, though when we spoke on the phone, I could tell she was badly shaken. She was staying in an apartment that didn't have cable television. As soon as she'd heard what had happened, she'd gone to the Hôtel Lutetia around the corner. The hotel staff were very kind to her, lending her a room to watch the news from America until the guests who'd checked out discovered that their flight to New York had been canceled and checked back in. She found her way to another hotel, the George V, and spent the rest of the day and evening in the business center following the heart-breaking coverage.

She and I were desperate to reach our sons. Both, I assumed, had been somewhere downtown. Jim worked on John Street, just blocks from the towers. He finally got through to me on the phone, which wasn't easy given the spotty cell service. He'd made his way through the smoke and ash from his building to another building on John Street, then, like thousands of other New Yorkers, he just kept walking uptown. Greg was a reporter for NY1, the local all-news cable channel. I had the advantage of seeing him live from the scene on TV, so I knew he was OK. Greg, I believe, was the first journalist to use the term "Ground Zero" to refer to the former World Trade Center site. That one certainly stuck.

*　　*　　*

When most people had left the office, I went over to the CNN bureau across from Madison Square Garden, where I shared my take on the day's events with Wolf Blitzer in Washington and Paula Zahn in New York. I thought it was important to add my perspective. I had, after all, been New York's police commissioner the last time terrorists attacked the city, striking the very same target. But, honestly, being a talking head on television wasn't exactly how I wanted to fill out my day. I didn't like watching the drama unfold from the nosebleed seats. After decades of running toward the action—whatever the action was—here I was offering commentary from afar.

"Terrorism is theater," I said that night, an expression I had used many times in the eight years since the last World Trade Center attack.

When I finished my TV segments for the evening, I walked a block up Eighth Avenue to a no-frills hotel room CNN had booked for me. I spent the rest of the night there by myself, watching television, making phone calls, and occasionally glancing out the window into the smoky night sky. Actually, I was lucky to have the room. There was no way I was getting back into our apartment in Battery Park City. Truly, I had no place else to go.

I checked in with some of my former law enforcement colleagues. I took calls from worried relatives and friends. No one seemed to know much more than what was being reported, including my police contacts, other than the fact that the loss of life was going to be horrific and al-Qaeda was suspect number one.

The next morning in Paris, Veronica made her way to the American Cathedral on avenue George V in the 8th arrondissement. They were having a special service in honor of the victims in New York. As she waited for the service to begin, she overheard one of the clergymen say, "All we need is someone to carry the flag."

Veronica spoke up. "I'm from New York," she said.

"Would you mind?" the minister asked, motioning to a large red, white, and blue flag leaning in a corner in the sacristy.

"I'd be honored," she said.

She joined the procession of more than a dozen clergy in white vestments, carrying the flag to the altar in her black suit. When the service was over, she led the procession back down the center aisle.

About halfway down, they stopped between the two rows of pews. A deacon leaned over and whispered to Veronica, "Can you swing that flag?"

She nodded.

With Veronica swinging the flag back and forth, the whole congregation sang "God Bless America."

Veronica told me later she didn't even try to hold back her tears.

*   *   *

On Thursday, September 13, the titans of Wall Street gathered in an executive conference room at Bear Stearns and mapped out the immediate future of America's financial markets. That's no exaggeration.

The heads of the leading investment banks were there. So were the chiefs of the major brokerage houses and stock exchanges. Representatives of the Treasury Department, the Securities and Exchange Commission, and other financial regulators attended as well. So was I. The meeting was hosted by Bear Stearns because the firm was located in Midtown and the downtown Financial District was still a civilian no-go zone. As the finance executives began their meeting, the New York Stock Exchange was closed for a third straight day, the longest interruption since the outbreak of World War I, when the Big Board was idled from July 31 to November 28, 1914. The pressing question for the assembled: When could the markets safely open again?

"We have to be certain that when we go, nothing brings us back down," warned NYSE chairman Richard Grasso. And that was far more complicated than unlocking the doors and switching the lights on.

Grasso's exchange and the Nasdaq Stock Market were both physically able to open and eager to do so. But some huge impediments remained. While the exchanges' internal technologies did not seem to have been damaged in the terror attack, their outside telecommunications connections were only beginning to be stitched back together two days later. Those data links are what allow investors to send buy and sell orders to the markets. Without them, the exchanges cannot operate.

One big worry was a Verizon switching facility. It handled more than three-quarters of the stock exchange's external data connections and was now running on backup diesel generators. Only thirty-six hours of fuel remained, though fresh supplies were being trucked in. The Financial District was still experiencing scattered power outages, including at the American Stock Exchange, just two blocks from the World Trade Center site. Hardwick Simmons, chairman and CEO of Nasdaq, which owns the American Stock Exchange, said his people had a contingency plan to shift options trading to exchanges in other cities. And Simmons had even bigger problems than that. At noon on Wednesday, his IT team had tested the electronic links to the thirty-two broker-dealer member firms that were located in the World Trade Center. "Nineteen were unable to respond," he said.

It was hard not to think the worst.

"I'm very worried about them," Simmons said. "We haven't heard from those firms in any fashion."

Meanwhile, 1 Liberty Plaza, directly across from where the towers had stood, partially collapsed on Wednesday, displacing 10 percent of Nasdaq's employees. Even with the staff moved to new locations, there was the question of how thousands of market professionals would get back into lower Manhattan, which was still filled with dust and debris and closed to nearly all traffic except for rescue workers. No one wanted an army of brokers, traders, and clerks interfering with the rescue and recovery efforts.

All of this was worrisome, and not just in New York. No one knew yet how the terror attack would affect U.S. stock prices. Immediately after the attack, equity prices plunged in Europe and Latin America, and on Wednesday they did so in Asia as well. But they stabilized Wednesday in Europe, leading to hopes that the damage would be limited when New York trading resumed. Still, some people were starting to question the whole idea of physical places where financial instruments were traded, especially physical places in packed urban neighborhoods. Had 9/11 revealed that the financial services industry, New York's largest employer and the single most powerful engine of the city's economy, didn't really need to exist in the city in its current physical form?

The Wall Streeters answered that with a resounding no.

The U.S. equity markets would resume trading "no later than Monday," Grasso said later to the media. "In the course of the next few days, we will do all the...stress testing that's required of our industry to make sure that by Monday morning the American people are served by the finest capital market the world has known."

Added Grasso, "New York is the financial capital of the world. It has been, it is, and it will remain so in the future."

Statements like that were hugely important. They told the world that New York might be down, but the city most definitely was not out. The markets opened Monday, right on time.

*   *   *

In the days that followed, I continued to take care of business at Bear Stearns, but I kept thinking about what had happened downtown. I shared my insights with the media. I was happy to do that. I thought it was important to remind people about the earlier attack and reflect on what it meant that the terrorists had returned. I sketched the history and motives of al-Qaeda and described what I knew about the inspirational power and twisted mind of Osama bin Laden. Everywhere I went, people had their own 9/11 stories. In countless conversations with friends and longtime colleagues, I traded stories about people who were missing and people who were found. The streets were eerily empty. People, serious people, were talking about leaving New York City and never coming back. *Shell-shocked* was the right term for how a lot of people looked, even those who hadn't been anywhere near the towers and didn't even know anyone there. At CNN, Paula Zahn reminded me that her husband, Richard Cohen, owned office buildings within blocks of Ground Zero. "How are the buildings?" she whispered to me during one of the breaks.

On September 14, President George W. Bush stood with Mayor Rudy Giuliani in the still smoldering pit and spoke through a bullhorn to the construction workers and rescue personnel.

"I want you all to know that America today—America today is on bended knee, in prayer for the people whose lives were lost here, for the workers who work here, for the families who mourn," the president said. "This nation stands with the good people of New York City and New Jersey and Connecticut as we mourn the loss of thousands of our citizens."

"I can't hear you!" one rescue worker called out from the back.

"I can hear you!" Bush called back through the bullhorn. "I can hear you! The rest of the world hears you! And the people, who knocked these buildings down will hear all of us soon!"

That was met with a loud, throaty chant.

"USA! USA! USA!"

Mayor Giuliani exhibited real leadership in those early days, I thought. In the years to come, many people, including me, would question some of his decisions and how well the city was prepared for a second attack. But in the crucial days and weeks after September 11, as a leader and a spokesman for New York, Giuliani projected strength and calm.

A few hours after President Bush had gone, I did manage to slip back into our downtown apartment and get a pile of clothes. A couple of my NYPD friends drove me down and walked with me through the security lines. The elevators in the building were off. I had to walk up sixteen flights of stairs. I grabbed some suits and shirts and toiletries. All flights had been grounded, and I didn't know when Veronica would get back to town. Unfortunately, I had left a window open in the apartment when I went to work on Tuesday morning. We faced south. The whole apartment was filled with a fine white dust. In my mind, I could already see the cleaning crews in their space suits.

I remained at the hotel for one more night and then stayed with a friend of mine, Michael Saperstein, and then at the apartment of my brother-in-law, Martin Clarke. Then I moved to other places and bunked with other friends. Like many New Yorkers that disconcerting month of September, I was somewhere between homeless and a nomad.

*   *   *

On the Sunday after 9/11, I was called to Washington by Norman Mineta, the secretary of transportation in the Bush administration. He told me he was putting together two small Rapid Response Teams to come up with safety improvements for America's air travel system and wanted me to be part of the process. Five days earlier, hijackers with box cutters had managed to commandeer four commercial airliners with devastating effects. Mineta was a very hands-on transportation secretary, and he was looking for practical reforms that could be instituted immediately, if not sooner.

He'd had his own harrowing 9/11 drama. As American Airlines Flight 77 approached the Pentagon, he'd been with Vice President Dick Cheney in the President's Emergency Operating Center. It was Mineta who made the white-knuckles decision to ground all aircraft coast to coast, the first unplanned, nationwide "ground stop" in U.S. aviation history. At that moment, there were 4,546 planes in the air. It was too late to do anything about Flight 77, which crashed into the Pentagon. But in a matter of minutes, pilots everywhere were seeking the nearest airports. Now, five days later, as the air travel system was groaning back to life, an obvious question had to be asked: What can be done to make the system safer? My four-person Rapid Response Team focused on airport safety, while the other team turned its attention to the planes. We were given two weeks to make our recommendations, an almost unheard-of timetable in bureaucratic Washington.

I was joined by Northwest Airlines CEO Richard Anderson, Chip Barclay of the American Association of Airport Executives, and, the one who did most of the talking, Herb Kelleher, the colorful cofounder and chairman of Southwest Airlines. The other group was similarly industry-heavy: American Airlines vice chairman Robert Baker, former Boeing vice president Robert Davis, Captain Duane Woerth of the Air Line Pilots Association, and Patricia Friend, president of the Association of Flight Attendants. Paul Browne accompanied me. As a former U.S. Customs commissioner, undersecretary of the Treasury, and New York police commissioner, I was the only member of either panel with a law enforcement background.

My impression was that the industry people, though concerned about safety, were even more concerned about interrupting the flow of the air travel business. So as I pushed for stricter background checks, closer body searches, and tighter luggage rules, Kelleher especially pushed back hard, emphasizing how challenging, expensive, or inconvenient each new step might be. I thought it was especially important that the government take the passenger-screening process away from the airlines, who'd overseen it for as long as anyone could recall. A federal safety agency should run that, I believed. I'd flown enough to know that as long as the airlines were in charge, the screeners would feel pressure to make sure all passengers reached the gate on time, whatever security shortcuts that might entail.

In the end, the two Rapid Response Teams came up with more than a dozen practical suggestions, many of which were quickly adopted or became part of a road map for future improvement: Wider use of passenger background profiles to catch people who pose potential security threats before they step aboard aircraft. Limiting carry-on luggage to one bag and one personal item per passenger. Requiring that some items be carried in clear plastic bags. Using Computer-Assisted Passenger Screening to check more people before they boarded the plane. Requiring airport and airline employees to undergo new criminal background checks. Scrutinizing travel patterns as soon as tickets are purchased. Fortifying cockpit doors. And perhaps most important of all, establishing a new federal agency, which became the Transportation Security Administration, to be in charge of air travel safety, taking that crucial responsibility out of the airlines' hands.

These measures would become part of an upgraded safety network for America.

As we began putting our proposals into practice, Mineta declared, "These are extraordinary times, and we are rejecting bureaucratic business-as-usual when it comes to transportation safety and security." Almost nothing in Washington had ever moved as swiftly as this.

*   *   *

Veronica had wanted to end her trip early and fly home from Europe as soon as the flight ban was lifted. Jim called and urged her not to. "Don't be ridiculous," he said. "There's nothing to come home to. Just stay there." She came back to New York in late September as planned. I was thrilled to see her. I was also tired of bunking with friends. So we checked into the Plaza Hotel, which wasn't quite as pricey as you might think. The Plaza was just about empty. Hardly any tourists were there. I think the staff were happy to see us when we arrived.

One afternoon soon after Veronica returned, she and I went down to our neighborhood. This time they wouldn't let us into our building, which was fully sealed off at that point. It wasn't until almost Election Day that we could get back inside. But we did manage to go up to the roof of another building in the area. By that point, I'd been down to Ground Zero a few times. Some of the cops had taken me to the edge of the hole for an up-close look. I thought I had a clear sense of what remained of the towers and all the damage that had been done there. But from the ground, there was simply no way to grasp the sheer size of it.

Standing on the roof with Veronica that afternoon, a hint of New York's crisp fall finally in the sour downtown air, I could hardly believe what I was seeing with my very own eyes. Just the breadth and the scope of it, the sheer magnitude, how much debris there was, how high the pile went, the number of people working down here, the enormity of removing collapsed office towers—every girder, every chunk of sheetrock, every ceiling tile—and knowing in my mind the great human loss that had taken place right there. We wondered what other names we would hear among the dead or the missing. We loved the area. We knew it the way you can know only your own patch of a city. It wasn't just the World Trade Center to us. It was part of our neighborhood. Thousands and thousands of facts, memories, preferences, and tiny little details.

Gone. All of it. Literally gone. With nothing but a pile of rubble left behind, the most enormous pile of rubble I'd ever seen in my life.

As we stood on the roof that afternoon, the sun setting against the west bank of the Hudson and New Jersey behind it, the pile straight ahead, Veronica started to cry. We tried to pick out familiar landmarks across the ruins. On the far side of the pile, we could see the top of the Millenium Hotel on Church Street and the top of the Woolworth Building up Broadway. It's not like I hadn't thought about any of this before. I'd thought about little else for weeks. But standing there, the whole scene crystallized for me. This was war, and I wanted to be in it.

CHAPTER TEN

Long Shot Mayor

As one of its many consequences, 9/11 upended New York City politics.

The Democratic and Republican primary elections for the mayoral race to replace Rudy Giuliani had been scheduled for September 11. Polls opened as planned that morning. They didn't stay open for long. Voting was halted shortly after the planes hit the towers, and the primary was postponed for two weeks, with a runoff sixteen days after that, if needed. But as the four Democratic and two Republican candidates tried to figure out what the delay meant for them, another unexpected question was dropped into the race: Would Giuliani really leave office?

On September 10, he was a lame-duck mayor who'd managed to exhaust New Yorkers with his acerbic style, his tumultuous personal life, and his zero-tolerance attitude toward anyone and anything he didn't like. What a difference a day can make. Suddenly Giuliani was "America's mayor" with soaring approval ratings. Some people were clamoring for him to remain in office even after his second term expired when the ball dropped at Times Square on New Year's Eve.

I didn't like the idea of Giuliani staying longer than the law allowed. I didn't believe—I still don't—that any individual is indispensable to the city of New York, even after a major catastrophe. Leaders come and leaders go. That's as it should be, the natural order of things.

At first, Giuliani brushed aside the suggestion that New York's election law be changed to accommodate a third term for him— or that he be given a few extra months of bonus time to steer New York's recovery. But as the hosannas grew louder—"Rudy the Rock," French president Jacques Chirac called him—the mayor seemed increasingly open to the idea. "I don't know what the right thing to do is. I really don't know," he teased just before Public Advocate Mark Green and Bronx borough president Fernando Ferrer finished first and second, respectively, in the delayed Democratic primary and headed to the October 11 runoff. "It's a very important decision and I need time to think about it, and I need time to talk to people about it, and I've not had the time to do that."

Giuliani's political allies began to lobby Albany, where the state legislature would have to bless any term extension. Governor George Pataki, who'd been at odds with Giuliani before 9/11 but was now a giant booster, was staunchly supportive. "I'll tell you," Pataki said in a press conference on September 21, "if I were a resident of New York City, I'd write him in" on Election Day. It wasn't just Giuliani's longtime allies who said he should stay. Two unlikely supporters jumped on board—Mark Green, the Democratic front-runner for mayor, and billionaire businessman Michael Bloomberg, the top Republican, both came out for more Rudy. Ferrer, the other Democrat in the runoff, was firmly opposed.

All this adulation must have been heady for Giuliani. One poll, from the Marist Institute for Public Opinion, found that 91 percent of New Yorkers rated his post-9/11 performance excellent or good. Still, that didn't mean most New Yorkers wanted him to remain at city hall. In the Marist poll, only 33 percent said they'd support changing the election law to accommodate him.

On October 3, eight days before Green and Ferrer were to meet in the Democratic runoff, Giuliani ruled out the third-term idea. But he would still like an extra three months in office, he said, if state legislators would go along with it.

"The offer is there," he said during a hastily called press conference. "If they want to accept it, they can."

This wasn't a power grab, the outgoing mayor insisted. It was "based on the good of the city." The next mayor, he said, "should have a longer—significantly longer—transition period. I think that anybody that thinks they're ready for this job on January 1, given the monumental tasks that lie ahead, doesn't understand this job really well."

And that's about where the idea died.

State assembly members, especially Democrats from minority districts in the city, were adamantly opposed. Assembly speaker Sheldon Silver said he was in no rush to consider anything of the kind. Somehow or another, the city would have to get along without Rudy Giuliani in charge.

* * *

While the Ground Zero recovery and Giuliani's machinations dominated the news, the actual mayoral race got relatively little attention. In the Democratic runoff, Green squeaked out a victory over Ferrer with 52 percent of the vote, though not before an ugly turn at the end. Green supporters distributed *New York Post* caricatures of Ferrer and the Reverend Al Sharpton in white sections of Brooklyn, leading to claims of racism. No one could prove the public advocate knew about the questionable literature, but he entered the general election with a sharply divided party and some angry African American and Latino Democrats.

Still, Green was widely expected to win.

Bloomberg, who'd rolled past former Bronx borough president Herman Badillo for the Republican nomination, had made a huge fortune selling financial data to Wall Street and vowed to spend whatever it took to get elected. But he had never run for public office before. He was not widely known. Green, by contrast, was a citywide officeholder, an energetic campaigner, and the nominee of the Democrats, who held a five-to-one registration advantage over Republicans. It's true, Giuliani had won as a Republican and then been reelected—but could lightning like that really strike again? Election Day was November 6.

A couple of weeks before the election, Bloomberg's campaign manager, Bill Cunningham, reached out to me. He wanted to know if I would consider endorsing Mike. I didn't know Bloomberg well, but we'd met a couple of times. I was impressed by him. Working at Bear Stearns, I knew how beloved his "Bloomberg terminals" were.

Several friends of mine warned me that an endorsement wasn't a smart idea. First of all, Bloomberg would probably lose, they said. Why attach myself to a loser? How did we know the Bloomberg campaign was anything more than an ego trip by another Manhattan billionaire? Did I really want to go along with that?

Those friends, some of them sharp political thinkers, had my best interests at heart. They didn't want to see me out on a limb I would later regret. I understood all that. But another consideration seemed more important. These weren't normal times. In such a moment of crisis, I thought the city could use someone who'd proven himself a savvy business leader. Bloomberg seemed smart, focused, public spirited, and eager to serve, even if he didn't have much special knowledge about municipal affairs. I just had confidence in him.

I endorsed Mike Bloomberg for mayor.

I didn't seek anything in return and nothing was offered. In my endorsement, I focused on his obvious strength. "The overriding issue in this election is the health of our economy, and there is no question that New York City needs Mike Bloomberg to prevent an economic catastrophe," I said.

That night, I attended the Alfred E. Smith Memorial Foundation Dinner at the Waldorf Astoria New York, an annual fund-raiser for Catholic Charities of the Archdiocese of New York. It's a formal affair that always attracts an elite group of business and political leaders. Veronica was busy, so Jim came with me. All night, people kept asking about the Bloomberg endorsement, the questions often accompanied by quizzical looks. At one point, Rosanna Scotto, a popular anchor at the local Fox affiliate, WYNY Channel 5, and now my son Greg's partner on *Good Day New York*, pulled Jim aside.

"What's he thinking?" she asked, motioning toward me. "Does Bloomberg really have a chance?" Rosanna was just asking. But if you'd polled the ballroom, I'm sure the yeses would have been a distinct minority.

I didn't care about the odds. I thought Mike was the better candidate. I attended a few campaign events and offered some issue suggestions to Jonathan Capehart, a former *Daily News* editorial writer who was advising the candidate on criminal-justice matters. Green's two most visible law enforcement supporters were Bill Bratton, Rudy Giuliani's first police commissioner, and Pat Lynch, president of the Patrolmen's Benevolent Association. The outgoing mayor waited a long time to make it official, but he also endorsed his fellow Republican Mike Bloomberg. Giuliani struck the same business chord that I had. "I am very, very confident that the city would be in absolutely excellent hands in the hands of Mike Bloomberg," he said. "If he can have half the success with New York City that he has had in business, New York is going to have an even greater future." Though the gap had been narrowing, the last *New York Times* poll of likely voters still had Green up by five percentage points.

On election night, I joined Bloomberg and a couple dozen of his supporters in a suite at the Hilton Times Square while other staffers and volunteers gathered for an optimistically billed "victory party" across West Forty-Second Street at the B.B. King Blues Club & Grill. Before any votes were tallied, Bloomberg said to me,

"I hope we can get jobs for everybody." He didn't mean jobs at city hall. He could read the polls as well as anyone. Bloomberg was clearly expecting to lose and eager to provide soft landings for the campaign staffers and volunteers. Even David Garth, Bloomberg's top strategist, seemed to be steeling himself for a loss. "Mike is a very big boy," Garth told the media. "He understands reality. He knew from the beginning what he was getting himself into."

But sometime after 10:00 p.m., I saw Mayor Giuliani and Governor Pataki sitting side by side in the hotel suite, poring over a long column of numbers. They were vote totals from Staten Island. Both men smiled. They nodded at each other. That was it, they decided. Bloomberg had won.

Everyone from the hotel suite walked across the street to the blues club, where Bloomberg delivered a victory speech, one of three versions he'd handwritten back at the hotel—win, lose, or too close to call.

There were several reasons Bloomberg was elected, I believe. The terror attacks made voters seek a more serious mayor, someone with a little extra gravitas. Some Democrats were still smarting from the bitter primary runoff. Giuliani's endorsement helped tremendously after his stellar post-9/11 leadership. And one other thing, more important than all the others combined: Bloomberg spent $74 million of his own money on TV ads, direct mail, and other campaign expenses, the most ever spent in a nonpresidential campaign. Had it not been for that and the terror attack, I'm certain New York would have been preparing for the New Year's inauguration of Mayor Green.

No one looked more surprised than Mike Bloomberg did as he stood in front of his cheering supporters at the blues club. "New York is alive and well and open for business," the next mayor declared. "The easy part is done. Now comes the hard part."

Later that night, I met Giuliani and a few others at Club Macanudo, a cigar bar on East Sixty-Third Street.

It was a heady evening that few people expected. To be with the winners on election night was a great experience. I stayed and enjoyed the scene long into the night. Late the next morning, I was walking on the street near my office at Bear Stearns when my phone rang. It was Mike Bloomberg.

"So," he said, getting right down to business with a minimum of pleasantries, an approach he would rarely veer from in the next twelve years. "You want to be police commissioner?"

We had never discussed that possibility, not in any explicit way. Somewhere in the back of my mind, I guess I had thought that, if by some odd chance Bloomberg actually got elected, my returning as police commissioner might be something to explore. I had no idea whether a similar thought had even occurred to him. One day when he and I were just talking, he had floated a totally different possibility, as if he were musing—the idea of my being schools chancellor.

That seemed like a stretch at the time. While I had several academic degrees—a bachelor's from Manhattan College, a law degree from St. John's, a master of laws from NYU, and a master of public administration from the Kennedy School at Harvard—I had never worked in education. I'd never taken an education course. I've never even taught second grade.

As I would discover later, Bloomberg is a big believer in the notion that a strong manager can manage anything. A lifelong investment banker and financial-data and media entrepreneur, he'd just gotten himself elected mayor of the nation's largest city, after all. But the schools musing had gone no further, and now he was offering something real—and right in my area of interest, experience, and expertise. I'd held the police commissioner job before. I knew that no one had ever done it for two nonconsecutive New York mayors. But I'd had a good run the previous time. I believed I had left with my reputation and integrity intact. I'd spent the eight years since broadening my experience with important federal responsibilities at the Customs Service, at the Treasury Department, and in Haiti. Since early 2001, I'd been learning Wall Street from the inside as senior managing director for corporate security at Bear Stearns. I certainly had the credentials, and I wasn't a stranger to New York politics. Bill Bratton, one of several other potential candidates, had backed Mark Green for mayor. If Green had won, Bratton would have a gotten a call like I just had.

Of course, the call from Bloomberg wasn't a total surprise. Veronica and I had kicked the idea around in a what-if kind of way. There were several arguments against taking the job, even if it was offered. After four decades of government work, we weren't exactly suffering, but we were far from wealthy. I still had to make a living. At Bear Stearns, I was finally making private-sector money. That was nice. The $150,500 police commissioner's salary would amount to a major pay cut. And there were other financial practicalities. I'd been receiving a police pension since I left the department at the end of 1993—a regular pension, not one of those tax-free, three-quarters disability pensions that top police brass had often gotten for themselves. But it was something, and if I went back to the department, those checks would stop coming in. Veronica had just retired from her job as an account executive at Tyco International. So we would be a one-salary family. But Veronica also knew how important I thought this mission was and how much the city needed to have the right people at the top during a time like this.

"It's not like it would be forever," I said, trying to convince myself as much as my wife. "How long would I really stay in the job? Realistically, I could be back in the private sector in a couple of years."

Veronica nodded.

She'd been with me every step of the way. She made clear, as she always had, that she'd stand with me 100 percent.

If the call came, I already knew what I would say. The real surprise on this postelection Wednesday morning was that the billionaire Republican and first-time candidate was in the position to make it—that he had actually won the race for mayor of New York.

I didn't ask for any time to consider the offer. "Sure," I said, answering as directly and as succinctly as I had been asked. "It would be an honor."

That was it. No sit-down meeting. No committee. No formal interview. No discussion of policing policies or the post-9/11 challenges ahead. None of that. Just a call and an offer. Just an unqualified yes—and a journey into the dark unknown.

I had to give credit to Mike for moving quickly. It wasn't like he had an appointments list drawn up in advance of the election, as the overconfident Mark Green apparently had. Even before the election, some top officials in the police department had met with Bratton to discuss their future assignments once Green won and brought Bratton back.

Mike was also fortunate to have Nat Leventhal in charge of his postelection transition. While the incoming mayor had no experience in city government and didn't know many people in New York politics, Leventhal had been on the inside of four city administrations, going all the way back to his youthful days as chief of staff to Mayor John Lindsay. He'd served as chairman of the Citizens Union and had recently stepped down after seventeen years as president of Lincoln Center. He was the ultimate New York insider. I believe he urged Bloomberg to fill the police commissioner job as quickly as possible, given the pressing need to rebuild public confidence that the city was safe to live and work in.

I knew—and I'm sure Mike did—that we didn't have a second to waste.

CHAPTER ELEVEN

Building the Team

M ike Bloomberg didn't announce my appointment for a week. But the morning after I'd accepted his offer to become police commissioner again, I was standing beside a metal easel in a brightly lit conference room at Bear Stearns headquarters on Park Avenue. A large flip pad was on the easel. I had a red Sharpie in my left hand.

It was still six weeks before the Bloomberg administration would take city hall, six weeks before I would return to my old fourteenth-floor office with Teddy Roosevelt's desk at 1 Police Plaza and the job I'd left with mixed feelings eight years earlier. There'd been three police commissioners since then: Bill Bratton (for twenty-six months), Howard Safir (four years, four months) and Bernard Kerik (sixteen months). My own previous term as police commissioner had ended after sixteen months, when Rudy Giuliani defeated David Dinkins for mayor in 1993.

Soon the responsibility would be mine again—but it wouldn't be the same job at all. The city was different now. The department would have to be different too. The crime drop we had set in motion with Safe Streets, Safe City had continued through the Giuliani years. September 11 changed nearly everything. There was no time to bask in my appointment. New York was still grieving. The city wasn't anywhere close to being back on its feet. The recovery had barely begun. Plenty of slogans were floating around: "Never forget." "Homeland security." "Rebuild better than ever."

"Let's roll." But there was no overall plan for rebuilding public confidence and no comprehensive strategy—not at the police department, not anywhere—for reducing the chance that the city would
be attacked by terrorists again. Devising that strategy, I knew, was
our first and highest priority.

To be certain, this would entail more than small changes at
the margins. It would require a fundamental rethinking of the
role of the police in New York City, a thorough reordering of
the department's priorities, and some genuine cultural change.
We'd still have to fight street crime. That challenge would never
go away. But moving forward, a large part of our responsibility—
maybe the largest—would be protecting the city against another
terror attack. No local police department had ever taken on that
responsibility. But no local police department had ever been in
the position the NYPD was in as 2001 came to a close. We had to
think creatively. We had to start—*now*. And I certainly couldn't
do it alone.

Four men in shirtsleeves and ties were with me that day in the
Bear Stearns conference room, sitting at a long glass table, looking up at the easel and at me. I began by drawing a sketch of the
police department's organizational chart.

"Commissioner's here," I said, drawing a small rectangle at
the top of the pad.

"Right below that, the first dep and chief of department," I
continued, putting two boxes below the one for commissioner,
connected to it with short vertical red lines.

Next I drew a row of boxes for all the deputy commissioners
and chiefs. "Besides the existing deputies and chiefs, two things I
want to add," I said.

The men in front of me nodded as I drew two additional rect-
angles on the pad.

"I want a counterterrorism bureau, and I want an expanded

intelligence division. I want a deputy commissioner in charge of each of them, and I want them both reporting to me."

The NYPD had never had a counterterrorism bureau, and the Intelligence Division had been overseen by a deputy chief, not a deputy commissioner. To someone outside law enforcement or the military, that might sound like a technical or trivial distinction. Inside a large police department, those differences can speak volumes—about power, resources, access, and priority.

I continued. "Let's significantly increase the NYPD component of the JTTF, and put that under the deputy commissioner for counterterrorism."

The Joint Terrorism Task Force had been created in New York City in 1980 amid a rash of political bombs by black nationalists, Puerto Rican separatists, and other radical groups, then replicated in dozens of other cities around the United States. The task force included personnel from various state and local law enforcement agencies, including the NYPD. But it had always been dominated and controlled by the FBI. I had learned from our experience at the first World Trade Center bombing in 1993. Since New York was the terrorists' prime target, I wanted to make sure the NYPD didn't get lost inside the task force.

"We need a much stronger role there," I said.

The men in the room nodded.

"And I want to do something about medical too," I continued. I didn't mean yearly physicals for department employees. I was thinking about the anthrax attack that had occurred in the weeks after 9/11, when letters containing the deadly spores were mailed to the Manhattan offices of NBC News and the *New York Post* and the Washington offices of Democratic senators Tom Daschle and Patrick Leahy, killing five people and infecting seventeen others.

"With the anthrax attack," I said, "we need an infectious-disease component in the counterterrorism bureau. It should be separate from the medical unit that is in personnel. That's for regular medical concerns. Chemical and biological weapons are part of the terror arsenal now." As an organization, we needed to learn more about that and be prepared for it. It's about protecting the public and protecting our officers. I didn't want people running into a scene of a chemical attack with no idea what they're facing.

As I spoke, I kept drawing new lines, making new connections, moving some boxes up and others down. One Sharpie mark at a time, I was reimagining the flow of power and information inside the New York City Police Department.

I was doing almost all the talking. The four other men in the room were my initial sounding board. I had history with all of them—and, more important, they had my trust. I wanted their reactions. There was Paul Browne, who'd been with me at the NYPD, the Customs Service, the Treasury Department, and with the police monitors in Haiti. He'd been my media spokesman and a whole lot more. I called him my wartime consigliere, not like Tom Hagen in *The Godfather*. There was Joe Wuensch, who had held one of the most important and least appreciated jobs in the NYPD, deputy commissioner of management and budget, until Bernie Kerik inexplicably asked him to leave. There was Mike Farrell, who started as a numbers whiz at the Department of Justice. He had been a top crime analyst, policy adviser, planner, and quality-control guy at the NYPD and then became deputy director of the state Division of Criminal Justice Services. Finally, there was George Grasso, who'd gone to law school as a police officer and then rose to deputy commissioner for legal matters at the NYPD. He was always a steady hand in the crisis of the moment.

These were intelligent, forward-looking people who knew the department intimately. They were all pros, not remotely political. They were able to make tough decisions when they had to. All four of them would play major roles in the department in the years to come.

As I laid out my vision, I could tell that all four of them liked what they were hearing, a sweeping overhaul of the department's mission reflecting the new generation of threats the city now faced. But there was also some concern in the air. Paul Browne addressed it most directly.

"I love the way this sounds," he said. "But some of it is going to be a heavy lift internally. How do we get people to buy into such a big change?"

It was an excellent question. Paul was right. This would be a heavy lift, and it would never be achieved without solid internal support.

"We'll need help," I said. "We will have to bring some people in whose credibility is so strong, who have such gravitas, who so obviously know what they're talking about that no one will be able to question them. We need some people whose competence is totally beyond doubt. This won't be a job for pretty-good people. Who do you know?"

*   *   *

Word of my return leaked first in *Newsday*. Citing unnamed sources, the paper reported on November 11 that Mayor-Elect Bloomberg had asked and I had agreed to come back as police commissioner. That day, Bloomberg's people refused to confirm, and so did I. But the mayor-to-be was asked about the report the following morning on NBC's *Meet the Press*. He didn't quite confirm it, but he left little doubt. "Well," he said, "I did read that in the papers yesterday. Stay tuned."

I'd like to think that the formal announcement, when it came two days later, calmed some nerves in the city. The message was, *You don't have to worry about the police department. It will be in experienced, competent hands.* This was important for Mike Bloomberg. No one doubted his expertise when it came to economic development. He knew Wall Street. He'd been a hugely successful businessman. He could certainly handle budgets, tax policy, bond ratings, and the whole money side of city government. He also seemed fairly conversant with health and education issues, two passions of his even before he began eying city hall. But he had never demonstrated any particular interest in public safety and law enforcement. Frankly, I'm not sure if he'd ever gotten a traffic ticket. After the terror attacks, he recognized that protecting New York was the greatest challenge facing the city. Clearly the police wouldn't just be fighting traditional street crime. The city's very survival had been threatened by terrorists. If people didn't feel safe living in, working in, investing in, or visiting the city, nothing else the mayor might achieve in office would be worth very much.

At the same time, some huge internal challenges awaited us. The Giuliani administration had made decisions that were sure to cause some difficulty for whoever came next. They'd spent massive overtime dollars beating the crime numbers down, levels of spending that were unsustainable. Then 9/11 came and police costs shot up even higher. For the first time ever, captains and above were paid cash for overtime. All those inflated paychecks had the additional effect of sweetening the pensions of veteran officers, giving them large financial incentives to retire within the year. To add to the pressure, low starting salaries were squeezing recruiting efforts. And right after the election, Bloomberg mentioned the possibility of a 10 percent budget cut for the police department.

Department insiders were abuzz about all this.

*   *   *

The truth was, we needed help. A lot of help. From top people both inside and outside the department. I saw no reason that a police department ought to be satisfied with anything less than the best. Organizations can't always do everything with the talent they have, especially when the most urgent issue at hand is something entirely different from what the organization is accustomed to doing. Hadn't they taught me that at Harvard? Wasn't that one of the lessons of Haiti? I was committed to bringing in a caliber of talent that had never before worked in a local police department—the kind of people who had probably never even considered police work before. Real world-class experts in their fields who could help me take the NYPD to a whole new level.

I was convinced that intelligence gathering and counterterrorism were going to become key features of the New York police mission. Those weren't skills we had in great abundance in the field or at headquarters. They weren't what the police academy specialized in teaching. You didn't learn that sort of thing running a Bronx robbery squad or supervising Brooklyn South narcotics. But I also understood something else: If we were going to bring in outside people and put them in charge of New York police officers, those outsiders had better arrive with unquestioned qualifications. Otherwise they'd never get beyond morning roll call. They would have to be so talented, so credentialed, so experienced that no police officer could possibly question their authority.

But who?

Actually, I had the profiles before I had the names. I wanted a top official from the CIA to run the Intelligence Division and a Marine Corps general in charge of counterterrorism. No one knew intelligence gathering like the CIA, and after thirty years of active and reserve duty in the Marine Corps, having retired as a colonel, I'd seen how impressive some of the generals could be. Tough. Focused. Driven. Fully grasping the importance of mission and refusing to accept any result short of success. Those were the kinds of people we needed to help create the post-9/11 NYPD.

There wasn't any precedent for this, bringing a former CIA espionage chief, a retired Marine Corps general, or similarly high-powered outsiders into the upper echelon of a city police department. I knew from the start it would make some people uncomfortable, in and out of the department. Civil libertarians might object that an ex-spy, an ex-general, or their ilk might not fully grasp the Constitutional limits of urban policing. I knew that entrenched police officials would not be pleased when outsiders arrived with high rank.

The NYPD is a very hierarchical place. Insiders rarely express their unhappiness directly to the boss. Complaints are usually muffled or shared in close circles. I picked up on the usual grumbling secondhand, but none of it changed what I knew we had to do. September 11 gave me some extra leeway. It really was a case of "Don't let a crisis go to waste."

I approached a couple of generals I knew, and they said no. One of them, Martin Steele, who was working at the Intrepid Sea, Air & Space Museum, said he couldn't do it, but "Why not ask Libutti?" That would be Marine Corps Lieutenant General Frank Libutti. Libutti was born in Huntington, Long Island. So he knew New York. Among many other stops, he had commanded FMF/Pac—Fleet Marine Force, Pacific, a force of ninety thousand marines. Now retired, he had just started as special assistant for homeland security at the Department of Defense. This was before there was a Department of Homeland Security up and running. Frank sounded like a man who knew counterterrorism from the battlefield and from Washington.

I called and asked if he might be interested. "Sure, I'm interested," he told me immediately. We met at the Roosevelt Hotel.

Frank was great to talk to—totally direct, a hard charger, a Silver Star awardee who'd been wounded in Vietnam. The man had presence. He'd done all these things I admired. I laid out a very abbreviated version of my counterterror vision. I asked if he'd like to join me. He said, "Yes, sir," and I had my new deputy commissioner to run the Counter-Terrorism Bureau.

Unlike Libutti, David Cohen was someone I knew. During

his thirty-five-year career at the CIA, he'd done a tour as station chief in New York, which is a much more public position than you would imagine. He actually had sit-down meetings, an administrative assistant, and a business card. Cohen had retired from the CIA and was in the private sector now.

He seemed to me like an ideal candidate to run the NYPD Intelligence Division, which my Sharpie and I had just elevated in the organization. I called him in December. He was working at AIG, the international insurance conglomerate run by Maurice "Hank" Greenberg. Cohen knew I was at Bear Stearns, whose chairman, coincidentally, was Alan "Ace" Greenberg.

"Congratulations on the new—" he began when I got him on the phone.

"Yeah, yeah, yeah," I said, cutting him off. "Let's cut to the chase. I'm looking to make some changes in the police department in this post-9/11 world. I'm looking for a deputy. Are you interested?"

"Definitely sounds interesting," he said. "But I'm working for Hank Greenberg now. Mr. Greenberg has been very kind to me and very generous. I am very loyal to him."

"Yeah, yeah," I said, laughing. "You have your Greenberg problem, I have mine."

We talked a little more about the job, what a unique moment it was in New York, and why I thought we needed a first-string intelligence professional near the top of the NYPD.

He said he wanted to speak with his wife and he'd call me back in a day or two. An hour later, he was on the phone again, saying yes.

"If I had said no to you," Cohen told me, "it would not have been possible for me, with my DNA, to continue living in New York. I would have had to leave. If I had refused to do this and stayed in New York, I would have felt like a traitor. I couldn't do that."

When I heard that, I knew Cohen and I would get along just fine.

*   *   *

Those were the two major components, intelligence and counter-terrorism. In the weeks and months to come, I intended a dramatic expansion of the resources devoted to these areas, including staffing and expertise. I knew that if we were going to fight this new enemy, we couldn't rely entirely on old policing techniques. What might be effective against burglars in Riverdale or chain snatchers in Crown Heights was unlikely to provide much protection against a truck bomb, an improvised explosive device, or an airplane turned into a missile. I also knew that the battle against terrorists couldn't begin in front of some high-profile New York target. It had to start far earlier than that. If we were going to protect this city against terrorists, we had to know who the terrorists were—their methods, their ideologies, their funding, and their associates. We had to know everything. And at this point, at least, the New York City Police Department knew hardly anything at all.

Cohen and Libutti weren't the only outside powerhouses we would bring in. Over time, those two would be joined by dozens and dozens of others who arrived with knowledge and relationships the department had never been able to access before. Counterterrorism pros like Michael Sheehan, Richard Daddario, Rebecca Weiner, and Richard Falkenrath. Defense-intelligence specialist John Decker. Top intelligence analysts like Mitchell Silber and Arvin Bhatt. Active CIA officer Larry Sanchez. Former FBI agents like Sid Caspersen and Ed Curran. Top-flight legal minds like Douglass Maynard, Stephen Hammerman, Andrew Schaffer, Katherine Lemire, David M. Cohen, Jessica Tisch, and jack-of-all-trades Rob Lewis.

Working in concert with the talent we already had inside the department, these new leaders would go on to achieve things almost unimaginable in any other local police department—or even in this one at an earlier time. People with their experience and backgrounds simply don't work in local law enforcement. And yet they did. Asked to join a crucial mission at a make-or-break time, every one of them signed on readily and then performed extraordinary services to New York and America. We truly could not have achieved so much without them. And it all started with the yeses I got from Cohen and Libutti before I was even sworn in.

*   *   *

I was able to give some hints of my plans at my formal swearing-in as New York's forty-first police commissioner. That took place on Friday, January 4, at Gracie Mansion, the mayor's official residence, which Bloomberg made clear he wouldn't be living in. (I was really sworn in at 12:01 a.m. on January 1.) For the first time, I laid out the three Cs that would guide my time as police commissioner—Counterterrorism, Crime Fighting, and Community Relations. But it was not even four months since the World Trade Center attack, so counterterrorism was the one on most people's minds.

"We will ensure that a strong relationship exists with federal authorities in our mutual desire to thwart terrorism," I told those present at my swearing-in, including former mayors Ed Koch and David Dinkins, former police commissioners Howard Safir and Bill Bratton, and the district attorneys of Manhattan and Queens, Robert Morgenthau and Richard Brown. Of course, Veronica and our sons Jim and Greg were there too, along with many of my relatives.

One of my first initiatives, I said, would be to create a high-level position to oversee New York's response to terrorism, a threat we would not be leaving solely to state and federal agencies anymore.

I explained that Veronica and I had only just gotten back into our apartment building in Battery Park City, across West Street from Ground Zero. "When we returned and looked from the roof down onto the devastation," I told those assembled, "a part of our hearts were ripped away."

*　　*　　*

A week before my tenure officially began, I visited my old office, which I hadn't seen for eight years. I met with Joseph Dunne, the first deputy commissioner for the outgoing administration, a real pro who a lot of people thought would himself make a fine police commissioner. And I set about trying to change the culture of the NYPD into something better suited to the post-9/11 New York.

"It's a big change," I conceded when we announced Cohen's and Libutti's appointments in late January, "but our whole world has changed as a result of September 11." I said I understood that counterterrorism had previously been left essentially in the hands of federal agencies. We wouldn't be doing that anymore, not when New York was "very high on the target list of terrorists."

I had no antagonism toward the FBI, the CIA, or other federal agencies, except when they behaved imperiously. They had good people. They had great equipment. They did fine forensic work. But for years, they had been dominating local law enforcement, and in our case, at least, that wasn't going to happen anymore.

I wasn't intimidated by these people. I knew them. I had spent nearly five years working in federal law enforcement at the Customs Service and the Treasury Department, where I oversaw the Secret Service, the Bureau of Alcohol, Tobacco and Firearms, the Customs Service, and other agencies. I understood the language they spoke, and I wasn't in awe of anyone.

And the NYPD brought a lot to the table.

We were bigger than the FBI. We certainly had a lot more diversity. We had sources on the street in New York and in immigrant communities, contacts the feds could only dream of. We had people who could work undercover with potential terrorists. The FBI had very few agents who could do that.

I knew some people would interpret this as a slap at the FBI or the CIA. But it wasn't. "Our intention is to work *more* closely with the federal government," I said. "To do that, we had to put in place a structure to train our officers and find people from outside the police culture to do it." These personnel were just the beginning of it, I emphasized. We also needed to get started immediately gathering our own intelligence—and analyzing it. The days of waiting for federal assistance and guidance were over. "We already have an Intelligence Division that is substantial," I said. "We need to do a better job in the interpretation of the intelligence that comes in."

Mike Bloomberg approved of the idea. He understood the advantages of recruiting outside expertise. That's routine in the business world. The mayor sounded proud. "This makes us the only police department, I believe, in the United States with somebody of this stature focusing on intelligence," he told reporters, singling out Cohen's arrival.

It was interesting to watch Libutti and Cohen navigate a roomful of New York reporters. Clearly media coverage wasn't something either man had ever sought. Quite the opposite in Cohen's case. He'd spent thirty-five years not just staying under the radar, but refusing to acknowledge that the radar waves even existed.

He wouldn't confirm even the most basic biographical details about himself. Asked his age, he said that he was between twenty-eight and seventy. Asked if he had ever worked in the CIA office at the World Trade Center, he answered, "You're going to have to ask CIA where their offices were."

Ever the spy.

Neither of those facts was an actual secret, of course. The

CIA office was listed in the Manhattan phone book, and Cohen certainly had a driver's license, a public record that any reporter could have researched, though it might have been a challenge pinning down which David Cohen he was. I think he was just setting a fresh tone—*things will be different now*—and enjoying his man-of-mystery persona. As the reporters were packing up to leave, the spymaster had a big smile on his face. "It's the first press conference I've ever been to," he allowed. "It was sort of like my bar mitzvah."

Wait, did he just acknowledge he was male *and* Jewish? I'm not sure he ever spoke with a reporter again.

CHAPTER TWELVE

Crime Fighters

While David Cohen, Frank Libutti, and the others were helping to establish the NYPD's new war on terror, I knew we also had to reinvigorate NYPD crime fighting and repair the police department's frayed relations with some of the diverse communities we served. We had to cover all three of the Cs—counterterrorism, crime fighting, and community relations. Those three together, I knew from the beginning, would be the central pillars of my time as police commissioner, however long that might be. Clearly New York City police commissioner was a job that required constant multitasking. It wouldn't be enough to succeed in one or two areas.

Eight years earlier, when the Dinkins administration came to an end, we left behind a generous gift for the incoming mayor and his team—a huge influx of police officers fully paid for with state and city dollars through our Safe Streets, Safe City program. The Giuliani administration had only to pass out the uniforms and send the new recruits onto the street. From his first year in office, Mayor Rudy Giuliani reaped huge benefits from those new hires. He'd run for mayor on a heavy law-and-order platform, portraying David Dinkins as a hapless protector of New York. And yet it was the Dinkins administration that handed Giuliani and Police Commissioner Bill Bratton the single most valuable tool for turning campaign rhetoric into practical policy.

The crime drop that started in the final three years of the

Dinkins administration continued and accelerated over the next five. The numbers proved it. In Giuliani's first year in office, 1994, New York City recorded 1,561 murders. The number fell to 1,177 in 1995, then to 983 in 1996 and to 770 in 1997, down more than half in just four years.

Success has many fathers. Mandatory prison terms, the decline in crack use, changes in the nation's demographics, and a brightening U.S. economy—they may all have played a role in cutting crime, as academic criminologists were quick to contend. Others pointed out that crime was dropping all over America, not just in New York. Some people even argued that after the U.S. Supreme Court legalized abortion nationwide in *Roe v. Wade*, fewer potential criminals were born. But still. New York was where the drop began, starting in 1991, and New York was where crime was falling the fastest. The city was on a truly impressive seven-year roll—three years under Dinkins and four under Giuliani—from 2,245 murders in 1991 to 770 in 1997.

Homicides declined again in 1998, to 633, after Giuliani won reelection against Democrat Ruth Messinger. But then, in the second year of his second term, midway through Howard Safir's time as police commissioner, the crime decline suddenly stalled. Six hundred and seventy-one New Yorkers were killed in 1999. In 2000, when Safir handed off to Bernard Kerik, there were 673. In 2001, the number was 649. That last number, of course, did not include the people killed in the World Trade Center attack, who, strictly speaking, were homicide victims.

That's where things stood when Mike Bloomberg was elected mayor and I returned as police commissioner at the start of 2002. Crime had stopped falling. It hadn't shot up, but it definitely wasn't still declining, and most of the experts said it wasn't likely to. In their view, New York had settled into a natural modern-age floor of six hundred to seven hundred murders per year. That was a little higher than the pace during the middle decades of the twentieth century, before the 1960s, heroin, and crack cocaine sent it on its maddening upward spiral. But at this point, how much lower could it go? These numbers seemed like they'd be very hard to reduce or even to maintain.

Some causes of homicide, the experts argued, were simply beyond the control of the police. However great a job the NYPD did, some New Yorkers were inevitably going to kill each other. Spousal abusers, the deranged mentally ill, drug-gang enforcers, angry people with knives in bars—can extra police officers really stop all of them? Not likely. That was the conventional wisdom, anyway, as I gathered my new team together and got to work.

Back when homicides were still hovering above one thousand, *New York Post* columnist Jack Newfield said if the number ever went below 600 a year, the city should hold "a ticker-tape parade up Broadway" for the police. But I saw no reason why the crime numbers couldn't continue to decline. As far as I was concerned, 649 wasn't close to low enough. Why not 550? Why not zero? Even if we never got there, wasn't setting bold goals better than simply throwing our hands up? This wasn't just some numbers game. These were real people. Every murder we prevented was one more New Yorker who was still alive.

I understood that crime fighting wasn't exactly Mike Bloomberg's top priority. That was just a fact. He had other issues on his mind. He certainly understood, taking office just months after 9/11, that New Yorkers needed to be protected from terrorism as well as traditional crime. But Rudy Giuliani had been the crime-fighting mayor. That was *his* turf. Mike Bloomberg was going to be the education mayor—or maybe the public-health mayor. He didn't get elected to preside over the third Giuliani term.

This meant I had a relatively free hand in running the police department as I saw fit. We got very little interference from city hall as long as we stayed within the tight resources and trimmed budgets we received. Much of my daily communication with city hall was through Deputy Mayors Ed Skyler and Cas Holloway and criminal justice coordinator Jon Feinblatt. There would be no new wave of Safe Streets, Safe City hiring to bail us out.

As things turned out, we had to do it all with six thousand fewer police officers than the department had during the Giuliani administration—and a thousand other cops assigned to counterterrorism duties. Essentially, Mayor Bloomberg shifted the money for those six thousand cops into the Department of Education. Mark Shaw, the deputy mayor for operations and first deputy mayor, agreed with this staffing reduction after some heated discussions.

There was another factor in the mix: the city's population was growing again. After some shrinkage in the bad old days of white flight, urban unrest, and fiscal crisis, people were moving back to New York City and staying here. This was great news. It was stabilizing the taxes and reviving neighborhoods. But just to keep the crime numbers even, we'd have to reduce the crime *rate*—the number of murders, rapes, robberies, burglaries, assaults, and so on per 100,000 residents. To promote fresh declines, we'd have to work that much harder.

This was just the reality: if we were going to keep crime down and fend off terrorism, we would have to do it with fewer police officers with more demands on them in a city where more people now lived. Too bad some outgoing mayor didn't leave us with an extra five thousand already-paid-for police. But none of this was cause for despair. It was cause to get focused. Thankfully, as we began this journey together, I had some ideas and some very smart people to help.

*   *   *

So how did we do it?

The basics of crime fighting were well established and well known. Be visible. Patrol. Interact with the citizenry. Don't be lazy.

Don't be corrupt. Be open. Be respectful. Be flexible. Interview witnesses. Gather forensic evidence. Respond quickly and appropriately when called. Keep reliable statistics. Allocate your resources accordingly. Fight crime by going where the crime is. Most important, be proactive.

No one needed to reinvent any of that. Our job was to do it. Constantly. Professionally. Sensitively.

We knew that. But some of those time-honored policing techniques needed to be reinvigorated, reimagined, and reenergized. It wasn't that they were wrong or outmoded. They had just drifted away.

To lead this effort among the uniformed ranks, I did something unexpected. I kept Joe Esposito as the chief of department, the highest-ranking uniformed position. Joe was Giuliani's guy, but unlike other administrations, I didn't believe in change for change's sake. You lose a great deal of talent and experience by taking that shortsighted approach. Joe had deep knowledge of the department. He'd entered as an eighteen-year-old trainee and worked almost everywhere, including the 10th, 34th, 66th, 77th, 83rd, and 109th Precincts, the Narcotics Division, and the Detective Bureau. He'd run the strategic and tactical command for Brooklyn North.

Could I have put someone new in the job? Sure. But I had to consider the environment I was in. We were already making a lot of people nervous inside the department. Clearly things were changing rapidly. People were thinking, *Who knows what the hell they might do next?* The police knew Rudy Giuliani. But who was Mike Bloomberg? No one really knew what his agenda might be for the police department. Joe had been chief of department for a year and a half already. I thought it was important to maintain some continuity.

Joe was a big believer in getting police officers out of the radio cars and onto the street, interacting proactively with crime suspects and other people behaving suspiciously. "We have to put our hands on more people," Joe told the commanders more than once at CompStat meetings, where precinct commanders were brought in to be grilled on the details of their crime-fighting strategies. When Joe retired, I replaced him as chief of the department with Philip Banks III, a smart, experienced executive who also understood the value of proactive policing.

One of the biggest challenges in leading any modern police department is keeping the cops constantly active and engaged. Police work, when it's done well, requires energy and initiative. To stop crime, you have to go where the crime is. To catch criminals, you have to look for them. To know what's happening on the sidewalk, you have to be out there. Any good officer is always on the lookout for people behaving suspiciously.

Whether a person was lurking in a dark alley, casing a potential mugging victim, approaching passersby in a drug-sale location, or checking the door handles on parked cars, we wanted our officers to be questioning them.

"How are you tonight?"

"What's going on?"

"You live around here?"

Depending on how the person responded and what evidence the officer discovered, the individual might be detained, arrested, subjected to a simple pat-down, or sent immediately on his way.

It's a legal, time-honored, and effective crime-fighting technique. There is nothing inherently oppressive about it at all. We used it to great effect at the NYPD, as have previous administrations and police departments in every city I'm aware of. That's why I was disappointed near the end of the Bloomberg administration when these street stops were wildly mischaracterized for political reasons and dragged into a drawn-out federal lawsuit. There was nothing inappropriate about the technique or how we executed it. But that didn't stop the sloganeering on the other side, starting with the critics' sneering term for the practice, *stop and frisk*.

Street inquiries would have been a more accurate description—

or, at most, *stop, question, and sometimes frisk*. The critics conveniently left off the "question" part because doing so made the police sound more overbearing and unfair, as if the cops were constantly grabbing and searching random citizens for no reason at all. That was the furthest thing from the truth.

These street inquiries were not by any means a be-all-and-end-all of our crime-fighting strategy. But they were part of it, a growing and valuable part. The stops were a tool we certainly believed in.

We required police officers to record all street stops in their activity reports, just as they recorded arrests and other interactions with the public. If you don't know what your people are doing, it's hard to help them do it better. As time went on, our stop-question-and-frisk numbers went up—in part due to increased activity, in part due to better record keeping. In only about half the stops did the officers conduct limited pat-downs.

Other measures of police productivity also improved. This enhanced activity was a good thing, as was the careful recording of it. It showed that the police on the street were doing their jobs.

We never relied on numerical quotas, despite complaints by the unions. But productivity goals are part of how performance is judged everywhere. There is clearly a difference between the two.

*　　*　　*

With six thousand fewer police officers, we needed to be more visible, especially in neighborhoods that had once had serious street-crime problems. We couldn't afford to have any of that return. Operation Impact, which we launched in early 2003, was a step in that direction. The idea was fairly straightforward: Take officers who had just graduated from the police academy and send them in large numbers into high-crime neighborhoods with experienced supervisors. Saturate those areas to the point where the recruits could actually see each other on the sidewalks. The young cops brought their energy and vitality. They got the chance to jump immediately into police work. They learned neighbor-hoods many of them had never visited before, much less worked in. They interacted with the people there, making note of every significant contact. The people, law-abiding and otherwise, got to meet them. Even though we were down six thousand cops, the average citizen would not have known there had been a reduction of that size. Day by day, the cops on the street were building their confidence and their skills. This paid almost immediate dividends.

When the Republican National Convention came to Madi-son Square Garden in the summer of 2004, we had a high-profile opportunity to test the department's improving street skills. I knew we'd be under a microscope. We started planning eighteen months in advance, and I held weekly meetings with our conven-tion team to make sure we were fully ready. In the end, the whole NYPD did an extraordinary job maintaining relative calm and order under difficult circumstances. Convention week included the largest protests at any political convention ever. Managing these took a huge commitment of resources, but our performance and professionalism were singled out for lavish praise—by CNN, the *New York Times*, and George W. Bush, the target of many of the demonstrators. We were sued anyway over the 1,800 arrests we made—New York and America being so ridiculously litigious.

At every turn, I wanted to send a message up and down the department: We are a big-league organization here. We can achieve remarkable things together. Nothing important is beyond our reach.

That's why we brought in a top-flight roster of guest speakers to address the NYPD executive staff—such as former secretary of state Henry Kissinger, former Israeli prime minister Ehud Barak, former British prime minister Tony Blair, foreign policy writer George Packer, Washington journalist Steve Coll, King Abdul-lah of Jordan, the emir of Qatar, and Robert Gates, who was defense secretary and director of the CIA. From a wide variety of perspectives, they shared their unique insights on modern policing and the state of the broader world. I wanted our people to think big, and we benefited from the spirited flow of ideas. Other visitors to the NYPD included journalists Peter Bergen, Richard Engel, and Ralph Peters and CIA director John Brennan.

All of this created an atmosphere where we kept coming up with fresh ideas, asking ourselves, "What are the biggest issues we have to face now?"—then facing them creatively. Operation Crew Cut was just one of many examples, but an excellent one.

We determined that 30 percent of the city's shootings and a similar share of the murders were the result of loosely knit crews of young people fighting over turf, usually competing for territories. We moved aggressively against them.

Doing this meant doubling the size of the NYPD Gang Division. We created a strong social-media contingent, trawling Facebook, Twitter, and the Internet for evidence of gang activity and coming turf fights. These disputes often first popped up online. We put a lawyer inside each borough's gang unit to interact between the police and the local district attorneys. Former Brooklyn prosecutor Brian Meagher, whose uncle was a legendary uniformed officer named Pierce Meagher, helped coordinate the program. We got great support from the city's five district attorneys, who worked with us to generate major felony cases. We put a uniformed police officer component in each precinct with the mission of disrupting gang activity.

Twenty-five major Operation Crew Cut investigations produced more than 450 indictments. The cases were painstakingly constructed. The vast majority were bolstered by incriminating Facebook updates, Twitter posts, cell phone videos, and other social-media self-incrimination. These were violent people. The city was demonstrably safer having them away in prison. Crew Cut was a major success and was a prime reason that we set record low numbers for murders and shootings in 2013.

*   *   *

I knew we had big work to do on the third C, community relations.

Some tension will always exist between police officers and the people they police. That comes with the territory. Everyone loves firefighters. They show up to save your house or save your life. What's not to love? The business of policing is more of a mixed bag. Police officers do things that sometimes make them popular—protect victims, clean up a troubled corner, locate lost children. Sometimes cops get hugs and handshakes and flattering letters to the editor. But not everything the police are asked to do is universally appreciated. Stopping speeders, arresting lawbreakers, hauling people off to jail—those are all important duties of modern policing. But a suspect who's just been handcuffed rarely appreciates the officer who is walking him to the radio car for a ride to central booking. Very few drivers say "thank you" after being cited for an illegal U-turn.

Then add race, culture, economics, alcohol, drugs, rage, politics, and a dozen other factors into the equation. Relations between police and citizens can sometimes grow testy or worse, igniting harsh feelings on both sides.

I knew that reestablishing community relationships had to be a high priority. Several high-profile cases in the Giuliani years had exacerbated the tension between the police and the community. Abner Louima's was the most shocking of them. Louima was arrested in 1997 outside a nightclub in East Flatbush and was sexually tortured in a men's room at the Seventieth Precinct. The incident provoked understandable outrage. Seven thousand demonstrators marched on the Seventieth Precinct in a "Day of Outrage Against Police Brutality and Harassment." The Louima case was cited in an Amnesty International report on police brutality, torture, and abuse. Midway through the trial, the main actor, Officer Justin Volpe, admitted to sodomizing Louima, pleaded guilty, and was sentenced to thirty years in prison.

The 1999 death of Amadou Diallo also produced great outrage. Diallo, a Guinean immigrant, was shot and killed in the Soundview section of the Bronx by four plainclothes officers, who fired a total of forty-one shots at him. Bruce Springsteen even wrote a song about the incident called "American Skin (41 Shots)." It's never good when Bruce is singing about your police brutality cases.

The following year, 2000, unarmed bar patron Patrick Dorismond was killed by undercover narcotics officers in a scuffle on a Midtown sidewalk after they asked him if he knew where they could buy drugs. That too produced public uproar.

These were not examples of typical police behavior in New York. All three were failures of policing. No one should ever be tortured, and unarmed people should not end up dead, even if they are suspected of wrongdoing.

When I came back to the job, we took a different approach, both symbolically and practically. Week after week, I made a point of visiting black and Latino churches. Recognizing the simmering tension inside the city's Islamic community, I added several mosques to my house-of-worship rotation and formed the Muslim Advisory Council, made up of leading voices in the Islamic community. We formed the Brooklyn Clergy Coalition, led by Bishop A. D. Lyons and Bishop Gerald Seabrooks, that provided the borough's clergy with up-to-date crime information. We then expanded that effort to other boroughs, as well. I turned up regularly at large community events, mixing with local leaders and regular citizens alike. People appreciated seeing the police commissioner. I didn't march only in the St. Patrick's Day Parade. I participated in Brooklyn's annual West Indian Day Parade, Manhattan's Puerto Rican Day Parade, and parades and celebrations for the Dominican, Greek, Korean, Chinese, Israeli, and many other communities, though I have to say the West Indian event was always one of my favorites, since they let me play the steel drums. We sponsored soccer leagues and cricket leagues in

Brooklyn, Queens, and Staten Island. The cricket leagues, especially, got publicity around the world. Media outlets across South Asia and other cricket-loving locales covered not just our matches but the curious fact that the New York City Police Department seemed to understand how important the sport was to their pride and their cultures. We provided halal food at the soccer and cricket matches for Muslim young people and their friends.

We also created a new Liaison Unit that reported directly to me. The unit was composed of police officers with direct lines of communication to the African American, African, Haitian, Asian, Jewish, Muslim and LGBT communities. I met with these officers on a weekly basis. This was an excellent vehicle for keeping up to speed with current issues in the diverse city of New York.

That sounds small, but it wasn't. People notice little things. They noticed enough to want to join the police department. New York is a highly complex city, tribal in many ways. The more closely a department reflects the city it serves, the better its understanding will be. Picking up from efforts I had begun in my previous run as commissioner, we put in place a robust recruitment program with a strong emphasis on diversity, and it was working. Not just with blacks and Latinos either. The already highly diverse population of New York was becoming even more so, and the police department's makeup was staying ahead of that growing trend. We ended up with police officers born in 106 countries. Nothing remotely close to this exists anywhere else in the world. It gave us enormous depth, understanding, and new lines of communication. Going forward, it's an absolute necessity in a city like New York to try to mirror the diversity of the citizenry.

Is community outreach a panacea? Not even close to it. But having a diverse police department really does enable the police to better understand who they are dealing with and makes it easier for the people to relate to and trust the police. It just helps.

In my time as commissioner, we had significantly fewer controversial shootings than in the previous years, and nothing, thank God, equivalent to the Abner Louima case, certainly nothing that produced that kind of uproar. But try as we did, we couldn't get the bad-shootings number down to zero. The fatal shooting of Timothy Stansbury was definitely one of our low points. Stansbury was nineteen years old. Around 1:30 a.m. on January 24, 2004, he was opening a door onto a rooftop in Bedford-Stuyvesant to get some CDs when he was shot and killed by a police officer. Stansbury lived in an adjoining building. He was unarmed. The officer was patrolling the roof with his gun drawn. Stansbury died from a single wound to the chest.

We got the facts out quickly. Rumors were flying around the neighborhood, and people were understandably upset. I was concerned about the possibility of retaliation. I met with the teenager's mother and apologized on the day of the shooting. That day, I called the shooting unjustified. It was rare for a police commissioner to speak so frankly and so swiftly, but Stansbury's shooting wasn't even a close call. That angered the Patrolmen's Benevolent Association, which passed a resolution expressing no confidence in me. It had no practical effect, but it certainly got across the union's displeasure. The Brooklyn grand jury did not indict the officer, accepting his story that the shooting was an accident. But it was still a bad shooting, and I said so.

If anything, the Sean Bell case was worse.

Early on November 25, 2006, a team of plainclothes detectives were investigating reports of prostitution at Club Kalua, a strip bar in Queens. Bell, who was getting married barely twelve hours later, was leaving his bachelor party with two friends. A confrontation erupted outside the club with another group of men. Ultimately five detectives fired a total of fifty rounds, wounding Trent Benefield and Joseph Guzman and killing Bell.

Clearly, the shooting was unjustified. Sean Bell and his friends weren't armed. They didn't threaten the officers. No one should have ended up dead.

Three of the detectives went to trial on manslaughter, assault, and reckless-endangerment charges. All three were found not guilty. However, they were ultimately forced to leave the department.

The Bell shooting produced protests. The case was widely considered an unjustified shooting. The controversy had racial overtones. It was bad. The facts were indefensible. But we did have better lines of communication by then, and that turned out to be a help. We had a strong foundation of trust with community leaders. We actually knew each other. That didn't protect the department from criticism, and some of the criticism was undeniably warranted. But it was on a different level than before.

I was convinced that our community outreach, along with Mayor Bloomberg's robust commitment to the effort, really did make a difference, even though this was sometimes hard to prove. But when an issue came up, we often had someone we could call, someone we'd already had positive dealings with. We weren't introducing ourselves for the first time.

*　　*　　*

When I was a police officer, detectives filled out reports by hand or sometimes pecked them out on Royal manual typewriters—and things hadn't changed all that much since those days. I was committed to bringing the department's technology into the twenty-first century, hopefully before the twenty-second arrived. The NYPD was a classic case of a large organization not knowing what it knew. It was considered a giant leap forward when IBM Selectrics showed up in some precinct squad rooms, just about the time corporate America was hauling its last typewriters to the Dumpster out back. We were, I am certain, one of the largest and latest users of carbon paper and Wite-Out in America.

Even after computers arrived, we stuck with the crudest models. When I returned as commissioner in 2002, the department was still using primitive green-screen technology. The NYPD, large and multitentacled as it was, held an awesome amount of information somewhere and was collecting more and more every day—but good luck finding any of it. We had twenty different databases that didn't speak to each other and were almost impossible to search. Each division, bureau, and unit had its own hardware and software and its own unique way of maintaining the files.

I sought advice from Lou Gerstner Jr., the chairman and CEO of IBM. I didn't expect Lou to come down personally and start installing PCs in every precinct, but I thought he might know someone who could spearhead a digital revolution at the NYPD. He did. That person was Jim Onalfo.

I think Jim was appalled by what he saw when he arrived. A former army captain who had guided information technology at Kraft Foods International and Stanley Works, he came on as our chief information officer, reporting directly to me. At the police department, two thousand communications and IT employees were placed under him, mostly people who were already on board and a handful of new high-level hires. Before Jim did anything else, we developed a Strategic Systems Plan for moving the NYPD into modernity. The basic question was an obvious one: What do we need to know, and when do we need to know it? The persistent answers: Everything, and now. Next question: Where do the officers need to know it? The answer to that was wherever they were.

I had the vision. Jim and his people had the architecture. Working together, we fundamentally changed how the department communicated with itself. Police are only as effective as the information they have at their disposal. So let's get it to them—now. We created a central information hub called the Real Time Crime Center, a name I came up with. The core of the Real Time Crime Center was a massive searchable database that gave our people up-to-the-minute reports on crimes, perpetrators, criminal histories, witnesses, court dispositions, prison records, and a vast amount of other information—across the entire city, twenty-four hours a day. What do we know about this victim? What other crime occurred at this address? Who's on probation or parole nearby? What's been going on in this neighborhood? What do we know about the relationships between the people involved? Those were the kinds of questions detectives started with. Knowing the answers from the beginning helped them solve more crimes. If someone was robbed in the Seventy-Seventh Precinct, detectives could find out immediately that there was an ex-con in the Seventy-Seventh Precinct with a long rap sheet of street robberies. He might be someone worth questioning. In the years since the center opened, smaller versions have popped up in police departments across America. We had the first one and the best, the one everyone else wanted to copy. But the crime center was just a start. Technology progressed, and so did we.

I ordered that video cameras be installed in virtually every precinct to record interrogations. That way, there would be no doubt what suspects said under questioning. Thanks to city hall, we achieved a top-to-bottom upgrade of the 911 emergency dispatch system, getting first responders to emergencies far more quickly and far more reliably. We put in place elaborate protection against cyberattacks, fending off millions of those each year. Whatever changes we were making, we couldn't afford to have them compromised by nefarious hackers or even giddy mischief-makers.

If the Real Time Crime Center was designed to push up-to-the-second information out to our people in the field, the new NYPD Command Center flowed the opposite way. It was a central hub for bringing live information back to the operations unit headquarters, located in a two-story space on the second and third floors of 1 Police Plaza. The software there could pull in video feeds from two thousand cameras around the city and crunch raw intelligence in a myriad of ways. This is especially useful during major events—when the president comes to town or something's happening at the United Nations or during an unfolding terror incident. Once the Command Center was up and running, it began hosting as many as a hundred representatives from different agencies, all sitting in that one big room, coordinating their security operations in ways they never could before. Richard Falkenrath led the effort to obtain funding for it.

We replaced the executive conference room on the fourteenth floor of police headquarters with another state-of-the-art command center. We installed computer terminals and live video feeds that gave us instant access to every corner of the department. By the time we were done, the room resembled something more like an airport control tower. Gone forever was the dowdy conference room furniture and decor. In its place was a high-tech venue for briefings, meetings, and worldwide video conferences.

And we just kept going. The Network Operations Center monitored our internal information-technology operations. The Facial Identification Unit used burgeoning technology to help identify crime suspects. The Lower Manhattan Security Initiative surveyed threats in the Financial District, a neighborhood where terrorists had already struck twice. The Enterprise Case Management System kept careful, searchable track of investigative developments in more than one million criminal cases. We set up full agency enterprise automation cloud modules, crime-data warehouses, evidence-tracking and case-management systems, motorized command centers, land and air surveillance robots, license plate readers, wireless hot spots, and narcotics bank account tracking systems. No longer was the police department a labyrinth of walled-off offices and padlocked file drawers. Now its open architecture encouraged free information flow.

As time went on, we took the NYPD from a technological laggard to the most advanced police department anywhere. With the help of data whizzes like Nick Donofrio, Rodney Rogers, Dan Reed, and Tony Salvaggio, we built a full web of new systems, many of them focused on very specific crime-fighting needs: a major contributor to all this was Chief of Detectives Phil Pulaski. Phil was a lawyer and an engineer and always open to innovative ideas. He was constantly pushing the Detective Bureau forward, developing new ways to harness burgeoning technologies to help us solve crimes.

*   *   *

Taken all together, our crime-fighting techniques along with the added boost of new technology did what hardly anyone thought was possible: they kept the numbers falling. In 2002, my first year back, New York recorded 587 homicides, 62 fewer than in Mayor Giuliani's last year, easily breaking Jack Newfield's farfetched threshold. I'm just sorry we never had that parade and let Jack lead it. After a tiny upward tick in 2003, the number kept falling. To 570 in 2004. To 539 in 2005.

The numbers stayed well below the 650 homicides a year that was thought to be the modern floor for New York City. We had 596 murders in 2006, 496 in 2007, 523 in 2008. In 2012, the number was 414. By 2013, my final year in the department, the number dipped below 400. New York recorded 333 murders that year—not even one-sixth as many as in the city's peak murder years, by far the lowest rate of all big cities in America.

It wasn't just the homicide numbers, by the way, that saw improvement. By 2005, New York had the lowest overall crime rate among the ten largest cities in the United States. The 2013 murder rate, below 4 per 100,000 people, was at its lowest level since at least the early 1960s and was the lowest for any major city in America. That year saw the lowest number of shootings ever recorded.

These numbers were gratifying and a credit to the entire department.

CHAPTER THIRTEEN

Bulking Up

O ur first test of how the NYPD could transform itself for the modern age came just a month after I took over as Mike Bloomberg's police commissioner and four months since the 9/11 attacks. The World Economic Forum was due to arrive at the Waldorf Astoria hotel on January 31, 2002. This high-level group of government leaders, global business titans, and academic experts usually gathered in Davos, Switzerland. As a gesture of post-9/11 solidarity—and because construction was going on at the Davos site—this year, they were heading to New York. Their single agenda item: confronting global issues raised by the terror attacks.

"In these extraordinary times," forum president Klaus Schwab said, "greater international cooperation is needed to reverse the global economic downturn, eradicate poverty, promote security, and enhance cultural understanding. As the world's financial capital and the site of the recent terrorist attacks, there could be no better place than New York City to confront these issues."

Which all sounded fine. But who was going to protect these people—high-value targets, all of them—once they arrived? They were sure to attract a rowdy crowd of protestors, including a fiery contingent of anarchists, some of them with a proven penchant for violence. Such a protest the previous summer had left one demonstrator dead at a summit of wealthy nations in Genoa, Italy. So were we ready here?

I called a planning meeting in the executive conference room at 1 Police Plaza with chiefs and commanders from the Intelligence Division and elsewhere. At that point, David Cohen hadn't yet come up from Washington.

I went around the long wooden table, asking basic questions and looking for information.

How many protestors were we expecting? What groups did they represent? What was being said on the Internet? What demonstrations did they have planned? Where would the attendees be eating? How would they get back to their hotels? Should we expect the protestors to arm themselves? If so, with what kinds of weapons? What had happened the past two or three times these two worldviews had clashed?

None of this required classified intelligence. Much of the information was available from open, public sources or a few hours of working the phones. From the answers I received, I didn't get the feeling anyone had scratched too hard. What I got from the people in the room were a lot of vague assurances and more than one uncomfortable stare. Perhaps we were still suffering from the aftershocks of 9/11.

I knew we had to spring into action before the leaders and the protestors arrived. We dispatched detectives to Seattle, Quebec, and Genoa to learn how demonstrations there had slipped into violence and vandalism. How had minor scuffles suddenly escalated into massive chaos?

From the information we gathered, we devised an overall crowd-control plan. We blocked off the streets around the Waldorf. We flooded the area with police. Once the protests began, we cordoned the marchers into clearly designated routes, giving them plenty of room to express themselves but blocking them from rushing the hotel. We stationed buses, motorcycles, and radio cars around the perimeter. We positioned video cameras on nearby buildings and flew helicopters overhead.

It did cost us a lot in overtime expenses, but I was fairly happy with the way things turned out. It showed the power of strong focus and fast attention, if not long, deep planning. We got through the summit with no major catastrophes—five days of loud demonstrations with the usual bevy of minor arrests, but nothing really bad at all.

"It was our intention from the beginning to set the tone and have a robust force in place...to show that we were prepared for anything," I explained to the New York media as the forum finally ended and everyone was heading home. "And I think that was very helpful in dissuading those people bent on causing a problem from doing that."

Mayor Bloomberg certainly sounded impressed. "People had the ability to demonstrate, people had the ability to say what they thought, and they did it generally without impinging on others' rights," he said. When the protestors became unruly, "the police department acted appropriately, with restrained but forceful consideration for the citizens of this city."

*   *   *

We appreciated the upbeat reviews from city hall, but these raucous New York anarchists had nothing on other potential threats facing us: suicide bombers. Overseas training camps. Sophisticated masterminds. A willingness to kill innocent civilians. Technical expertise. Powerful religious fervor. A fully developed concept of martyrdom. Money and a communications network. A large immigrant population in America easy to hide within. Taken all together, the new breed of Islamic jihadists were more daunting than anything America had seen before.

The only way to handle that threat, I was convinced, was to create our own full-scale intelligence and counterterror operation inside the NYPD, overseen by David Cohen, Frank Libutti, and me. Every day, I wanted to increase the chance that the terrorists would fail. That required constant vigilance. We couldn't rely entirely on others to protect the city. We'd seen how that had worked out—twice. We had reached the era of self-help now.

I instituted a morning meeting every day with Cohen and Libutti. I didn't want a single day to begin without my being fully informed about terror threats, cases, and investigations in New York City and around the world. If terrorism was going to be our top priority, we couldn't afford to miss any important developments in that arena.

So we took on an enormous challenge. We built something that no city, including New York, had ever attempted before— our own highly trained, well-staffed, fully integrated counterterror capacity. Then again, there had never been another American city that faced New York's threats.

There were always unknowns in this business, but Libutti had a stock way of answering when people asked about the prospect of another attack. "I believe the bad guys have us on their mission profile," the retired general said. "They attacked us one time in the nineties, when they didn't do as much damage as they wanted. They attacked us again in 2001, when they did a lot of damage. If they have the means to come and attack us, don't you think they'll try again?"

With his military bearing and Marine Corps background, Libutti made the new bureau his next mission. We carved out space at 1 Police Plaza for the offices and set up a working facility at a large, out-of-the-way location in Brooklyn. We didn't want to call attention to ourselves. We had electronic maps on the walls and digital readouts from foreign capitals such as Moscow, London, Tel Aviv, and Riyadh. We set up a global intelligence room with twelve large flat-screen TVs mounted from the ceiling. Via satellite, we could instantly access live broadcasts of Al Jazeera and other international programming. I assigned George Brown, a three-star chief, to work with Libutti.

We made a major new commitment to the FBI's Joint Terrorism Task Force. Prior to 9/11, there were 17 New York City police detectives assigned to the task force. We upped that to 120. We expanded our role in the task force for several reasons. We wanted to be sure the bureau had the staffing to protect us properly.

We also wanted our people involved in everything going on at the JTTF. I liked having the power of numbers on our side. Part of Libutti's job was finding qualified people in the department who could be assigned to the task force, then coordinating the flow of information from them back to the NYPD. When Libutti left after two years to become undersecretary of the new U.S. Department of Homeland Security, Michael Sheehan, another first-class professional, replaced him as deputy commissioner for counterterrorism.

Some of our counterterrorism efforts had to be handled discreetly. But others, our Hercules teams along with our critical response vehicles—as many as a hundred at a time—were purposely visible. The elite, heavily armed convoys moved around the city, arriving in black Suburbans and other vehicles with armor-plated vests and submachine guns, sometimes with air or sea support. They popped up without warning at the Empire State Building, Times Square, Columbus Circle, the New York Stock Exchange, Bloomingdale's—you never knew quite when or where or why they had suddenly converged on a particular location. They showed that the NYPD could turn out massive force in a hurry, and that was a good message to send. Clearly part of the purpose was to intimidate potential terrorists. New York was not an easy target, we wanted to continue reminding them.

At the same time that we were building the Counter-Terrorism Bureau, David Cohen was launching a series of new initiatives that completely reorganized and reshaped the NYPD Intelligence Division. One thing that reorganization involved was getting our people into the neighborhoods of Brooklyn and Queens. Intelligence Division detectives worked the blocks of New York as a source of tips and intelligence. There was no nation on earth that didn't have some immigrants in New York. These people often knew things that could help protect America, and most of the time they were perfectly happy to help. The point for us was never to trample on anyone's culture or religion. We were there to follow evidence of potential threats from anywhere in the world. Sometimes, though, there was still no substitute for being there.

That was the thinking behind our decision to station as many as a dozen NYPD detectives in terror-prone locations overseas. No local police department had ever attempted anything like it, but it turned out to be a useful tool for us. When I was Customs commissioner, we had legats, legal attachés based at U.S. embassies overseas. They fed us valuable information from a perspective we did not otherwise have. I wanted to embed our people as listening posts inside the police departments in other cities in order to protect New York. So we did.

Starting in 2003, we stationed New York police detectives in Tel Aviv, and the program grew to include detectives stationed in Abu Dhabi, Lyon, Amman, Madrid, London, Tel Aviv, Paris, Toronto, Montreal, Singapore, and the Dominican Republic, listening for anything that might have an impact on New York. The terrorists knew no national boundaries. Why should the New York City police?

Our people got some pushback from U.S. ambassadors in certain countries. "You have to report here," they said.

"Why?" we asked.

"You're not federal employees," we were told.

"So?"

Part of the duty involved constantly working with local authorities, obtaining valuable information. Part of it involved rushing in wherever a bombing or another attack had just occurred, then relaying the details back home. After the bombings in Madrid in 2004, in London in 2005, and in Mumbai in 2008, our detectives were on the street in less than twenty-four hours, funneling up-to-the-minute information back to New York.

This wasn't mere curiosity on our end. As we kept learning, terrorism is in many respects a copycat business. Ideas, trends, and inspiration travel around the globe. We could have waited months for Washington to summarize the events in London or Madrid or wherever they happened. Or we could get our people there serving only us. If New York was on someone's target list, we didn't want to wait for their boys with box cutters to start boarding planes.

Singapore, Jakarta, Tel Aviv—wherever the trouble was, we could have New York City police detectives on the ground in just a few hours. They did a terrific job wherever they went, providing us with real-time, granular information that we never would have gotten before. Who was responsible? What did the local police know? What contacts, if any, did the suspects have in New York? No one but the NYPD would make the effort to find out these things. Wherever terrorists struck, we wanted to know: What does this mean for New York?

We kept getting better and better at our techniques. When ten Islamic militants from the Pakistan-based Lashkar-e-Taiba terrorist organization carried out a multi-day assault of shootings and bombings at hotels and other prominent sites in Mumbai in November of 2008, killing 164 people, we had three Intelligence Division detectives on the ground immediately. They sent back constant updates. Less than a week later, the detectives had prepared a seventy-five-page report, detailing everything that was known and how it connected to us. Based on that, we conducted our own tabletop command exercise at 1 Police Plaza and a larger training scenario at Floyd Bennett Field. We also brief four hundred members of NYPD SHIELD, the security directors of major companies. This was all done within a week's time of the events in Mumbai. The efforts were designed to get people thinking strategically about how to handle what we now knew were realistic terror scenarios, bouncing ideas off each other, reacting in the pressure of the moment, and facing the immediate consequences of the decisions that are made. These role-play exercises can be highly valuable in focusing people's minds. We shared the results of our examination with the FBI, who took months to finish their own report on the attacks. I was concerned that we might not have a sufficient number of qualified people to respond to our own Mumbai-style attack. I decided we should train two hundred members of our Organized Crime Control Bureau in heavy-weapons tactics as a backup to the Emergency Service Unit. In addition, we filmed the lobbies of major hotels in the city as a resource for police officers, in case they had to respond to a major event inside.

This was a whole new frontier for the NYPD, and we didn't want these overseas assignments to be subject to the budgetary whim and whimsy of the city council. To pay for the postings, we turned to the New York City Police Foundation, the only authorized charitable arm of the department, which had supported NYPD programs for more than thirty years. Given the diversity of the department, we had no trouble finding people with the language and cultural backgrounds to make these foreign assignment postings effective.

We received warm welcomes from most overseas law enforcement agencies. Many in the U.S. government encouraged our efforts as well, although there was always some sensitivity about turf. FBI director Robert Mueller came to support us, too.

We just pressed ahead.

In 2005, we started the Lower Manhattan Security Initiative, a unique private-public partnership designed to bring extra protection to the Financial District, one of the most tempting terror targets on earth. There were so many entities operating on that tiny patch of densely packed real estate, truly the home office of American capitalism. Wouldn't it be better, we asked, if everyone cooperated?

Mayor Bloomberg and I floated the concept to Hank Paulson, chairman of Goldman Sachs, whose firm had a major presence downtown. He liked the idea, and so did other key Wall Street figures. Participants included the New York police, the Port Authority police, the Metropolitan Transportation Authority, and corporate security officials from some of the largest companies downtown. Our goal was to make the 1.7 square miles south of Canal Street the safest business district in the world.

We created the Lower Manhattan Coordination Center, manned twenty-four hours a day by police officers and representatives of private firms and governmental agencies in the area. We installed hundreds of security cameras in lower Manhattan, as well as license plate recognition scanners, which fed those images into a central database. We set up posts with uniformed police officers near sensitive locations. We had special radiation and nuclear-material detectors, which we installed on boats, helicopters, and trucks. We equipped some of our officers with detectors on their gun belts. For all this, we got terrific support from downtown companies and other law enforcement organizations.

We kept deepening our ties with the city's—and the nation's—corporate community. When it came to technology, and especially security, we found plenty of overlap. Later, in cooperation with Microsoft, we created the Domain Awareness System, which we licensed out to other cities around the world, with New York getting 30 percent of the profits. This important effort was coordinated by Deputy Commissioner Richard Falkenrath and Director of Counterterrorism Policy Jessica Tisch. When a threat call came in, an alert would pop up on a computer screen, instantly showing officers an interactive map of the neighborhood, footage from nearby security cameras, radiation-level readings, and whether any other threats had recently been received.

Some of our activities were controversial, even the ones that shouldn't have been. This being New York, there are always people willing to criticize and often people ready to sue. We got some of both on a counterterror campaign. One unexpected flash point was our small Demographics Unit, which was part of the Intelligence Division.

The idea was a simple one: We should know who lived where. That could help us in many ways. People are drawn to the familiar. They often live near people like themselves. This is especially true of immigrants getting settled in a new, foreign land. That's one reason people say New York is made up of many "communities." If a Chechen brother left a bomb at the Boston Marathon and began driving toward New York, wouldn't you want to know that there are Chechen immigrant communities in Brooklyn and New Jersey—and not have to launch a panicked scramble in search of them? (The stated intent, by the way, of the Boston Marathon Bombers was to go to New York and plant explosives, but they were cornered by Boston-area police before carrying out this plan.) If one small town in Libya produced twelve suicide bombers, wouldn't it be worth knowing where their cousins lived in New York? If you came to the city from Moldova, chances are you know some other Moldovans—probably on the same two blocks in the Bronx. Should the police have pretended that wasn't true?

Our Demographics Unit officers gathered their information by walking around and talking to people in the diverse neighborhoods of New York. They didn't sneak in anywhere. They identified themselves. It was done out in the open. They recorded accurate information about what they saw and heard. It's hard to imagine police work much less intrusive than this.

Nonetheless, in a breathless series of articles, two reporters from the Washington bureau of the Associated Press made the Demographics Unit sound like a massive intrusion into people's private lives, something out of North Korea or *1984*. Matt Apuzzo and Adam Goldman filed more than fifty articles in all and repurposed the pieces in a book titled *Enemies Within: Inside the NYPD's Secret Spying Unit and bin Laden's Final Plot Against America*. The work won a rash of journalism awards including the Pulitzer Prize. Frankly, I don't care if they wrote a thousand articles and won the Nobel Peace Prize. Their work was deceptive, imbalanced, and wildly overhyped. The reporters fundamentally mischaracterized what the Demographics Unit was all about. The pieces actually read like they'd been dictated by disgruntled federal law enforcement officers in Washington.

The reporters' basic claim was that the Demographics Unit

violated the rights of Muslims in our information-gathering process. In fact, everything the unit did was legal, appropriate, and fully vetted by NYPD attorneys. In addition, the information-gathering techniques were explicitly permitted under the federal-court guidelines known as the Revised Handschu Agreement. That agreement, first signed in 1984 and overseen by U.S. District Judge Charles Haight, settled a lawsuit that came out of a 1971 prosecution of twenty-one members of the Black Panther Party who were acquitted of conspiring to blow up police stations and department stores in New York. That agreement laid out which techniques the NYPD could and could not use in investigating crimes connected to political activity. In 2002, at my direction, NYPD General Counsel Stephen Hammerman asked Judge Haight to approve a revision of Handschu in light of the new threats the city faced in the post-9/11 world. The judge agreed. He decided that a criminal predicate was not always needed for police to gather information. He recognized that it might be too late for that. The revised guidelines explicitly permitted the NYPD investigators to attend meetings open to the public, to review websites available to the public and to produce reports and studies that would help us better protect the city—the very techniques that the Demographics Unit and others in the Intelligence Division were employing. In many of the articles, the AP reporters didn't seem to have ever heard of Handschu. The misunderstandings ran deep. The reporters complained that the unit's work didn't result in any arrests. Well, that wasn't the point. The investigators were gathering information. They weren't supposed to be making arrests. Paul Browne had a perfect answer to that. Said Paul: "That's like saying Derek Jeter 'admitted' to having never scored a touchdown."

The bottom line? Despite all the hype, the Demographics Unit continued its important information gathering. We eventually changed its name to the Area Assessment Unit, but its important work stayed the same. New York City was safer as a result.

CHAPTER FOURTEEN

Terror Never Sleeps

The terrorists didn't rest on their laurels after 9/11. They didn't take a victory lap through the streets of Karachi or Kabul and call it a day. As far as they were concerned, September 11, 2001, was the spectacular start to an endless barrage of attacks on America and, especially, New York City, target number one. Their goal: obliterating public confidence, wrecking the U.S. economy, and fatally undermining what in their view were the godless values of the West.

This wasn't just our speculation. We learned it through painstaking intelligence gathering, daily experience, and often from the terrorists themselves, who ended up turning on their cohorts far more often than you might expect. We had plenty of evidence to judge from. They kept coming at us, confident that they would score a string of victories or at the very least would ultimately wear us down.

We counted sixteen attempts in all—genuine, active terror plots launched by Islamic extremists intent on causing damage and killing people in New York City, all potentially deadly, many possibly catastrophic—during my twelve years as the city's police commissioner. The plots started with Iyman Faris and his aborted attack on the Brooklyn Bridge—and just kept rolling from there.

That's where the vigilance really came in.

We knew all along that the law of averages was against us: We had to beat them every single time. They only had to beat us once. Painful as 9/11 was, the consequences of a repeat performance were almost too terrible to contemplate. And we knew the threats could come from nearly anywhere. There was an almost infinite array of variables we had to guard against.

The sixteen plots to attack New York City were not just the wide-eyed rantings of zealous believers or the harmless fantasies of the mentally ill. Let me be clear about this: they were live, active conspiracies, perpetrated by people intent on mass murder, stopped somewhere on the road to execution by diligent law enforcement and, yes, quite a bit of luck.

Some of these plots were more ambitious or better financed or more sophisticated than others. None of them was a joke. Some, like the scheme to breach the PATH train tunnel below the Hudson River and flood lower Manhattan, were hatched in distant countries. Others, like Shahawar Siraj's plan to put a bomb in a Macy's bag and blow up the Herald Square subway station because "Jews shop at Macy's," were 100 percent homegrown. Some of the plots—the transatlantic airliner attack, the Times Square truck bomb, the one we call the Florida-to-New-York plot—got disconcertingly close to succeeding. Some, like Najibullah Zazi's cross-country quest to place bombs on moving subway trains in New York, got terrifyingly close. All sixteen were tied in one way or another to the cause of radical Islam.

To understand how we were able to protect the city and the region, we have to dig into the frightening details of these individual conspiracies, climbing inside and taking the plots apart. Every one teaches an important lesson going forward, including the biggest one of all: in the years and decades that are coming, we must never drop our guard.

One: THE BROOKLYN BRIDGE PLOT

We were lucky, I suppose, that Iyman Faris came first. We learned so much from his aborted plot to destroy the Brooklyn Bridge. As the first post-9/11 sleeper agent captured inside the United States, Faris perfectly illustrated the importance of the counterterror measures we were rolling out then and the kinds of enemies we would be facing in the years to come. Zealous. Motivated. Willing to commit mass atrocities. Free to move around. The Ohio truck driver's plot to blow up the "*Godzilla* bridge" in New York approached the operational phase before he and his handlers decided to pull the plug. But they didn't pull back for reasons entirely of their own. They canceled the bridge attack because of the visible security precautions we had put in place in the first half of 2002. "The weather," Faris communicated to his handlers, was just "too hot." We learned about that lifesaving assessment only after Khalid Sheikh Mohammed was arrested in Pakistan in March 2003. But it was sincerely gratifying to see that the decision had been made as a direct reaction to the precautions we had put in place.

Faris's journey from cheerful young immigrant to heartless terrorist also turned out to be highly instructive. His path would be followed by many other aspiring terrorists in the years to come. Born June 4, 1969, in Azad, Pakistan, Faris was only twenty-four when he arrived in Ohio on a student visa. He never enrolled in college, but given the looseness of immigration enforcement in those pre-9/11 days, no one followed up on that.

A friendly young man with an easy smile and an occasional volatile streak, Faris got a job as a cashier at a gas station, where he met an American woman named Geneva Bowling, who worked at a local auto-parts company and stopped in regularly for discount gas. The daughter of a Kentucky preacher, she was twelve years older than Faris, had been married at least twice before, and had a ten-year-old son named Michael. Iyman and Geneva married in a Muslim ceremony in 1995 and moved into her townhouse in Columbus.

At first, Faris seemed well on his way to achieving the American

dream. His wife's family liked him. He got along well with his stepson. The two of them watched movies together and played *Coman-
che: Maximum Overkill.* One of their favorite movies was *Air Force
One*, in which Harrison Ford plays the president and Gary Oldman
a terrorist leader who holds the First Family hostage. Faris became a
U.S. citizen in December 1999, five years after arriving in America.

But there were problems beneath the surface. Neighbors
heard the couple fighting. Faris sought counseling from a local
imam, reporting thoughts of suicide. The young immigrant was
briefly hospitalized for psychiatric evaluation when he tried to
jump off a bridge. He told his wife he'd been having blackouts and
hearing voices. His main tormentor, he said, was a half man who
looked like Faris and would speak to him from the branches of
a tree.

The five-year marriage ended in 2000, the same year Faris's
father died. Faris and a friend traveled to Pakistan and Afghanistan. The friend knew people who were involved with the militant
Islamic group al-Qaeda. In late 2000, nearly a year before 9/11,
the friend brought Faris to meet Osama bin Laden, al-Qaeda's
fanatical leader, at a training camp in Afghanistan.

On a trip to Karachi in early 2002, Faris was introduced to
bin Laden's lieutenant Khalid Sheikh Mohammed. "How else can
you help al-Qaeda?" Mohammed asked.

Faris described his work as a truck driver in America and his
access to American airports and cargo planes. After weighing a
grander plan for simultaneous attacks in New York and Washington, he and the bin Laden lieutenant settled on the idea of
severing the cables on the Brooklyn Bridge. In all future communications, Faris was told, he should refer to gas-powered cable
cutters as "gas stations."

I'd been back in the role of police commissioner for three and a
half months when Faris returned to America in April 2002. As he
resumed his life in Ohio, no one suspected a thing. But between

then and March 2003, Faris sent several coded messages to his al-Qaeda contacts in Pakistan, often going through an intermediary in the United States. He reported that he was still trying to locate the "gas stations."

On March 19, 2003, after Khalid Sheikh Mohammed was in custody and had begun providing information, FBI agents approached and briefly interviewed Faris at a hotel in Cincinnati. They questioned him again in Columbus and at the FBI Academy in Quantico, Virginia. He admitted he'd returned to America as a sleeper agent and described making trips to New York in order to case the Brooklyn Bridge. He explained how the NYPD's intense security measures had caused him to doubt the wisdom of the plan. The radio cars on the bridge, the Harbor Unit boat in the water, the attention he had not expected to find.

After many hours of questioning, Faris agreed to work as a double agent. With FBI agents monitoring his communications traffic now, he continued exchanging e-mail messages with his al-Qaeda handlers. On May 1, he pleaded guilty at U.S. District Court for the Eastern District of Virginia to providing material support to a terrorist organization overseas. U.S. district judge Leonie Brinkema sentenced him to the maximum term he faced, twenty years in federal prison.

After the bridge plot was foiled and Faris was safely in custody, the NYPD tightened security even more. I made my tour of the cable shed, now far more heavily fortified. We took additional measures to secure the access points to the bridge's cables. The new rules mandated that no work could be done on the bridge without prior approval of the NYPD Intelligence Division.

Two: THE MUBTAKKAR PLOT

As Iyman Faris was casing the Brooklyn Bridge, a CIA mole inside al-Qaeda reported that the terror network had plans to place poison-gas devices on New York City subway trains. If the terror network's technicians could achieve something like that, we knew, the damage could be catastrophic. The subway at rush hour is a very crowded place. The plot talk, which started as a rumor, was confirmed in early 2003 when Bassam Bokhowa, a jihadist from Bahrain, was captured in Saudi Arabia. On his laptop, Saudi security forces discovered detailed plans for building what the terrorists were calling a *mubtakkar*, the Arabic word for "new invention." This case showed vividly, as others would later, how intelligence gathering abroad can be hugely valuable in protecting a city like New York.

As the Saudi interrogators tried to find out more, using whatever techniques they used, technicians at a CIA laboratory in Virginia began building a prototype from the laptop schematics. It wasn't all that difficult. The plans showed a cantilevered device with two interior chambers. One was for sodium cyanide. The other was for hydrochloric acid. Both chemicals were widely available and legal to possess. The same way a cell phone could trigger a hidden explosive, a remote signal would break open the seal between the two chambers. That would create hydrogen cyanide, a highly volatile colorless gas with the faint odor of peach pits or bitter almonds.

Once the gas was inhaled, the symptoms would come on quickly. They included nausea, disorientation, burning eyes, fever, chills, skin irritation, and, with a sufficient dosage, swift death. The only protection was a gas mask. It was hard to imagine distributing one of those to each of the subway's five million daily riders.

But here's the good news about chemical and biological terror attacks and why, though certainly alarming, this wasn't the most likely of the sixteen plots to succeed. To be effective, the poison has to be airborne. It has to disperse. It has to be dense enough to do the intended damage but diffuse enough to reach more than a few potential victims. This is a very difficult balance to achieve. In the annals of terrorism, there have been very few successful large-scale poison-gas attacks. Even in military warfare, poison gas is a weapon of intimidation as much as it is one that succeeds in practice.

Still, the FBI and CIA, with on-the-ground investigative backing from the NYPD Intelligence Division, squeezed hard for more details. The Saudi interrogators said they had gotten all they could from Bassam Bokhowa. The CIA mole, whose name was Ali, identified the key creator as Yusuf al-Ayeri, nickname "Swift Sword." Ali said the target date was forty-five days off.

According to Ali, al-Ayeri had visited Ayman al-Zawahiri, a fast-rising al-Qaeda leader, in January 2003 to describe the *mubtakkar* and tell him about the plot to drop the devices in the New York subway and other high-traffic spots.

But al-Zawahiri had balked.

The terrorist leader called the device unlikely to create a sufficient number of casualties. He said a gas attack in the subway was not spectacular enough to follow the triumph of 9/11. Al-Qaeda blinked again.

We were lucky that the terrorists decided in the end to pull back. Unfortunately, that string of retreats could not continue forever. But in this long-running fight of ours, we were happy to take our victories any legal way we could get them.

Three: THE ELECTION PLOT

Fighting terror is much too important and too delicate a duty to be used as a tool of partisan politics—by any side. That has always seemed obvious to me. That's why I was made distinctly uncomfortable by what I came to think of as the 2004 election plot.

On July 28 of that year, delegates at the Democratic National Convention in Boston nominated John Kerry as the party's candidate to challenge President George W. Bush. Four days later, on August 1, the U.S. Department of Homeland Security raised the terror threat level to orange—"high alert"—for cities with major financial institutions across the East Coast. White House spokeswoman Erin Healy cited disturbing intelligence that was "very new, coming in during the last seventy-two hours."

This was based on the arrest in the United Kingdom of Dhiren Barot, an Indian-born midlevel al-Qaeda operative known by his nickname Issa al-Hindi, "Issa the Hindu." Barot had compiled fifty-one compact discs that contained terror-planning reports and research. On a computer hard drive in London, investigators also found an eighty-minute video from a reconnaissance trip Barot had made to New York, Washington, and Newark, New Jersey. During the trip, he had visited numerous sites, including the New York Stock Exchange, the Federal Reserve Bank of New York, the Citicorp building, the World Trade Center, the Prudential building in Newark, and the International Monetary Fund and World Bank buildings in Washington. A portion of the video zoomed in on the Trade Center. An unseen man in the background mimicked the sound of an explosion.

"*Ka-boom!*" the man said.

The footage was spliced into a videotape of the Bruce Willis movie *Die Hard: With a Vengeance*.

Undeniably frightening material. The only problem? It was all three or four years old. The minute we were notified, I wanted to know: What was so urgent about raising the terror alert *now*?

I had my doubts.

I couldn't help but notice the political calendar. Did raising the threat level have anything to do with the president's reelection campaign? Was someone in Washington trying to gin up public anxiety about an imminent terror attack? I wasn't certain, but the thought did cross my mind.

As soon as we got word that the threat-assessment material

was available in Washington, we arranged through the Joint Terrorism Task Force to have the documents rushed up to New York. The material arrived that night. By then, Michael Sheehan, a former U.S. Special Forces officer and ambassador-at-large for counterterrorism at the State Department, had taken over from Frank Libutti as our deputy commissioner for counterterrorism. Sheehan was another world-class expert who agreed to serve in the police department. He had taken a rare weekend at the beach. When we notified him, he drove straight back to police headquarters. He and David Cohen stayed until way past midnight, reviewing every page of the threat reports so they could brief me first thing on Sunday morning. I wanted to hear straight from them what the documents said, how the heads of our intelligence and counterterrorism divisions interpreted them, and what we should do about it.

These guys never said no when something came up. Like me, they hardly ever took a day off. And when they did, they were inevitably rushing back to 1 Police Plaza to deal with one issue or another. I was blessed to have these two seasoned professionals constantly available to us, able to read complex intelligence documents and interpret them, independent of whatever the Washington intelligence community might have to say.

Between them, they probably had seventy years' experience doing just that. That is what they were there for. I knew they would have their own thoughts, informed by long careers at the highest levels of the diplomatic and intelligence worlds.

"We don't doubt the importance of the plot," Cohen said the next morning. "We do doubt its imminence."

"There is nothing here to suggest that this activity, however genuine it might have been, has any active component at this point," Sheehan said.

Their recommendation? No need to raise the terror level now. It was good to hear that Barot was finally in custody, they agreed.

Age six at our summer
bungalow in Island Park.

The Kelly family circa 1949.
Standing, left to right: Donald,
Leonard, Kenneth. Seated: Mary,
Dad, Mom, and me.

With Veronica at Island
Park Beach, 1963.

Our wedding reception
at the officers' club at
the Brooklyn Navy Yard,
December 14, 1963.

Aboard the USS *Monticello* after Operation Harvest Moon, Vietnam, 1965.

After returning from Vietnam, I fed five-month-old Jim for the first time in Laguna Beach, California, 1966.

Our young family in Baldwin, New York, 1969.

My reward for graduating at the top of my police academy class was the Hiram C. Bloomingdale Trophy, an engraved revolver. *NYPD*

Graduating with my JD from St. John's University School of Law, 1971.

With Jim in a radio car on Fifth Avenue in the Twenty-Third Precinct in East Harlem, 1971.

As captain of the Emergency Service Unit, I reported to the scene of a double homicide in an East Harlem grocery store, 1980. *NYPD*

Speaking with a community leader in the 106th Precinct in Queens—known as the Stun Gun Precinct. *Mike Lipack/ New York Daily News*

Being sworn in by Mayor David Dinkins as the thirty-seventh New York City police commissioner in 1992. *City of New York*

The cover of *New York* magazine, February 22, 1993. *Harry Benson/New York magazine*

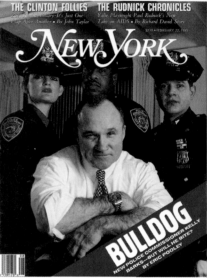

Testifying at my Senate confirmation hearing for the U.S. Customs commissioner post in 1998. *U.S. Customs Service*

Following a 1993 gun bust, I held a press conference with Manhattan district attorney Robert Morgenthau. *Betsy Herzog*

With Greg in Cité Soleil, Haiti, 1994.

After a firefight between U.S. Army and Haitian troops in 1994, Marine reserve Major Mario LaPaix and I carried a wounded man.

After the peaceful transfer of power in Haiti, we caught a ride back to the U.S. on Air Force One with President Clinton. *The White House*

In Paris in 1998 in the office of Felix Rohatyn, then U.S. ambassador to France, with stolen religious artifacts recovered by the U.S. Customs Service. *U.S. State Department*

Recovering the remains of a fallen NYPD officer at Ground Zero in 2002. *NYPD*

President Bush visited the NYPD Command Center in 2004. Mayor Bloomberg and Governor Pataki are on the right. *NYPD*

In 2011 President Obama visited us at the Real Time Crime Center at police headquarters. *NYPD*

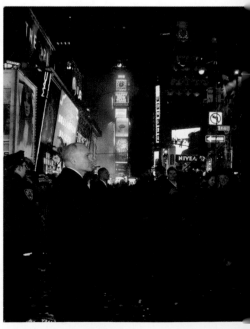

Keeping watch in Times Square, New Year's Eve 2011. *NYPD*

Opening day at the 2011 NYPD United Cricket Youth League in Kissena Park, Queens. Hundreds of city teenagers have competed in the popular police-run cricket and soccer youth programs since 2008. *NYPD*

In 2013 I served as grand marshal of the St. Patrick's Day Parade and posed for pictures on the cathedral steps with two cardinals, Timothy Dolan and Edward Egan. *Timothy A. Clary/Getty Images*

Conferring with Mayor Bloomberg at the city's Office of Emergency Management as we prepared for the arrival of Hurricane Irene in August 2011. *NYPD*

Visiting with members of the NYPD Bomb Squad and their bomb-sniffing dog, Winston. *NYPD*

Playing the bongos at a benefit for New York's famed Apollo Theater at Ron Perelman's home in the summer of 2011. *Kevin Mazur/WireImage*

Meeting Pope Benedict in 2008 at the papal nuncio's residence in New York. *NYPD*

Manhattan College celebrated the dedication of the Raymond W. Kelly '63 Student Commons on October 15, 2014. Manhattan College president Brennan O'Donnell is on the left; Tom and Mary Alice O'Malley are on the right. *Chris Taggart/ Manhattan College*

The family at the Waldorf Astoria for the 2012 New York City Police Foundation Gala. From left: Jim, his wife, Jennifer, me, Veronica, and Greg. *NYPD*

But there was simply no evidence, Sheehan and Cohen said, that his reconnaissance trip had led to any further action.

From police headquarters, Sheehan, Cohen, and I went to the FBI command center at 26 Federal Plaza, where we joined a secure conference call in Washington. U.S. Homeland Security Secretary Tom Ridge and Defense Secretary Donald Rumsfeld were on the line. FBI director Robert Mueller also participated in the call.

"Why do we need to raise the threat level?" I asked.

The Washington officials repeated the list of targets and reiterated their importance to the financial system. But no one on the call was able to offer any evidence that the threat was remotely imminent. It had potential for being current, of course. All threats do. But it certainly didn't seem immediate to me.

I expressed my reservations. I passed along the analysis of our two deputy commissioners. Everyone responded politely. The Department of Homeland Security went ahead and raised the threat level to orange.

In a briefing with journalists later that day, Ridge made the threat sound quite ominous. "The preferred means of attack would be car or truck bombs," he said. "That would be a primary means of attack."

It would be up to New York City, he went on, to consider moving its own threat level to red, the highest level. Ours had been at permanent orange since September 2001. "This is not the usual chatter," Ridge cautioned. "This is multiple sources that involve extraordinary detail."

Asked about the chain of decision, White House spokeswoman Healy said this: "The president made the final decision today agreeing with the recommendation of Secretary Ridge to go ahead and raise the threat level in these select areas."

And that was that.

The threat level stayed elevated until November 10, eight days after President Bush handily defeated John Kerry. Only after he'd left office did Tom Ridge publicly acknowledge that the terror-threat level could be a political—as well as a security—decision.

He wrote in his book, *The Test of Our Times*, that he was pressured by other members of the Bush Administration to raise the national terror-alert level again just before the 2004 election. Such pressure, he said, contributed to his decision to resign on November 30 of that year.

For his part, Barot was indicted in the Southern District of New York along with his friends Nadeem Tarmohamed and Qaisar Shaffi. But they were never tried in the United States. They and four other codefendants were charged and convicted in London for their terror plotting. Barot was sentenced to forty years to life in prison.

Four: THE HERALD SQUARE PLOT

Shahawar Siraj was just a neighborhood blowhard, a loudmouth clerk in a Brooklyn bookstore, not the kind of individual worthy of federal investigation—or so the FBI believed.

We took a different view. An Arabic-speaking detective from the NYPD Intelligence Division heard Siraj's violent ramblings, noting that they frequently veered into threats of terrorism against Americans. To us, the America-hating bookstore clerk seemed like someone to keep a careful eye on.

I am very happy that we did. The twenty-two-year-old Siraj earned the distinction of being the first fully homegrown terrorist intent on killing New Yorkers after 9/11. Unlike fellow American Iyman Faris, Siraj didn't have to travel to the Middle East to get radicalized, and his timing couldn't have been much more disturbing: he threatened to hit Herald Square just as the 2004 Republican National Convention was coming to Madison Square Garden, two blocks away.

The Siraj case demonstrated the core value of the NYPD Intelligence Division's deep undercover efforts in the fight against terrorism. It showed how effective undercover detectives with diverse backgrounds can be. And it showed the importance of not leaving terror fighting entirely in the hands of the FBI. The FBI took a pass on Shahawar Siraj. We didn't. We were right.

Much credit goes to an undercover officer who used the pseudonym Kamil Pasha. Born in Bangladesh, he became a New York City police officer and was assigned to the Intelligence Division. There, he used his training, his street smarts, and his own cultural understanding to help foil this potentially catastrophic terror plot.

When Pasha walked into Islamic Books & Tapes on Fifth Avenue, next door to the Islamic Society of Bay Ridge mosque, he recognized immediately that Siraj was a whole lot more than a neighborhood loudmouth. Pasha introduced Siraj to Osama Eldawoody, an Arabic-speaking man who had worked with us as a paid confidential informant. Thankfully, Pasha's colleagues and supervisors in the Intelligence Division understood how to use the informant effectively, how to analyze field reports, and how to protect the undercover, the informant, and their families as the case slowly unfolded. This is what experienced detectives do.

Siraj had come to America from Karachi, Pakistan, six years earlier, entering the country illegally through Canada. His parents and young sister were already here seeking asylum. His uncle owned the bookstore. In April 2004, Siraj introduced our informant to James Elshafay, a heavyset nineteen-year-old high school dropout who lived with his mother and aunt in the Rossville section of Staten Island. He'd clearly had a troubled young life, failing the eighth grade three times and sniffing glue and using drugs as a teenager. When Elshafay tried to join the U.S. Army, he was rejected because of a "personality disorder." His mother was Irish, his father Egyptian. In the previous eighteen months, he had developed an interest in his Islamic heritage. He'd grown a beard. He'd begun to pray. And he'd started to notice a lot of anti-Muslim prejudice, which he said the police never did anything about. Elshafay said he'd seen a sign that read GOD BLESS AMERICA on one side and KILL THE ARAB BABIES on the other.

Eventually Elshafay confided that he had drawn up a list of targets to attack. They included subway stations on Forty-Second and Fifty-Ninth Streets in Manhattan, the Verrazano-Narrows Bridge, and Staten Island's three police precincts, the 120th in St. George, the 122nd in New Dorp, and the 123rd in Tottenville.

Soon Siraj was showing Eldawoody CDs with bomb-making instructions. "I want at least a thousand to two thousand to die in one day," Siraj said. "I'm going to fuck this country very bad."

The men settled on the busy Herald Square subway station at Sixth Avenue and Thirty-Fourth Street, beneath Macy's department store. They decided to tour the targeted location on Saturday, August 21. The Republican National Convention was set to open nine days later, on August 30. For their reconnaissance visit, Siraj assumed a disguise, a do-rag and baggy pants. He said he wanted to look less Arabic and more hip-hop. When they got to the subway station, Siraj, Elshafay, and Eldawoody split up, each doing his own recon, taking special note of where the benches and garbage cans were.

The plan they developed was for Siraj to place the bombs in the subway. Elshafay would stand as his lookout. They would go in the Thirty-Third Street entrance and come out on Thirty-Fourth Street. But when the three of them met two days later to finalize their plans, Siraj seemed to get cold feet. "I'm not ready to die," he said.

After all their discussion and planning, maybe the attack was off.

But Elshafay spoke up. "I'll do it," he said. "I'll place the bombs in the subway."

And he had his own idea for a disguise. When the day came, he said, he would wear the black hat, long coat, and side curls of a Hasidic Jewish man " 'cause they know the Jews aren't the ones doing it."

Siraj suggested his friend put the explosive devices in a Macy's bag: "Jews shop at Macy's," he said.

At this point, supervisors in the Intelligence Division decided they had more than enough evidence to move in. On August 27, Siraj was arrested outside the bookstore in Bay Ridge. In his pocket was Elshafay's diagram. Elshafay was taken into custody at the Noor Al-Islam mosque on Staten Island. Before the police cuffed him and put him in a patrol car, the devout Muslim asked if he could have a cigarette.

Elshafay pleaded guilty and agreed to testify against his friend, who went to trial in front of U.S. District Judge Nina Gershon. Siraj was convicted of all charges. Before he was sentenced, he made a statement to the court. While claiming to feel remorse, he tried to shift some of the blame to others. "I am taking responsibility for Thirty-Fourth Street, but I was manipulated."

Judge Gershon didn't buy it.

"They had the potential, if not thwarted, to wreak havoc with the New York City transportation system, indeed, the tristate-area transportation system," she said, sentencing him to thirty years in federal prison.

Five: THE FAKE-IDENTITY PLOT

Majid Khan had a problem.

The veteran al-Qaeda operative was sitting in Karachi, Pakistan, 7,500 miles from the United States. He'd left America secretly in violation of U.S. immigration law. Now he had direct orders from Khalid Sheikh Mohammed to bomb underground storage tanks at gas stations in Maryland.

Khan needed a way back in.

That's when he met twenty-three-year-old Uzair Paracha and proposed a deal. Uzair's father, Saifullah Paracha, owned a business in New York, marketing apartments in Karachi to Pakistani American families. Khan offered to invest $200,000 in the business—in return for a favor.

A series of favors, actually.

Small, personal favors, we knew, often help to lubricate international terrorism, similarly to religious zeal and large piles of money. Families like the Parachas—affluent, educated, international, traveling frequently back and forth—are valuable assets to organizations like al-Qaeda. They help to get the murderous business done.

Though he spent much of his childhood in Pakistan, Uzair was highly Americanized. As a young child, he attended the Rainbow Montessori preschool in Queens. He managed a New York gas station during his summer breaks from college. He wore designer jeans and pricey sneakers. He always had the latest cell phone.

During a meeting at an ice cream shop in the Pakistani capital in early February 2003, Khan detailed his request. Uzair, a legal permanent resident of the United States who could travel between the two nations without raising suspicion, would return home to New York. There he would undertake a series of actions designed to fool immigration authorities into believing that Khan was still in the United States.

To execute this ruse, Uzair would use Khan's credit card and deposit money into Khan's bank account. He would call U.S. immigration officials, pretending to be Khan, to inquire about the status of Khan's pending passport application. Once the passport was sent, Uzair would use the key Khan gave him to retrieve the passport from the Maryland post office box Khan had given as his mailing address. Impersonating Khan, Uzair would close the postal box and hand-deliver the passport to Khan in Pakistan.

The al-Qaeda man could then return to the U.S. to execute Mohammed's murderous plan.

To make sure the job got done, Khan provided handwritten instructions to Uzair. Each item had a star in front of it.

*Always call from a pay phone.
*Put money in the bank account.
*Use the card at any gas station.
*Practice the signature.

To help Uzair pull off the identity ruse, Khan also included his father's and mother's names and gave Uzair his Maryland driver's license, his Bank of America ATM card, his social security card, and a high school ID bearing Khan's name and photograph.

Uzair returned to America and followed Majid Khan's script. He made the calls. He added the deposits. He used the credit cards. In phone calls to U.S. immigration officials, he pretended to be Khan, helping the al-Qaeda operative lay his phony trail. But on March 28, 2003, members of the Joint Terrorism Task Force, including FBI agents and New York City detectives, arrested Uzair Paracha in New York and searched his home.

The presence of NYPD detectives in large numbers gave the terrorism task force the benefit of street smarts, investigative experience, and diverse relationships that the FBI agents seldom had. Many of the federal agents came from other places. They'd been in New York on relatively short tours between transfers in and out of other postings. They were talented investigators in their own right with access to the deep resources of the FBI. But I would match our seasoned detectives against most of them.

In his possession, Uzair still had the items Khan had given him. He admitted that his father, Saifullah, had told him of Khan's ties to al-Qaeda. This information couldn't have been jarring to Uzair. He already knew his father admired Osama bin Laden.

After a two-week trial, during which he testified and tried unsuccessfully to disavow the confession he had given over the course of several days, Uzair was convicted of providing material support to a designated foreign terrorist organization and four other charges. Judge Sidney Stein sentenced Uzair to thirty years in prison.

His father, Saifullah Paracha, accused of using his business connections to help smuggle bomb-making chemicals into the United States, was sent to military custody at Guantánamo Bay.

Majid Khan pleaded guilty on February 29, 2012, in a military court at Guantánamo Bay to working with al-Qaeda. He admitted to the gas-station plot, to complicity in the 2003 bombing of a Marriott hotel in Jakarta, Indonesia, and to planning to assassinate Pakistani president Pervez Musharraf.

Six: THE TUNNEL PLOT

Think of lower Manhattan, and particularly the World Trade Center, as a giant bathtub. Deep in the middle. Shallower around the edges. The only thing missing is the water, and that's waiting right nearby. Billions and billions—no, trillions—of gallons of water. In the Hudson River. In New York Harbor. In the Atlantic Ocean beyond that. So much water, it's almost impossible to quantify. It's the job of the bedrock and the earth and some landfill and a lot of tall buildings with deep foundations to keep all that water out. Otherwise lower Manhattan would drown. If someone could somehow pierce the wall of the bathtub, then you'd be getting into the realm of big-budget disaster movies.

In 2005, we learned with considerable alarm that someone was plotting to do exactly that—drown us from thousands of miles away.

Operation Life Raft. That's what we called the case. Although the plotters schemed with each other entirely overseas, their multinational conspiracy made clear to everyone: you don't have to be in New York City to threaten New York City. Had it succeeded, the PATH train plot could have been truly devastating.

In summer 2005, FBI counterterrorism agents picked up some disturbing messages in online chat rooms, detailing a planned attack on the Hudson River PATH train tunnels that link lower Manhattan and northern New Jersey. The agents tracked some of the web postings and e-mail messages to Assem Hammoud, a thirty-year-old economics and computer science instructor at the Lebanese International University.

When Lebanese armed forces showed up at his door on April 27, 2006, Hammoud admitted to exchanging detailed maps and other information about the tunnel plot with like-minded unaffiliated terrorists around the world.

The FBI kept the arrest a secret, not wanting to alert the other plotters. It was a serious plot with catastrophic potential. Those tunnels, century-old cast-iron tubes that rest on the river bottom under a thin layer of silt, are a crucial part of the metropolitan region's commuter transportation network.

As the FBI and foreign agents worked diligently overseas, NYPD detectives surveyed the highly tempting underwater target. The PATH tunnels were easily accessible. Nearly 250,000 people ride those trains every weekday. Maritime engineering experts had chilling warnings about how much of a charge of explosives would be needed to pierce the tunnel walls and flood a major part of lower Manhattan south of Fourteenth Street.

Without divulging an inappropriate level of detail here, the answer was "Not much." An unbelievably small blast could do it, breaching the tunnel and delivering a devastating torrent of water into the low elevation of the crowded city.

Proof of concept would come years later with Hurricane Sandy. Lower Manhattan, which began to fill with water, really was like a bathtub. The Port Authority has since fortified the tunnel with a bank-to-bank bomb-resistant covering.

As part of Operation Life Raft, the NYPD and Port Authority police put extra security on the tunnel, while authorities overseas continued mining data off Hammoud's computer. They found maps, bomb plans, and intricate descriptions of the tunnels, stations, and trains—a full digital compendium of deadly and incriminating details.

The conspirators got into some highly precise detail. According to their plans, they would enter Canada first, crossing into the United States from the north. Once in New York, they would board PATH with backpacks full of explosives, which they planned to detonate while the trains were inside the Hudson River tunnels, drowning those passengers who were not killed in the immediate blast. The plotters even mentioned a strike date for October or November of 2006.

Cracking the case was an excellent example of international law enforcement cooperation. Not only did the FBI and the New York City police play a crucial role, so did law enforcement agencies in six other countries.

Two men were arrested in England and Canada. The conspirators from the other countries were not arrested.

Lacking an extradition treaty with Lebanon, we could not get Assem Hammoud back to New York for prosecution. Given the realities of the Lebanese justice system, he ended up serving only three years in prison. If he'd been prosecuted and convicted in America, he'd have faced thirty years or more.

But there was a clear lesson to be learned from the case. Several of them, actually.

One was that rail and transit systems made very inviting targets. Huge damage could be achieved with relatively modest effort. And while airports were vastly more secure since the 9/11 attacks, relatively little attention or resources had gone toward keeping America's urban and suburban transit systems safe.

Another lesson had to do with the importance of international cooperation. Without that, this plot could have gone much further than it did.

Finally, we were reminded again that law enforcement had to become even more vigilant in monitoring blogs, websites, chat rooms, and other digital forums. They provide an easy way for our enemies to organize themselves. Plots that used to require face-to-face meetings, international rendezvous, and in-person recruitment campaigns can now be launched with a few short keyboard strokes or one click of a mouse.

Seven: THE BUCKEYE PLOT

Russell Defreitas had what he was convinced was the perfect terror target: the underground pipeline that delivers jet fuel to John F. Kennedy International Airport.

Part of a large national energy network known as the Buckeye Pipeline, this underground section runs from northern New Jersey, beneath some of the busiest parts of Manhattan, and into Queens, with branches feeding the needs of LaGuardia and Kennedy airports.

The deadly possibilities were a cause of glee for the former JFK baggage handler and his coconspirators. An underground conflagration raging across the region, propelled by igniting jet fuel, sending high-energy fireballs toward New York's international transportation hub—that sounded positively spectacular to these America-hating terrorists.

"Anytime you hit Kennedy, it is the most hurtful thing to the United States," Defreitas was caught on tape bragging to an informant run by a veteran NYPD detective with the Joint Terrorism Task Force. "To hit John F. Kennedy, wow… They love JFK like he's the man. If you hit that, the whole country will be in mourning. It's like you can kill the man twice."

"Even the twin towers can't touch it," one of his coconspirators agreed. "This can destroy the economy of America for some time."

Defreitas, an American citizen who came from the South American nation of Guyana, concocted the plan in early 2007 with other terror-minded extremists from that part of the world. Joining the conspiracy were two other Guyanese men, Abdel Nur and Abdul Kadir. Kadir was a former member of the Guyanese National Assembly. The fourth conspirator was Kareem Ibrahim, who came from Trinidad. The investigation was led by the JTTF, but it was a senior NYPD detective who ran the probe. That made perfect sense, since Defreitas was so well wired into the underbelly of life around the airport.

In his job at the airport, Defreitas claimed to have observed weapons being shipped to Israel and became outraged that they might be used to harm Muslims. That, he asserted, was what spurred him to act.

The plotters conducted extensive surveillance of the pipeline and related targets. They carefully reviewed satellite photos. They attempted to make contact with another Islamic terrorist group. We even had reports of a possible Iran connection, though that was never proven.

When I was first briefed on the details of the plot, I knew immediately how horrendous a pipeline explosion could be, especially in a crowded part of Manhattan. With hundreds and hundreds of miles of potential access points, it was nearly impossible to secure them all. This was a terror conspiracy that would have to be foiled by solid detective work with informers and cooperators and reports from the inside, not by placing patrol cars on every corner in New York. Thankfully, given the depths of NYPD contacts in these communities, we were able to get that detective work done.

Defreitas was arrested in Brooklyn in early June 2007. His

three coconspirators were taken into custody in Trinidad and extradited to New York in June 2008, where they were indicted for conspiring to cause "death, serious bodily injury, and extensive destruction" at Kennedy Airport. "One of the most chilling plots imaginable," said U.S. Attorney Roslynn Mauskopf of the Eastern District of New York. "Had it succeeded," she said, "it could have resulted in unfathomable damage, deaths, and destruction."

Some people in the media tried to minimize the plot. The *New York Times* buried the story on page 37, noting that no explosives had been purchased and the plotters hadn't actually blown up anything. *Time* magazine asked pointedly, "The JFK Plot: Overstating the Case?" *Wired* magazine portrayed the plot as a joke: "Portrait of the Modern Terrorist As an Idiot."

But it's easy to shrug off a plot that never happened. And these conspirators certainly had the motive, the inside knowledge, and the energy. We are fortunate they were caught in time.

Thankfully, New York congressman Peter King, who chaired the House Homeland Security Committee, understood all that. "We've gone from criticizing them for not doing enough immediately after 9/11 to now criticizing them too much." He called such reactions "the price of success when you haven't been attacked in six years."

Defreitas, Ibrahim, and Kadir were convicted at trial and sentenced to life in federal prison. Nur pleaded guilty and was sentenced to fifteen years. Their appeals were all denied by the U.S. Court of Appeals for the Second Circuit. The judges there seemed to get the seriousness of the plot. The conspirators intended "to explode pipelines and jet-fuel tanks at JFK Airport in order to kill countless Americans and other travelers, disrupt air travel, and harm the American economy," the judges wrote. "The gravity of the crimes for which they were convicted easily justifies the life sentences that were imposed."

Eight: THE TRANSATLANTIC PLOT

One way to kill Americans is to come to America and do it in person. Another way is to explode liquid bombs aboard international flights bound for New York; Washington, DC; Chicago; and other cities.

That was Rashid Rauf's preferred method.

Born in 1981 to religious Pakistani parents, Rauf was raised in the northern factory city of Birmingham, England. His father, who'd been a sharia judge back home in Kashmir, worked as a baker in Birmingham. The city was rife with fundamentalist Islam that often collided with the traditions of the Christian faith. Rauf attended Washwood Heath Secondary School, where Israr Khan, a Muslim teacher, leaped up during Christmas carols one December day and shouted: "Who is your god? Why are you saying Jesus and Jesus Christ? God is not your god. It is Allah."

Seven months after 9/11, when he was twenty-one, Rauf moved to Bahawalpur, Pakistan, leaving England amid reports that he was wanted for questioning in connection with the murder of his uncle. Soon Rauf was traveling to Afghanistan, where he formally signed on with al-Qaeda. Increasingly devout, the intense young man married the daughter of Ghulam Mustafa, founder of a local Deobandi madrassa, Darul Uloom Madina. Through his new wife's family and his own networking skills, he got to know several top al-Qaeda leaders and got busy working his way up the terror organization.

By 2005, Rauf had assumed an important role in the group: He was responsible for shepherding recruits who arrived from England and other Western countries. He would meet the wide-eyed newcomers. He would assess whether they were serious candidates for jihad. He would pass promising ones on to senior al-Qaeda leaders, who would try to persuade them to launch suicide missions back home.

Among Rauf's prized protégés were Mohammed Siddique Khan and Shehzad Tanweer, perpetrators of the horrific 7/7 attacks on the London transportation system in July 2005. Fifty-two commuters were killed that day. After helping to recruit the killers, Rauf managed the bombing plot from afar via Yahoo messages, e-mails, and mobile phones.

He eventually began handling some of the persuasion himself, never forgetting to mention the seventy-two dark-eyed virgins who awaited male Muslim martyrs and how badly Muslims had been treated at Abu Ghraib prison in Iraq. He was a friendly face who could easily relate to disaffected young Muslims from the West. Later he would play exactly that role with Long Island Rail Road bombing conspirator Bryant Neal Vinas and New York subway bomb plotters Najibullah Zazi, Adis Medunjanin, and Zarein Ahmedzay. But in late 2005 and early 2006, Rashid Rauf was focused on blowing planes out of the sky.

It wasn't as easy as it would have been a few years earlier.

Since 9/11, thanks in part to Transportation Secretary Norman Mineta and our Rapid Response Teams, security had been vastly improved in America's and the world's air travel systems. Airport screening was far more effective. Tighter carry-on restrictions were in place. While some people complained that the searches were intrusive, the U.S. Transportation Security Administration and many parallel agencies abroad did a far better job than the airlines had. Cockpit doors had been hardened, and armed air marshals were aboard many flights. But no security system is unbeatable, and the terrorists were constantly dreaming up new ways to overcome whatever we thought to put in place. The latest idea from Rauf and his coconspirators in Britain and Pakistan: liquid explosives.

For many months, the British intelligence service MI5 was picking up chatter about an air travel terror plot, an especially bold one. The plan was to start with the powdered soft-drink mix

Tang, then add in some other chemicals. The mixture would be hidden in soda bottles and sneaked aboard transatlantic flights, ready to be combined and ignited in the air. One trip to the restroom later, there would be a ready-mix bomb on board.

As the British investigators followed their leads, all the evidence pointed in one direction: at mastermind Rashid Rauf.

The chatter was right. He had a plan. It targeted seven transatlantic flights on three airlines—American, United, and Air Canada. The flights would leave London's Heathrow Airport, bound for New York, Washington, Chicago, San Francisco, Toronto, and Montreal. Suicide bombers on board would mix the explosive cocktails and set the bombs to explode. The seven planes were scheduled to depart within a 155-minute window, ensuring that once the bombs began detonating, there would be no way to stop the other bombers.

Had it been executed, Rauf's scheme would have caused "mass murder on an unimaginable scale," one British official warned as the details leaked out. On August 9, 2006, twenty-four people were arrested in London and Birmingham, England. Rauf was picked up in Pakistan.

Immediately, British and U.S. authorities raised the threat level on transatlantic flights to "critical" and "red," the highest on each nation's risk chart, and tightened airline baggage rules. International air travel was thrown into turmoil for days. From that week forward, only small quantities of liquids were allowed on board, and then only in clear plastic bags.

"I have done nothing wrong, but I have been framed," Rashid Rauf told a Pakistani court in December. "Everything against me is based on lies, lies."

He needn't have worried. Unfortunately, the justice system in Pakistan didn't take terrorism as seriously as we did. Rauf was never extradited to England, as authorities there were requesting. Instead, a judge in Rawalpindi found insufficient evidence that the al-Qaeda operative had been involved in a terror plot and reduced the charges to forgery and possession of explosives.

A year later, in December 2007, Rauf escaped from custody under highly suspicious circumstances. On his way back from a court hearing, Rauf was allowed to enter a mosque for prayer while the police officers who were transporting him stopped for lunch at McDonald's. Not surprisingly, Rauf took the opportunity to escape.

He didn't enjoy his freedom for long. On November 22, 2008, he was killed by a U.S. drone strike in Pakistan.

Rauf's legacy, however, has been a lasting one for the traveling public. As a result of his plot, the TSA limited the total volume of liquids each passenger may bring aboard an aircraft and instituted the 3-1-1 rule: Liquids, gels, aerosols, creams, and pastes must be transported in quantities of 3.4 ounces or less. They must be sealed in one-quart clear plastic zip-top bags. Each passenger is limited to one bag.

Nine: THE LIRR PLOT

Bryant Neal Vinas was a nice Catholic boy living in the Long Island suburbs of New York, an average student at Longwood High School, a Sunday congregant at St. Francis de Sales Church, a dedicated fan of the hapless New York Mets.

But then something changed. Vinas's case vividly emphasized what can happen when even a seemingly normal American kid falls under the influence of radical ideology.

Vinas wasn't the first to walk down this frightening path from American boy to terrorist operative. The short list already included al-Qaeda propaganda chief Adam Gadahn, "American Taliban" John Walker Lindh, and former California street-gang member Jose Padilla. But al-Qaeda leaders were still very much on the lookout for white Westerners who could be recruited as suicide bombers, people who could travel freely back to America and easily blend in.

Vinas left Long Island for Pakistan in 2007 to study religion, he said—but he was already a committed jihadist on a gradual path to violent action. Born December 4, 1983, to immigrant parents from South America, both Catholic, Vinas loved *G.I. Joe* and wrestling. After high school, like a lot of kids, he had trouble figuring out what came next. He joined the army but was discharged three weeks into boot camp at Fort Jackson, South Carolina. He worked as a truck driver and in a car wash and was in and out of technical college.

Sometime in 2003, the brother of a friend gave Vinas a copy of the Koran and spoke with him about Islam. Vinas converted in 2004 and began attending services at the Al Falah mosque in Queens. He spent time with some of the hardliners at a mosque in nearby Selden, joining a discussion group called Islamic Thinkers Society, where people spoke approvingly of jihadist groups including al-Qaeda. Like many young men who would later turn to terror, Vinas watched videos of Anwar al-Awlaki, a charismatic New Mexico–born imam sometimes described as the "bin Laden of the Internet."

Vinas left for Pakistan in September 2007, ready to join the fight against America. In late March 2008, he trained in the mountains of Waziristan. He traveled through the tribal areas in the spring and summer, and met some of al-Qaeda's most senior leaders. The al-Qaeda operatives persuaded Vinas to return to the United States and carry out an attack there. The target he and his handlers settled on was the Long Island Rail Road, the commuter train system that served the area where he'd grown up. Vinas proposed detonating a bomb aboard a moving train, timing the explosive so that it would inflict maximum damage, inside the East River tunnel as the lines converge on Manhattan.

All that must have been enticing to al-Qaeda's upper echelon.

But plots like this can only be successful if the planning is kept secret, and Vinas was not very good at that. Before he even left Pakistan, local authorities had learned about his plotting and arrested him in Peshawar. The Pakistanis turned him over to the FBI—American radicalized, Pakistani trained, and ultimately neutralized before he was able to strike.

New York was fortunate Vinas couldn't keep his mouth shut. All we could do was learn from his path to terrorism. Vinas got radicalized to violence before he ever left home in quiet North Patchogue, escaping the notice of his local police department while becoming enamored with al-Qaeda terrorism.

This happened outside the jurisdiction of NYPD. Nevertheless, we redoubled our efforts and cooperation with the many suburban police departments that ring New York City, in Long Island's Nassau and Suffolk Counties especially. They understood the importance of working cooperatively with the NYPD. Our worlds were deeply intertwined. Their counties were more diverse than ever. Many of their residents worked in the city. Anything that happened in the boroughs would surely affect their suburban economies. Vinas's hometown police in Suffolk County took the case extremely seriously, vowing to make sure the next Bryant Neal Vinas didn't escape detection.

Ten: THE BRONX SYNAGOGUE PLOT

They hated Jews and also America, and they were more than ready to act on it. They conspired in 2009 to bomb two synagogues in the Bronx and fire a Stinger surface-to-air missile at a military plane near the Air National Guard station in Newburgh, New York.

The good news was that James Cromitie, David Williams, Onta Williams, and Laguerre Payen, petty criminals from lower Westchester County, New York, seemed to have no ties to any international terror groups. The bad news was the viciousness of their intentions.

There wasn't much doubt what the men hoped to accomplish. They were caught on tape repeatedly spouting incendiary threats against America in general and Jews in particular. "I don't give a fuck if a bunch of Jews are in there," ringleader Cromitie said about planting a bomb outside one of the synagogues. "I will let it go off. Jews are the wickedest people that Allah has created."

This case, like several others, emphasized the importance of using credible confidential informants. Shahed Hussain was a Pakistani national who was granted asylum in the United States based on a claim of political persecution. Like many cooperators, he had his own issues. In 2002, he was convicted of fraud based on misconduct as a translator at the Department of Motor Vehicles in Albany. Nevertheless, he was an effective confidential informant. He befriended Cromitie and his fellow plotters, pretended to sympathize with their extremist views, and let them think he would facilitate their conspiracy. In fact, he was reporting back to us every step of the way and making sure that the homegrown jihadists didn't succeed.

The plot took a while to hatch. At times, the informant had to nudge, focus, cajole, and even urge the suspects. But in the final analysis, they were perfectly clear on what they were doing, and they agreed. They staked out their targets carefully. With a digital camera they purchased at Walmart, they took photos of the locations. On May 6, they drove to a warehouse in Connecticut to pick up what they believed was a surface-to-air guided missile and three improvised explosive devices, all of which were actually duds. They brought the weapons back to a storage facility in Newburgh, keeping them there until the night of the planned attack, May 20, 2009. That night, they placed what they thought were homemade bombs, each packed with thirty-seven pounds of phony C-4 plastic explosives, into two cars already parked outside the Riverdale Temple, a Reform synagogue, and the nearby Riverdale Jewish Center, an Orthodox synagogue.

The men were arrested literally as the plot was going into effect. By the time NYPD detectives and FBI agents moved in, Cromitie and the other three conspirators had gone so far as to plant bombs—or what they believed to be bombs. The men were taken into custody as they were about to leave the block and drive to the National Guard base to shoot down the military aircraft. On the way, they planned to detonate the synagogue bombs with a signal from a mobile phone.

I watched the various transactions on a live video feed and went up to the scene with Joseph Demarest, the assistant director of the FBI, to brief reporters personally.

"There was a driver who was a cooperator, and there was the individual who placed the bombs in the vehicle, and then there were three lookouts," I explained to reporters after the arrests. "As everyone was going back to the car, that is when the signal was given to the emergency service officers to move in." They used a tractor-trailer to block the street and prevent the plotters' escape.

The men "stated that they wanted to commit jihad," I continued. Arresting them, I added, "speaks to our concern about homegrown terrorism."

The relationship between the four men and the undercover informant would become a key dispute among the lawyers in the case. But no one made the defendants do any of this, and given all the evidence we helped amass, there couldn't possibly be any doubt about the violent intentions of James Cromitie and his friends.

On June 29, 2011, when three of the men were set to be sentenced in federal court, Judge Colleen McMahon said they weren't "political or religious martyrs," but "thugs for hire, pure and simple." She probably should have added, "thugs who were caught trashing Jews, spouting violent Islamic rhetoric, planting what they thought were bombs outside synagogues, and preparing to fire a Stinger missile at a U.S. military aircraft on American soil."

The judge also objected to the ways the informant manipulated ringleader Cromitie. "The essence of what occurred here is that a government, understandably zealous to protect its citizens from terrorism, came upon a man both bigoted and suggestible, one who was incapable of committing an act of terrorism on his own. It created acts of terrorism out of his fantasies of bravado and bigotry, and then made those fantasies come true." She added, "The government did not have to infiltrate and foil some nefarious plot—there was no nefarious plot to foil."

Despite her florid language, Judge McMahon ruled that the convictions were all appropriate under the law. She sentenced Cromitie, Onta Williams, and David Williams to twenty-five years in prison. Two months later, she gave Laguerre Payen the same sentence. The Second Circuit Court of Appeals later confirmed that the district judge was right.

Eleven: THE SUBWAY PLOT

There was no doubt that Najibullah Zazi had what it took to commit mass murder in the name of Allah: zeal, dedication, top-flight terror training, and some genuine organizational skills. Of all the plots we faced in New York after 9/11, none came closer to deadly results than this one. Stopping Zazi and his two young immigrant friends from detonating bombs in the subway took everything we had.

Zazi's family had moved from Afghanistan to Pakistan and then to Queens, easily New York's most diverse borough, arriving when he was fourteen. At the Abu Bakr mosque, young Zazi got to know two other immigrant teenagers, Bosnian-born Adis Medunjanin and Zarein Ahmedzay, whose family had followed the Zazis' path from Afghanistan to Pakistan to New York.

Together, the three friends spent hours watching videos of two radical clerics—Anwar al-Awlaki and Abdullah el-Faisal, a Jamaican-born preacher who'd been convicted in London of stirring up racial hatred and urging his followers to murder Christians, Hindus, Americans, and Jews. All three became convinced they had a personal duty to defend Islamic lands against foreign invaders.

Soon they decided to act on that belief.

In August 2008, they flew to Pakistan, planning to enter Afghanistan. There, they hoped to fight with the Taliban forces against U.S. military and allied troops. They would stay, in Zazi's words, until "the country was liberated" and "ask God to give us martyrdom while fighting."

Zazi's cousin helped connect the young believers to al-Qaeda operatives, who passed them along to Rashid Rauf, the terror network's designated wrangler of Western recruits. Rauf and others, including Adnan Gulshair el-Shukrijumah, ultimately persuaded the three young friends to return to New York and conduct a suicide mission. They discussed possible targets. Grand Central Terminal, Times Square, Penn Station, the New York Stock Exchange—each had its own attractions as a terror target. But el-Shukrijumah cautioned the men not to overreach. Other missions had failed because the overly grandiose suicide bombers had tried to do something too big. A mission that succeeded in setting off a bomb in a movie theater, the terror leader told the young men, was preferable to one that failed to bring down the Federal Reserve.

The three friends from Queens all assumed *kunya*s, al-Qaeda terror names. Medunjanin became Mohammed. Zazi became Salihuddin. Ahmedzay took the name Omar. They headed off to a training camp in North Waziristan, where they fired heavy weapons and watched other propaganda videos.

Well versed in the art of terror and fully motivated to act, the young trio needed only to settle back into life in the United States. Medunjanin returned first, arriving in New York on September 25, 2008. Ahmedzay traveled to Afghanistan to spend time with his wife. In November 2008, Zazi went for further training on how to build and detonate explosives. At another al-Qaeda camp in North Waziristan, he learned how to mix chemicals to create different kinds of detonators and how to make and ignite a main charge. Before he left Peshawar, Zazi recorded his own martyrdom video, e-mailed his bomb-making notes to himself, and worked out a secret code. When the plan was entirely in place, Zazi agreed to e-mail that the "marriage" was ready.

Zazi returned to Queens on January 15, 2009. Ahmedzay followed from Afghanistan a week later. Zazi, Ahmedzay, and Medunjanin decided they were less likely to attract attention from law enforcement if they weren't all in New York. So Zazi moved to Colorado, where his uncle's family lived, and started acquiring what he would need to build an acetone peroxide detonator. Some things he was able to get at Lowe's Home Improvement. Other items he purchased at Walmart. But for the concentrated hydrogen peroxide that was a key component of the detonator, Zazi shopped at various beauty-supply stores around Denver, a shopping spree caught on videotape and later shown repeatedly on cable news. When asked by a clerk why he needed so much hydrogen peroxide, he replied, "I have many girlfriends."

Zazi visited New York in August. There, he, Ahmedzay, and Medunjanin narrowed down the targets they would hit. The subway seemed promising. A Manhattan line at rush hour—maybe the 3 or 4 train—would offer the greatest number of victims, they decided. Each of the three men would strap on a bomb and go to a different location.

Zazi returned to Denver, where he continued to perfect the formula for the explosive. He called Ahmedzay and, using code, shared the news: He had fixed the wire on his computer, he told Ahmedzay. Had he fixed the *whole* computer, meaning the detonator and the main charge, Ahmedzay wanted to know. Zazi responded that he hadn't fixed the whole computer. He had fixed the wires.

But for one slipup, Zazi, Ahmedzay, and Medunjanin might well have succeeded, their plan causing vast casualties in the New York City subway. However, the notes Zazi took at explosives-training camp in North Waziristan were incomplete. Unsure of the proportions of the components for the main charge, he grew rattled. Using the code they had devised in Pakistan, Zazi e-mailed his al-Qaeda contact and told him that the wedding was ready. That e-mail and others that followed caught the attention of law enforcement. The FBI began following Zazi.

Before sunrise on September 9, 2009, Zazi left Denver for New York City in a rental car. The acetone peroxide, hydrochloric acid, scale, scotch tape, goggles, and Christmas tree lights Zazi had with him couldn't all be brought on an airplane. He planned to drive straight through. Once in New York, he and Ahmedzay would buy the other items they needed for the main charge—hydrogen peroxide, flour, and ball bearings—as well as batteries for the detonators and backpacks to hold the completed bombs. Medunjanin would join them to finalize their targets. Zazi believed he was no more than five days from completing the mission.

The FBI asked the Port Authority police to stop and search Zazi's car before he entered New York City. They asked the Port Authority, I am convinced, so that the NYPD would not be involved.

The Port Authority police did as the FBI had requested. Zazi was stopped as he drove onto the George Washington Bridge on September 10. As Zazi sat in the driver's seat, the officers searched the rental car. Zazi didn't resist. He just sat there. He didn't run. He didn't jump. He didn't make a move of any sort. But for reasons

I'm not sure I'll ever understand, the Port Authority police found none of the bomb-making material he had in the trunk—not the acetone peroxide, not the hydrochloric acid, not the scale, not the tape, not the goggles, not the Christmas tree lights—none of it.

How could they miss all that? I don't know. But they allowed a would-be terrorist onto the streets of New York carrying a trunkload of bomb-making equipment. Zazi said later that he would have jumped off the bridge if the Port Authority police had found the bomb-making materials. He never had to. They didn't find a thing.

With that stop, Zazi knew he'd been made. The first chance he had, he dumped the chemicals and other bomb ingredients he had brought with him from Denver.

The *New York Times* and others reported widely—and incorrectly—that the three men abandoned their plan on September 11, once Zazi learned from Ahmad Wais Afzali, an imam at a mosque Zazi had attended, that the NYPD was asking questions about Zazi and his two friends. Afzali had worked as an NYPD informant and was told by an NYPD deputy inspector he worked with that the FBI was interested in Zazi, Ahmedzay, and Medunjanin. The press blamed Afzali—and therefore the NYPD—for tipping Zazi's father off that law enforcement was onto him. The *Times* published two front-page, above-the-fold stories asserting this. I took the allegation seriously. It forced me to transfer the deputy inspector.

However, the *Times* story simply wasn't true. Zazi later testified that what actually tipped him off was the bridge stop on September 10. This is an example of how a leak put out by federal law enforcement and believed willingly by the *New York Times* could unfairly besmirch the image of the NYPD and a police executive.

The next day, September 11, the JTTF seized Zazi's car in Queens while he took the subway to lower Manhattan and the area near the New York Stock Exchange. The car was towed to the 109th Precinct, where investigators copied the contents of his laptop computer and put the computer back in his car. After retrieving his car at the 109th Precinct, Zazi flew back to Colorado on September 12.

He agreed to be interviewed by the FBI in Denver the following week. He was questioned about the bomb-making notes on his computer and denied they existed. He was arrested on September 19 and charged with lying to federal agents.

Ultimately, Zazi, Ahmedzay, and Medunjanin were indicted on terrorism-related charges in the Eastern District of New York. Zazi and Ahmedzay pleaded guilty to charges that subjected them to terms of life imprisonment. However, they entered into cooperation agreements to try to lessen their sentences. Both testified at Medunjanin's trial. He was convicted of nine charges and sentenced to a term of life.

Of all the plots, none came closer to being realized than this one. These three young men had the training, the patience, and the skill to pull it off. Had they succeeded in detonating their subway bombs, the results could truly have been catastrophic. Their plan was to perpetrate the attack on September 14, 2009—and it just so happened that President Obama was in New York City that day.

Twelve: THE TIMES SQUARE PLOT

If you see something, say something.

The NYPD was constantly urging citizens to alert authorities about suspicious activities. Several Times Square street vendors seemed to have taken that message to heart.

Alioune Niass, a Muslim immigrant from Senegal, was selling framed photographs of the New York skyline on Saturday, May 1, 2010, outside the Minskoff Theatre at Seventh Avenue and West Forty-Fifth Street, where *The Lion King* would be staged that night. He noticed smoke rising from a 1993 Nissan Path-finder parked near his table and alerted mounted police officer Wayne Rhatigan. (Later, several other vendors would also boast they were the first to alert police: Lance Orton, Duane Jackson, and Wayne Robinson.) Officer Rhatigan saw the smoke, caught an aroma that smelled like gunpowder, and radioed for help, sum-moning the NYPD Emergency Service Unit, the bomb squad, and the FDNY. Quickly, police closed off Times Square from Forty-Third to Forty-Ninth Streets. The mammoth Marriott Marquis hotel was also evacuated.

The bomb unit brought in a remote-controlled robotic device. After a careful search of the smoking vehicle, officers inventoried three propane tanks, two five-gallon canisters filled with gaso-line, several plastic bags of fertilizer, 152 M-88 fireworks, and two alarm clocks connected to wires.

Joe Esposito and David Cohen reported immediately to Times Square. Mayor Bloomberg and I were at the White House Correspondents' Association dinner in Washington that night. We left promptly and flew back to New York. "Had it detonated," I said to reporters when I got back to New York, "it would have caused casualties, a significant fireball."

In the years since 9/11, most of New York's terror plots were busted by early detection, investigators uncovering incriminating evidence at home or abroad. The Times Square bombing attempt fell victim to the perpetrator's own incompetence.

We had no advance warning of the plans in this case. Despite all our efforts and resources, we picked up nothing from inter-national communications or well-sourced investigators in New York neighborhoods. Nobody did. We learned about the plot only after the perpetrator, Faisal Shahzad, parked his dark-blue SUV with tinted windows on one of the most crowded corners in all of America, then failed in his carefully planned attempt to make the vehicle explode.

Sometimes the incompetence of our adversaries is the best weapon we have.

Painstaking investigative work by NYPD detectives and FBI agents reconstructed exactly what happened here. The patterns Shahzad followed were familiar. But it was crucial nonetheless—maybe even more so in this case—that we piece together every scrap of evidence we could find.

Born in Pakistan in 1979 to a well-off family, Faisal Shahzad attended primary school in Saudi Arabia and came to America at age eighteen in 1998 to study at Southeastern University in Washington, DC. He transferred to the University of Bridgeport in Connecticut, where he earned a bachelor's degree in computer applications and information systems. He went on to earn a master's degree at the same university, working part-time as a junior accountant for the cosmetics company Elizabeth Arden in Stamford, Connecticut.

By all appearances, Shahzad was living the immigrant's American dream, getting a good education, building a promising career, and buying a home in the suburbs. In 2006, he got his green card as a lawful permanent resident and went to work as a junior accountant at Affinion Group in Norwalk, Connecticut. On April 17, 2009, he became an American citizen. With that, he had truly completed his successful immigrant's journey.

But something was obviously going on beneath the surface. He'd apparently been listening to al-Awlaki tapes. A few weeks after becoming a citizen, he stopped paying his mortgage and defaulted on the loan. On June 2, 2009, he called from the airport to tell his wife, who'd been resisting his pressure to wear a hijab, that he was moving to Pakistan. She declined to join him and moved with their two young American-born children to Saudi Arabia, her family's home.

Shahzad got on a flight to Dubai, then arrived in Pakistan on July 3, 2009, and quickly found his way to a terror-training camp in Waziristan. It wasn't al-Qaeda he was training with but the Tehrik-e-Taliban, an extremist group known in the West as the Pakistani Taliban.

In the camp, he received training in weapons and explosions. He recorded his own forty-minute martyrdom video, discussing his plan to attack the United States and encouraging other Muslims to follow suit.

That tape provides a chilling look into the mind of a would-be terrorist. "A Brave Effort by Faisal Shahzad to Attack United States in Its Own Land," the video is titled. It is produced by Umar Media, the communications arm of Tehrik-e-Taliban. The video opens with Shahzad cradling then firing a machine gun. He speaks directly to the camera and explains himself.

"We decided we are going to raise an attack inside America," he says in clear, confident English.

The goal, he says, is to "incite the Muslims to get up and fight against the enemy of Islam."

He goes on to explain that jihad is one of the pillars that holds up Islam. "I've been trying to join my brothers in jihad ever since the 9/11 happened," he says. "I am planning to wage an attack inside America."

He certainly seemed to mean it.

His radicalism complete, Shahzad returned to the United States on February 3, 2010. Over the next three months, he purchased the bomb components he would need: fertilizer in Connecticut, fireworks in Pennsylvania, other items elsewhere. However, he changed the formula to avoid suspicion. He received $12,000 from Tehrik-e-Taliban, on top of $5,000 he had received while he was still in Pakistan. He bought the Pathfinder through an ad on Craigslist on April 24, paying $1,300 in cash, and got the windows tinted.

In searching for an appropriate target—somewhere that was accessible and very crowded—he watched real-time live video feeds from Times Square. He decided Saturday night was the busiest time of all.

Security video shows that Shahzad arrived in Times Square at 6:28 p.m., parking at Seventh Avenue and West Forty-Fifth Street. The bomb components were laid out carefully. In case he was confronted, he had with him a folded semiautomatic rifle in a laptop bag.

He lit the fuse, grabbed the laptop bag, shut the car door, and walked briskly away, confident that the SUV would explode shortly and dozens of people would be killed. He walked west on West Forty-Fifth Street then made his way to Grand Central Terminal.

But the vehicle only smoldered. Somehow, the fuse failed to detonate the intended explosion. The bomb never went off. The street vendors sounded their various warnings, and no one was hurt. All Shahzad's plans had come to nothing.

On his way to Grand Central, he stopped for a moment, waiting to hear the horrific explosion. He heard nothing at all. Once Shahzad got home to Connecticut, he turned on the television and heard about the vehicle bomb that forced the evacuations in the Theater District but failed to explode.

It was a fast but intense investigation. The NYPD and the FBI were both deeply engaged. Investigators reviewed E-ZPass records, which showed when Shahzad had driven into Manhattan, and gathered footage from near one hundred security cameras tracing his arrival and getaway. Shahzad fled quickly, but the case was broken by tracing the ownership of the SUV. The plates on the Pathfinder had been stolen from a Ford truck, so that went nowhere. And the vehicle identification number had been removed from the dashboard and the door. But investigators found the number hidden beneath the engine block. That was traced to the last registered owner, a female college student. She said she'd sold the SUV to a man whose name she didn't remember, but she did have a cell phone number, which was traced to a disposable phone that also had registered calls to Pakistan and to a fireworks store in Pennsylvania. Investigators also found a set of keys in the Pathfinder that were ultimately traced to Shahzad's house in Connecticut and to the 1998 Isuzu Rodeo he had parked eight blocks from Times Square for his getaway.

FBI surrounded Shahzad's house in Bridgeport, but somehow he managed to slip away. Through a federal terrorist database, we got word he was already at Kennedy Airport. He had driven with his 9-millimeter rifle, which he left in the car, and boarded a flight to Pakistan via Dubai. After the plane had left the gate and was about to taxi onto the runway, authorities boarded, pulled him off, and placed him under arrest. He refused to express remorse for his actions, and he pleaded guilty at his first court appearance and was ultimately sentenced to life in prison.

Thirteen: THE MANHATTAN SYNAGOGUES PLOT

Not all terrorists are fueled by deep religious fervor. Some are small-time, racist criminals seeking easy profit and infamy by killing people or blowing things up. Ahmed Ferhani and Mohamed Mamdouh never gave much indication that they believed in anything, other than taking what didn't belong to them and hating people different from themselves.

Born in Algeria in 1985, Ferhani moved with his family to New York as an eight-year-old. He was arrested in October 2010 for a robbery in Manhattan. It was then that an NYPD detective overheard him saying he hated Jews and was angry at the terrible way Muslims were treated around the world.

"They're treating us like dogs," he complained.

He also mentioned an interest in jihad and said he might like to become a martyr.

There's nothing illegal about crazy boasts or strong opinions, even ugly ones. But the apocalyptic, racist talk from the twenty-five-year-old robbery suspect convinced detectives to keep an eye on him. He definitely seemed to be a troubled young man, suffering from bipolar disorder and living in his father's basement in Whitestone, Queens.

We brought the case to the FBI's Joint Terrorism Task Force, but the supervisors had no interest in Ferhani's racist blathering. There wasn't sufficient connection, they said, to overt criminal acts. Who could possibly know if he was just another hothead racist or someone with truly dangerous intent? To us, that was the point. He was someone worth watching. We pressed the case on our own. That judgment paid off.

By April 12, 2011, Ferhani was telling an NYPD undercover detective that he wanted to blow up the biggest synagogue in Manhattan, musing that he might disguise himself as a Hasidic Jew. He said he'd sell drugs to raise the money for the operation. He also introduced the undercover to a young friend from Queens.

Mohamed Mamdouh was just twenty years old and seemed to share Ferhani's anger and prejudices. Zionists, he said, look like "little fucking rats." He was working as a taxi dispatcher, but he'd had his own scrapes with the law. He'd pleaded guilty to stealing jewelry, a laptop, and a bottle of vodka from a girlfriend and kicking her four-year-old poodle Lulu so hard he bruised the dog's ribs.

Mamdouh said he wanted to blow up ten synagogues one at a time. "Hell, yeah, I would love to blow that motherfucker up," he said about one of them.

Ferhani claimed to have some weapons but said he wanted to purchase more.

One undercover introduced the young man to another undercover, who posed as a gun dealer. The three of them met on May 11 at Twelfth Avenue and West Fifty-Eighth Street, where

Ferhani gave a $100 down payment for three semiautomatic handguns, three boxes of ammunition, and what he believed to be a hand grenade. He asked about buying a bulletproof vest, a police scanner, and a full box of grenades.

Ferhani was arrested at the scene. Mamdouh was arrested several blocks away. Once the FBI had shown no interest, the U.S. attorney's office seemed uninterested too. We brought the case to Manhattan district attorney Cyrus Vance. Ferhani and Mamdouh were arraigned May 12 on New York State terrorism charges, which were enacted after 9/11. This was the first time ever that New York State terrorism charges rather than federal charges were brought against terror plotters. Ferhani and Mamdouh were held without bail.

After much legal wrangling, Ferhani pleaded guilty to ten charges, including conspiracy as a crime of terrorism and criminal possession of a weapon as a crime of terrorism. Mamdouh pleaded guilty as well. Ferhani got ten years in state prison. Mamdouh got five.

Fourteen: THE MOM'S-KITCHEN PLOT

In the view of Jose Pimentel, the list of potential targets was long.

"People have to understand that America and its allies are all legitimate targets in warfare," he wrote on his website, trueislam1 .com. "This includes, facilities such as army bases, police stations, political facilities, embassies, CIA and FBI buildings, private and public airports, and all kinds of buildings where money is being made to help fund the war."

Alarming as his words were, this was another case the FBI wasn't interested in. We ran with it alone.

Pimentel wasn't a likely terrorist. He was born November 8, 1984, in the Dominican Republic, and moved to upper Manhattan as a child. He didn't convert to Islam until he moved upstate to Schenectady for college. His marriage had dissolved. He was smoking a lot of marijuana. He was spending way too much time on the Internet. He found his way to *Inspire*, the English-language online propaganda magazine run by al-Qaeda in the Arabian Peninsula.

Among the articles he read and linked to at his own website were "The Preparatory Manual of Explosives" and "How to Build a Bomb in the Kitchen of Your Mom." He also posted fifteen video clips of senior al-Qaeda motivational speaker Anwar al-Awlaki to his YouTube account.

Pimentel had moved back to New York and was living with an uncle at Broadway and West 138th Street when Pimentel's online activities attracted our attention. An undercover NYPD informant got to know him.

"We really have no excuses as Muslims here, you know, like, as jihadi Muslims in the West, we don't have any excuse for not to be blowing shit up," Pimentel said in one rambling conversation caught on tape by the informant. "At the end of the day, you know what I'm saying, when you can make a bomb with, like, twenty to thirty to forty dollars."

It wouldn't be that hard to take down a building with a bomb, he said. "All we got to do is put it in the basement. And I was thinking, like this is what we should do: If we put it, the car has to be facing the direction that we're going to exit. You feel me? And we should put it in a bag that doesn't look too suspicious, like a garbage bag."

We stuck with him as he rambled on. When he stopped trusting one confidential informant, two other confidential informants and an undercover detective stepped in.

Pimentel wasn't all talk either. What he lacked in proper diction he made up for in follow-through. By August of 2011, he began plotting his own bomb attack. He got more focused after September 30, when al-Awlaki was killed in a U.S. drone strike in Yemen.

Pimentel and the informants collected the components to build three bombs. At a 99 Cent store in Manhattan, he bought a clock similar to one he'd seen on the *Inspire* site. He found elbow joints, work gloves, Christmas lights, and nails at Home Depot.

Using step-by-step instructions from *Inspire*, he began drilling holes in the pipes, preparing the incendiary powder from six hundred matchstick tips and doing everything else needed to assemble the bombs. I watched him do all this on video. He considered various potential targets, including police cars and postal vehicles, but settled on U.S. troops returning home from Iraq and Afghanistan, considering them the most potent target imaginable. On November 20, 2011, when Pimentel was one hour away from having the bombs fully assembled, we moved in, taking him into custody.

Pimentel was prosecuted not by the federal government but by Manhattan district attorney Cyrus Vance. Although the would-be bomber insisted he'd been entrapped by our undercover informant, he pleaded guilty at New York State Supreme Court in Manhattan to a state terrorism charge and was sentenced to sixteen years in prison.

Fifteen: THE FINANCIAL DISTRICT PLOT

Unlike many future terrorists, Quazi Mohammad Rezwanul Ahsan Nafis didn't immigrate innocently to America and then become radicalized once he was here. The twenty-one-year-old left his native Bangladesh on a student visa in January 2012 with a single-minded plan.

Jihad.

He brought bomb-making instructions on his hard drive and tried to recruit willing coconspirators in New York. One of the people he approached turned out to be an FBI informant. In a recorded telephone call, Nafis asked for help launching a terror attack on American soil. The informant introduced him to an undercover FBI agent.

"We just want to meet our lord as soon as we can," Nafis told the agent at a meeting in Central Park on July 24, six months after he'd arrived. He said he intended to commit a suicide attack, something "very, very, very, very big that will shake the whole country."

One possible target, he said in August, was the New York Stock Exchange. Our cameras captured him scouting out the building at Broad and Wall Streets. By mid-September, he had switched his focus to the Federal Reserve Bank of New York on Liberty Street, less than a five-minute walk from the World Trade Center. A date was chosen: October 17.

"We will not stop until we obtain victory or martyrdom," he declared.

He said he hoped the attack would disrupt America's upcoming presidential elections. He wrote an article that he gave to the undercover, which he hoped *Inspire* magazine would post after the attack. Nafis wrote: "All I had in my mind [was] how to destroy America...I came up to this conclusion that targeting America's economy is [the] most efficient way to draw the path of obliteration of America as well as the path of establishment of Khilafa," Islam's dominance of the world.

Nafis's final plan called for assembling a thousand-pound bomb in several plastic trash bins inside a van and then attaching a detonator. On the day the attack was set to occur, Nafis drove to a warehouse, where he filled the garbage cans and loaded them into the van. He drove to the lower Manhattan Financial District and parked outside the Federal Reserve. The JTTF followed him all the way.

He walked to the Millenium Hotel on Church Street, where he had already booked a room. From the hotel, Nafis repeatedly tried to detonate the bomb with a remote-control device.

Of course, nothing went off. What he thought was a thousand pounds of explosives was, in fact, inert material provided by the JTTF. The remote detonator didn't detonate anything.

Nafis was arrested at the hotel, a man with murderous intentions who failed to achieve his goal.

He pleaded guilty at U.S. District Court in Brooklyn to attempting to use a weapon of mass destruction. On the day of his sentencing, Judge Carol B. Amon said she was convinced that the young Bangladeshi "would have executed this plan or a similar, perhaps less grand one, had he not been discovered."

She sentenced him to thirty years.

Sixteen: THE FLORIDA-TO–NEW YORK PLOT

Raees Qazi was at home in Fort Lauderdale, Florida, when he first tried to contact terror leaders in Yemen. Just nineteen years old, he sent word that he was prepared to lay his life on the line fighting the Western infidels in Afghanistan.

No, thank you, he was told. The terror network had enough fighters in that war zone. Do something in America instead.

So Qazi came up with a plan, and it wasn't to attack the Galleria at Fort Lauderdale. New York was the target he quickly settled on, following in the footsteps of many would-be terrorists before him, all of them eager to make a violent splash on the world's top stage.

Like Faisal Shahzad, Qazi wanted to attack somewhere crowded and public. Like Jose Pimentel, he consulted the *Inspire* article "How to Build a Bomb in the Kitchen of Your Mom." Like almost every other aspiring young jihadist in the United States and Europe, he'd been listening to the stirring sermons of Anwar al-Awlaki.

Qazi recruited his thirty-year-old brother, Sheheryar Qazi, to help plan a mission. He figured his older brother could help with some money too. After researching volatile chemicals and the methods for making explosives from household items like

Christmas lights, Raees was ready to proceed. In Sheheryar's words, his younger brother "would be a lone wolf" like Shahzad, who'd attempted to set off the SUV bomb in Times Square.

Born in Pakistan, the Qazis were naturalized U.S. citizens who'd spent most of their lives in South Florida's Muslim community. Raees made a living selling bicycles on Craigslist and doing maintenance work at a local mosque. Sheheryar worked as a cab driver.

On November 23, 2012, after shaving his beard to be less conspicuous, Raees got a ride to New York City with a friend. For several days, he pedaled a bicycle around Manhattan scouting possible terror targets, including Wall Street, Times Square, and the Broadway Theater District. But we were onto him, thanks to the excellent street sources of our NYPD detectives at the JTTF and especially the in-depth knowledge of NYPD intelligence chief Tom Galati. Galati recognized a phone number that Raees had dialed, connecting it to the National Street Mosque in Flushing, Queens. From that point forward, we shadowed his target-hunting trip around New York.

But Raees wasn't able to organize the actual attack yet. He ran out of money first. He had no organizational help. He headed back to Florida disappointed. On his way from New York, he phoned his older brother. "Continue to practice," Sheheryar said. "We can raise money. Then, you can return to carry out your attack."

We weren't ready to move in yet. We wanted to see how the brotherly plot developed. But the FBI and NYPD were definitely all over the Qazis.

Back in Florida, Raees continued collecting bomb-making components that he stored at the Qazi family apartment in Fort Lauderdale. By this point, his e-mails to the Middle East were also being monitored. "When Raees gets his first chance, he's going to do it," the brother said in a secretly recorded conversation with one of our informants. "He has taken his covenant and written down his life in the name of their God, Allah."

There didn't seem to be much wiggle room there.

Convinced the plot was an immediate threat, FBI agents arrested the two brothers on November 29, 2012, in Florida. In a search of the Qazi family apartment, agents found batteries taped together, stripped Christmas lights, and parts of a remote-control toy car that could have been used to set off a bomb. On the younger brother's computer, agents detected searches for PETN, the explosive used by Richard Reid, the so-called shoe bomber who tried to blow up a jetliner three months after 9/11.

Both brothers pleaded guilty to federal terrorism charges, admitting they plotted a terrorist attack on landmarks in New York City and later assaulted two deputy U.S. marshals while in custody. Raees also pleaded guilty to a charge of attempting to provide material support to al-Qaeda. Both got the maximum penalties allowed by law—thirty-five years for Raees and twenty years for Sheheryars.

*　　*　　*

It's a record we have a right to be proud of—sixteen serious terror plots against New York City, none of them successful. The perpetrators were discovered and brought to justice. The city remained safe. It was a massive effort that required the commitment and dedication of thousands of people and numerous law-enforcement agencies—police and prosecutors, local, state and federal—and the cooperation of decent citizens in New York, America, and abroad. We also got lucky a few times.

I have no illusion that this job will be completed any time soon. Certainly our counterterror campaign must continue for many years to come. The terrorists aren't through with us, and we mustn't be through fighting them. New plots are being hatched right now. I am certain of that. All we say with certainty is this: our vigilance has paid off so far, and the battle presses on.

CHAPTER FIFTEEN

Target Tower

Nothing anyone could do would bring back the people who died on 9/11 or ease the pain of their suffering loved ones. But those of us involved in the long recovery, it seemed to me, had an ongoing responsibility to do everything imaginable to reduce the chance of a repeat attack. Our many NYPD counterterror measures were a big part of that. So was an ancillary campaign we took on, a fight never before waged by the New York City Police Department or police departments anywhere. We sought to fundamentally alter the design and location of a massive skyscraper.

Such decisions have always been the prerogative of architects and engineers, developers and politicians, zoning and building officials—not the police. But this was the future of Ground Zero, a piece of Manhattan real estate with huge security implications. Far too much was at stake this time for us to stay silent.

From September 12, 2001, pretty much everyone had an opinion about what should be built at the former World Trade Center site—or whether anything should be built there at all. Governor Pataki, Mayor Bloomberg, the Port Authority of New York and New Jersey—they all had opinions. So did the people who lived nearby and the relatives of the people killed there, each claiming a privileged role in the decision-making process. Various civic groups, land-use review committees, and newspaper editorial boards had their own views as well. The city council, the state legislature, the mayor's economic-development team, and the governor's economic-development team—they had opinions too, as did the one-and-only Donald Trump, who took to the media to insist that the old twin towers be replaced with new twin towers just like the ones terrorists had managed to knock down.

This was New York. Everyone had an opinion.

Larry Silverstein's view mattered more than most. He was the Manhattan real estate developer in control of the site. Just one month and eighteen days before the terror attacks, Silverstein had signed a long-term lease for the World Trade Center with the Port Authority of New York and New Jersey, the government agency that owns the site. After the towers were destroyed, Silverstein had collected hefty insurance payments, capped at nearly $4.7 billion, and was eager to put the property back into a leasing mode. He also had Governor Pataki on his side.

Amid all these competing visions, various slogans found their way into the debate. "Sacred ground" was one of them. This was the belief that nothing should ever be built on the footprints where the Trade Center's twin towers once stood. "Showing the terrorists" was another common refrain. This was the notion—advanced primarily by those who wanted the most in-your-face design possible—that the new structure should somehow thumb its nose at the radical Islamists who had attacked the buildings on September 11, 2001, and might very well be thinking of attacking America again.

By December 2003, Silverstein, with Governor Pataki's backing, settled on a design called the Freedom Tower. A grand collaboration between master planner Daniel Libeskind and lead architect David Childs, this Freedom Tower was a piece of politics as much as a piece of architecture. It had to be, taking into account the opinions of all those competing constituencies as well as the usual tussles between New York politicians and business-people when billions of dollars are at stake.

Now that Mayor Giuliani was out of government, Governor Pataki was flexing his role as the single public official with the greatest control over the site. The New York City Economic Development Corporation, which Mayor Bloomberg controlled, was essentially letting Pataki and Silverstein have their way.

From top to bottom, the proposed building was dripping with post-9/11 symbolism, a loud expression of confidence for an otherwise troubled age. Even the name, Freedom Tower, was meant to send a message to America's friends and enemies. The new building would be the tallest in the Western Hemisphere, a mammoth glass-sided tower 1,776 feet tall (once the Statue of Liberty–inspired spire was factored in), even the measure of its height a patriotic nod to the year of America's birth. All this, I suppose, was about "showing the terrorists."

To avoid "sacred ground," Silverstein's Freedom Tower was placed in the northwest quadrant of the sixteen-acre World Trade Center site, near the corner of West and Vesey Streets. The building would stand as close as twenty-five feet to the northbound lanes of West Street, a six-lane thoroughfare that is the southernmost portion of the West Side Highway, New York State Route 9A.

The minute I saw the building's design, two words entered my mind: *security nightmare*.

A glass-clad tower? Immediately beside a busy highway? A structure whose predecessor had already been struck by terrorists twice, the second time catastrophically? This was not a good idea.

Not that anyone sought the opinion of the New York City Police Department. Of all the official agencies, boards, and celebrities who had been weighing in on the future of the World Trade Center site, the one organization whose views hadn't been solicited or considered was the one with prime responsibility for keeping the complex safe. It wasn't from lack of trying to share our expertise.

In 2003 and early 2004, as the plans took shape, we kept asking questions and requesting additional information from the developer, the governor's office, and the Port Authority. We got little more than boilerplate responses and thinly veiled brush-offs. Some of our requests were ignored entirely. It was hard to avoid the distinct feeling that someone was purposely hiding the ball from us, as if we were a bunch of knuckle-draggers who had no business in an arena as subtle and complex as skyscraper design.

*   *   *

The Freedom Tower's cornerstone was laid in an emotional ceremony on Sunday, July 4, 2004, with Governor Pataki, Mayor Bloomberg, developer Silverstein, planner Libeskind, and relatives of some of the 9/11 victims.

"Today," Governor Pataki said, "we take twenty tons of Adirondack granite, the bedrock of our state, and place it as the foundation, the bedrock, of this new symbol of American strength and confidence. Today, we lay the cornerstone for a new symbol of this city and of this country, and of our resolve to triumph in the face of terror."

An inscription on the cornerstone read, "To honor and remember those who lost their lives on September 11th, 2001 and as a tribute to the enduring spirit of freedom—July Fourth, 2004."

Well said, but we still had very few answers to how we were going to protect the safety of this obvious target of a building. We had no good explanation for why the dead should be honored and the tragedy recalled by a building as plainly vulnerable as this one. What we kept seeing in the public reports—beautiful drawings of a glimmering glass tower right beside a busy highway—seemed like an invitation for the terrorists to return. It was an attractive building. I could see that. But it wouldn't be so pretty lying in a pile of rubble on the ground.

Michael Sheehan, our deputy commissioner for counterterrorism, made it his business to get some answers. This, he and I decided, was a top priority. We met regularly to discuss progress and, time after time, had little progress to discuss. Neither one of us could understand why we weren't getting the information we needed. We were being rebuffed at every turn.

Sheehan, a former Army Special Forces officer, White House national-security aide, and Bill Clinton's ambassador at large for counterterrorism, is a pretty aggressive guy, and he wasn't getting anything. I told him, "Send the letter to Seymour." Joseph Seymour was executive director of the Port Authority. "Let's press the Port Authority on this."

Once you put something in writing, it has a way of changing things. Suddenly people are on notice and at risk. If an official ignores a warning and something catastrophic occurs, that person may suddenly face a torrent of uncomfortable questions. That's not a happy position for any public official to be in. I thought it was time to create a paper trail.

Writing August 31, 2004, Sheehan reminded the Port Authority director that the building's cornerstone had already been laid. "I believe it is important therefore that we expedite our discussions of these security and design issues before the construction proceeds any further," he wrote.

Still Sheehan got no response. He wrote again on October 1. "I believe this is a crucially important matter that we are duty bound to address in a timely manner," he emphasized. "I urge you to enter into a dialogue with the N.Y.P.D. as soon as possible." This time, Sheehan cc'd Charles Gargano, chairman of the Empire State Development Corporation, and Kevin Rampe, president of the Lower Manhattan Development Corporation—two top Pataki appointments whose responsibilities extended to the World Trade Center site. He also copied Silverstein.

When that produced no action, the next step, I decided, was to meet in person with Silverstein.

I didn't doubt the developer's motives any more than I doubted the governor's. I knew both of them wanted to erect a world-class structure that would deliver a powerful statement around the world. But before it was too late, I wanted to make as clear as possible that the police department had several reservations about the safety of this Freedom Tower design. I was eager to deliver that message personally and directly. Frankly, I wasn't sure how much thought had gone into the building's security—beyond the impulse to "show the terrorists."

Before the meeting with Silverstein, I asked David Kelly, a lieutenant with the Counter-Terrorism Bureau, to prepare an official NYPD report, laying out all our concerns in a single document. With powerful data and clear arguments, he did so eloquently. The full confidential report, titled "The Freedom Tower Security Assessment and Recommendations," was delivered to Silverstein on April 8, 2005.

We pulled no punches.

"The Freedom Tower is a special requirements building," he wrote on behalf of the department. "Its very purpose is a political statement against global terrorism. Its name, size, design and history make it, when completed, the number one terrorist target in New York City (which is arguably the number one target city in the world)."

The building, he said, had a high likelihood of attack.

"In the estimation of the NYPD, the Freedom Tower is a far more likely target of terrorist attack than the newly constructed US Mission to the United Nations on First Avenue that is being built at a far greater standard of security."

What this requires, he wrote, are "design criteria more consistent with federal government buildings than commercial buildings."

On several counts, he concluded, the building's security standards were too low, falling far short of FEMA, Defense Department, State Department, and other federal standards, making the building even more of a target. "Designing a building that is recoverable and does not sustain major casualties for the designated threat would provide a powerful deterrence to would-be attackers— as well as provide a reasonable level of safety for future inhabitants of the building that is commensurate to a realistic threat."

The report even laid out some specific recommendations. If it couldn't be located at the center of the World Trade Center site, it should be "at least 100 feet and perhaps 200 feet" back from the surrounding roadways. It should be able to withstand a truck bomb "with the explosive equivalent of 10,000 pounds to 15,000 pounds of TNT"—two to three times the envisioned 5,000 pounds. The glass should be strengthened. Recessed windows should be considered. The developers should "recognize that the Freedom Tower is a special requirements building and provide it the commensurate level of security features to make it reasonably safe for its inhabitants and structurally recoverable from a predictable threat."

Was that too much to ask? I'm not sure how much plainer we could have made it.

Our meeting with Silverstein was held at the Federal Reserve Bank of New York, 33 Liberty Street, four blocks east of Ground Zero. I didn't want to meet at the developer's office or at police headquarters or anywhere we might attract media attention. I wanted a private exchange.

I did not go alone.

We knew the developer would show up with his usual team of architects, engineers, contractors, and consultants, including people from Ducibella Venter & Santore, the project's security consultants. I'm sure they expected me to walk in with one or two deputy commissioners and maybe a couple of police officers. With their high-powered phalanx, it would be no contest.

So before the meeting, David Cohen and I devised a plan. We had to make the strongest case possible to the Silverstein team. This meeting, we thought, might be our best and final chance. To level the field a bit, even tilt it in our favor, Cohen assembled what I can only describe as a counterterror all-star team, including Cofer Black and Brian Jenkins.

Black had been George W. Bush's ambassador at large for counterterrorism, director of the counterterrorism office in the U.S. State Department, and director of the Counterterrorist Center at the CIA, where he'd spent twenty-eight years in the war on terror. A world-renowned expert on terrorism and transportation security with four decades of experience, Jenkins had provided terror-fighting advice to everyone from the U.S. military to the State Department to the Nuclear Regulatory Commission and the Catholic Church. No one had to explain to either man why a high-profile, vulnerable building shouldn't stand right next to a busy highway or why a glass facade at sidewalk level might not be such a fine idea.

Besides Cohen, Sheehan, and me on our side of the table, we also had a representative of Lawrence Livermore National Laboratory, the premier research-and-development institution for national-security science and technology, and someone else from the CIA. I don't think Silverstein's people expected any of this.

The Silverstein team certainly looked surprised when they saw who walked into the Federal Reserve conference room and full introductions were made. These were not people they could easily ignore. The conversation was animated. But the comment that lingered in the air most potently was one made by Cofer Black. He looked straight at Larry Silverstein and said, "We guarantee you that in the next ten years this building will be attacked—one hundred percent. You are not remotely prepared for that."

One of our primary arguments was that the building they envisioned simply could not be protected from a truck bomb. That was no abstract threat, of course. A 1,500-pound bomb inside a Ryder truck was detonated in the 1993 World Trade Center attack when I was police commissioner. The new design's open lobby and glass-paneled facade simply had to go. They were like a terror magnet, almost daring someone to attack. Then the discussion turned to building access. How would deliveries be handled? Where would taxis drop off? How would entry to the parking garage be controlled?

We asked far more questions than they had answers for. Nothing was actually resolved in the meeting, though I could tell Black, Jenkins, Cohen, Sheehan, and the rest of our team had made a genuine impact. Silverstein promised to consider what we had said and get back to us.

Before we left I spoke privately with Silverstein in the hallway. "You really have to move this building," I said. "And the lower floors have to be reinforced somehow."

The developer seemed to be listening intently, but he still didn't sound entirely convinced.

"This is a political decision," he said. "It is not really something we can easily do."

"This has to be more than a political decision," I told him.

*　　*　　*

On May 4, 2005, I went to the governor's Midtown office for a meeting with Governor Pataki, Mayor Bloomberg, Larry Silverstein, and officials from the Port Authority. That's where I learned that Silverstein was finally ready to abandon the old design.

That evening, Governor Pataki put out a statement saying that, because of security concerns, the Freedom Tower would have to be redesigned. "A new design for the Freedom Tower is required in order to meet NYPD's security standards," the governor said. "Larry Silverstein's team will continue to work with the NYPD over the course of the next several weeks. I have no doubt that David Childs will come up with yet another magnificent new design."

Given all that came before, it was truly stunning and truly gratifying to read those words.

Pataki's aides made clear that the governor wasn't altogether pleased about this change of direction. The delay was sure to cost money and time, they noted. Silverstein, I had to assume, was not happy either.

John Whitehead, a Wall Street legend who'd been appointed by the governor to chair the Lower Manhattan Development Corporation, grumbled to reporters about the safety concerns that were raised by the NYPD. "I wish they had called attention to the seriousness of the problems earlier, rather than at this late stage." That complaint was undercut a bit when some of Mike Sheehan's increasingly urgent e-mails were made public, spanning back many, many months. The media did not know about David Kelly's frank report.

For his part, Mayor Bloomberg stood behind us firmly. "In 1993, there was a bombing at the World Trade Center, and we did not learn our lesson, and we paid for that with close to three thousand lives," the mayor said, quite eloquently, I thought. "This is a building, particularly the Freedom Tower, that is built to be a symbol, and symbols are great if you are encouraged by the cause, and they are potentially a target by people that hate the cause."

He got it.

Whatever was built there, the mayor said, should be no less a fortress than a U.S. embassy on the foreign soil of an unfriendly nation. That was just the reality. "We are going to build a building to embassy construction standards, which nobody has ever built [into] a building this high before," the well-traveled mayor said.

Once things got rolling, they rolled fast. On May 12, the governor brought in my friend James Kallstrom, the former assistant director of the FBI who had run the investigation into the crash of TWA Flight 800, to oversee Freedom Tower security. He'd be part of a new Ground Zero management team that included the governor's chief of staff, John Cahill. Pataki said that having Kallstrom on board would keep the project moving while also keeping it safe.

"I know if there is ever a security issue, it won't take weeks or months to address," Pataki said.

June 29, 2005, was a good day for New York.

That's when Governor Pataki and Mayor Bloomberg unveiled a fundamental redesign of the Freedom Tower, six weeks after they had promised a change was on the way. At least, terror-age security would no longer be an afterthought. The new version was a seventy-seven-story glass-front skyscraper sitting above a two-hundred-foot steel-and-concrete pedestal—set back another sixty-five feet from busy West Street. The new ninety-foot set-back was a huge improvement from the original twenty-five feet, though still shy of the "at least 100 feet and perhaps 200 feet" David Kelly had called ideal. But with the new setback and that huge, solid pedestal, a truck bomb couldn't do nearly as much damage as before the changes in design.

The redesign, which Silverstein's architects boasted they had whipped up at lightning speed, was clearly not something they'd wanted to do. It came, the *New York Times* said, after "an embarrassing setback for the trade center redevelopment, when the NYPD deemed the first version of the Freedom Tower too vulnerable to attack by car or truck bomb."

The change was truly dramatic.

Now, no tenants at all would have offices in the building's large pedestal. The first 30 feet would be nothing but base, totally solid. The next 50 feet would have sufficient openings to pull light into the lobby, but not more. The building's mechanicals would be housed in the next 120 feet, a minimum of 80 feet above the sidewalk.

Now *that* was a fortified building.

And that wasn't all. The windows facing West Street would be made of tempered, multilayered glass. The elevators, sprinkler systems, and electrical conduits would now be protected in a central core of super-dense steel-reinforced concrete. An extra stairway would allow rescue workers to go up in an emergency while evacuating tenants were going down.

Suddenly all the people who hadn't seen any need to change the old design were publicly enthusiastic in their praise for the new one. "I think it will be very safe," Governor Pataki said, adding that if his own children got jobs in the tower, he would be "confident in their safety."

"There is no question that it is a more secure building," said Kenneth Ringler from the Port Authority.

Silverstein said the revised design had "embraced very significantly" the stringent safety recommendations from the National Institute of Standards and Technology.

The design was an extraordinary victory for post-9/11 sanity. I skipped the self-congratulatory announcement event. I had a previously scheduled appearance with the Lieutenants Benevolent Association. But I had Paul Browne put out a written statement noting that the enhanced design "provides for a level of bomb blast mitigation consistent with the N.Y.P.D.'s report on the Freedom Tower and adequate to the threat."

Architect David Childs had even agreed to give up some of the flourishes he had once touted as integral to the building's soaring design. Gone was the parallelogram floor plan. Gone was the open-air superstructure filled with energy-producing wind turbines. Even Libeskind's beloved asymmetrical spire, which was supposed to recall the sweep of Lady Liberty's extended arm, was replaced. Now, there'd be a central antenna that harkened back to the former 2 World Trade Center. Libeskind said he could still see a hint of the Statue of Liberty's torch in the antenna's sculptural enclosure, though I'm not sure anyone else could. "The tower we have now is even better than the tower we had before," the master planner declared. "It asserts what the site is all about. The tower relates to the memorial, and rises in a symbolic way."

"The building is simpler, architecturally," Childs said of the revised design. "It is unique, yet it subtly recalls, in the sky, the tragedy that has happened here."

One thing didn't change: when the new antenna was counted, the building still topped out at 1,776 feet.

*　　*　　*

Thanks to those efforts, the building and the neighborhood were safer. Because of the expense involved, not every building at the site could possibly afford to be as fortified as the Freedom Tower. For the immediate area, we worked with Port Authority personnel to devise a state-of-the-art "campus security plan" and "smart car system." Richard Falkenrath, who replaced Mike Sheehan as deputy commissioner for counterterrorism in 2006, deserves a lot of credit for that. The plan included underground screening for truck deliveries. All vehicles that drove onto the sixteen-acre site would be inspected, weighed, photographed, and turned back if necessary. Other methods would be used to check black cars, taxis, and food deliveries.

At the same time, we made sure some broader lessons were learned. With Falkenrath leading the effort, we wrote a whole book about this, *Engineering Security: Protective Design for High Risk Buildings*, showing other developers how to build safer skyscrapers in the post-9/11 world. Not perfectly safe ones—that's not possible—but safer ones. And now the New York City Police Department can be part of the conversation—to make suggestions and, when necessary, sound warnings—whenever a major building is planned. David Kelly, who rose to assistant commissioner for counterterrorism, was instrumental in that.

Many, many people were involved, and the results were worth being proud of, what we had all achieved together. Had it not been for our persistence and our willingness to use the power that we had—had we not been willing to stand up to those around us—none of this would have occurred. The city would have been more dangerous as a result.

CHAPTER SIXTEEN

Reasonable Suspicion

This might be a surprise to some people, considering my chosen career and how I have been portrayed at times in the media, but I consider myself a civil libertarian. I am wary of governmental power and overreach. I believe citizens should never be subjected to harassment or unlawful invasions of privacy. I cherish the U.S. Constitution. In every job I've ever held in the public arena, from Marine Corps officer to police commissioner, I have sworn to "serve, protect and defend the Constitution of the United States of America against all enemies, foreign and domestic." That, to me, is a sacred duty, and I have always fulfilled it to the absolute best of my ability. I don't believe in cutting corners. Not in my personal life. Not professionally. And certainly not with the law. I am also a lawyer.

Which brings me, of course, to the policing tactic that is sometimes wrongly labeled "stop and frisk."

One of my biggest frustrations as police commissioner was how my views on this subject were so badly misconstrued. Some of this was just a matter of public confusion. Phrases fly around. People pay half attention. Being "stopped and frisked" by a police officer certainly doesn't sound like any fun. But much of this distortion, I came to believe, was purposeful. It occurred, I am convinced, for cynical, political reasons by politicians and activists who wanted to advance their own ambitions and didn't care about the facts—or the life-or-death consequences to the public.

I could handle the public relations heat. My poll numbers stayed high. So did the NYPD's. In January of 2013, the start of my twelfth year as police commissioner, as the so-called stop-and-frisk debate was really heating up, the department had a 70 percent approval rating, according to the widely respected Quinnipiac University Polling Institute. My personal approval rating was even higher at 75 percent. "Whether Democratic or Republican, white or nonwhite, male or female, wealthy or not, New York City voters overwhelmingly like Police Commissioner Raymond W. Kelly and would prefer that he remain in the job under the next mayor," wrote *New York Times* reporter Wendy Ruderman in her piece on the Quinnipiac poll. Those numbers, in a city as complex and contentious as New York and after eleven-plus years on the job, were extremely gratifying. What bothered me—what still bothers me—is that the stop-and-frisk controversy managed to undermine a valuable, appropriate, and legal—let me emphasize *legal*—tool of modern law enforcement, one that had helped to save literally thousands of innocent lives.

You want the police to stop and question people who are behaving suspiciously on the street. That's what we pay them for. Even the politicians who complain most loudly about "stop and frisk" want it. You'll notice they almost never demand that we quit stopping people behaving suspiciously. They call for "a more appropriate number of stops" without ever detailing how many that might be. The practice must be event driven, not numbers driven. To anyone concerned about crime today, ending these street stops would make no sense at all.

The reason is obvious: If a police officer stops someone acting suspiciously, someone whose behavior suggests the person is planning to commit a crime, we will have prevented that crime. There will be one less crime victim as a result. It is really no more complicated than that—at least, it shouldn't be.

Now, what do I mean by acting suspiciously? Here is a classic example, one that actually plays out every day in New York City and in other cities and towns everywhere. A person is walking up and down the street and attempting to open car doors, seeing if any of them is unlocked. Now, it is theoretically possible that this person owns every car on the street. It's possible he is an undercover block-patrol volunteer out on his daily rounds. I suppose that has happened once or twice in the history of the universe. But it is extremely unlikely. It is far more likely that the individual is looking for a car to steal or an unlocked vehicle with something valuable inside. At the NYPD, we would call this suspicious behavior, the same phrase the U.S. Supreme Court has used in decisions resoundingly approving of the practice. Under our guidelines, the officer should stop that person and ask a few questions. If there is some reason to believe the person may be armed or otherwise dangerous, a light pat-down is also permitted for safety's sake.

Keep in mind, trying car door handles is not illegal, even on cars that don't belong to you. You won't be arrested for that alone. But it is suspicious behavior, warranting an additional inquiry from the police. It's exactly the kind of activity an engaged police officer should confront.

Respectfully. Professionally. Firmly.

If the individual has no gun and no drugs and offers no other evidence of committing a crime, there is no basis for arrest. That person will be sent promptly on his way. But aren't you glad the police officer didn't stand by and do nothing? I think most people are.

This is what New York City public advocate Bill de Blasio, the New York Civil Liberties Union, the Center for Constitutional Rights, and various other litigators and critics couldn't or wouldn't recognize: They insisted that in cases like this, perfectly innocent people were stopped and harassed for no good reason. I believe differently. I believe the police just prevented a crime.

Lawfully. Appropriately. Doing exactly what we should want them to do.

I don't like to question anyone's motives. I believe most people try to do what they think is right. But these street stops have been so profoundly mischaracterized, I also believe there has to be something political behind the attacks.

*   *   *

The concept behind these street stops goes all the way back to English common law, the very basis of the American legal system. Back then, it was the constable who would see something suspicious and could intervene. In our country, the U.S. Supreme Court has validated the practice repeatedly, most prominently in the landmark 1968 case *Terry v. Ohio*, and it is enshrined in state and federal law. John W. Terry and two friends were pacing back and forth outside a downtown jewelry store as if "casing a job, a stick-up," when a veteran Cleveland detective confronted them. Asked to identify themselves, the men "mumbled something." In a brief pat-down, the detective felt a pistol in Terry's overcoat. Once the case got to court, Terry's lawyer argued the gun should be suppressed as the product of an illegal search. The court's eight-to-one majority, with only Justice William Douglas dissenting, was clear and unequivocal: The Fourth Amendment to the United States Constitution, which prohibits unreasonable search and seizure, is not violated when a police officer briefly stops and questions someone—so long as the officer has a "reasonable suspicion" that the person has committed, is committing, or is about to commit a crime. The pat-down during such a stop must be limited—not a full-on body search but a quick check of the outer clothing to be sure the individual isn't carrying a weapon and everyone is safe. *Terry v. Ohio* is why in many states these are called "Terry stops." In some way, shape, or form, stop-question-and-frisk is authorized in every state in the country and used by virtually every police department. It's what cops do when they are doing their job.

Let me clear up a couple of other facts about street stops. At the NYPD, there is no street-stop unit or street-stop program or Operation Street Stop. There never has been. Briefly stopping certain people, questioning them, and patting them down when appropriate is something all officers are expected to do. It is what proactive policing is all about, getting cops to get out of their cars, engage with the public, and be police. It is as fundamental a part of the job as knowing how to pull over a speeding vehicle or how to place a pair of handcuffs around a suspect's wrists. In my time as commissioner—and in other administrations, I presume—there were never any quotas or specific numerical targets for street stops, despite occasional claims to the contrary from the unions. The officers were simply expected to stay active and do the job they were hired to—all parts of the job, including engaging lawfully with people acting suspiciously on the street.

There is no need to exaggerate the importance of this one tactic. No one in policing considers it the be-all-and-end-all of crime fighting. But in conjunction with a variety of other methods and strategies, it has helped to drive crime down in New York City and to make the streets safer for everyone. It's hard to prove a negative, so we may never know for certain how many weapons weren't carried, how many muggings didn't occur, how many shootings or burglaries were avoided, how many people weren't killed because of those street stops. But we know this: In the twelve years of the Bloomberg administration, the city had nearly 9,500 fewer murders than in the twelve previous years, and the vast majority of the lives saved were those of young minority men, if history is any guide. Street stops certainly weren't the only reason for the steep decline, but they just as certainly played a role. In the final year of the Bloomberg administration murders and shootings were at record lows.

*　　*　　*

This didn't mean we wouldn't get sued, of course. In this litigious era, the city of New York constantly gets sued, the police department especially. The first big legal challenge to the street stops came in 1999, nearly three years before I returned as commissioner. That case, *Daniels v. City of New York*, was brought by one of the groups that sues the city often, the Center for Constitutional Rights. The matter was assigned to U.S. district judge Shira Scheindlin, who was nominated by President Bill Clinton to fill a slot at Manhattan's federal court that was vacated when Louis Freeh left to become FBI director. Lawyers for the group argued that under the Giuliani administration, the department's street stops amounted to illegal racial profiling, since the majority of the people stopped were either African American or Latino, a far higher percentage than in the population at large. They also complained that the NYPD kept inadequate records of these stops.

The suit came at a dicey moment for the Giuliani administration, right at the peak of protests over the fatal police shooting of Amadou Diallo, the unarmed African immigrant street peddler shot forty-one times outside his apartment in the Soundview section of the Bronx. The lawyers sought to channel the Diallo outrage into their own big victory in court, but that never happened. The *Daniels* case didn't ever go to trial. It inched along on Judge Scheindlin's lengthy calendar as the Giuliani administration ended and the Bloomberg administration came in. The city law department, led by corporation counsel Michael Cardozo, settled the case at the end of 2003, promising that the NYPD would keep clearer records and make sure people weren't being stopped based on their race. The city also agreed to conduct regular audits of the street stops, reporting how closely the law was being followed.

We lived under that agreement for the next several years,

following the procedures as we had promised to. People were stopped because of suspicious behavior—not based on race, ethnicity, national origin, or any other similar factors. We made sure the stops were being recorded. This was certainly not a practice that had been adhered to in the past. After every stop, the officers were required to fill out a UF-250, the Stop, Question and Frisk Report Worksheet, noting why the stop was made. The revised form was a product of the *Daniels* case with input from all sides, including the judge. The information was input into department computers after every shift.

But no legal fight is ever really over in New York. So it was with the *Daniels* case. The plaintiffs asked Judge Scheindlin to extend the settlement period beyond its 2008 expiration date. She declined but came up with a novel way of keeping the issue in her court. She invited the plaintiffs to bring another lawsuit and mark it as related to *Daniels*. That way, she would get to hear that one too.

I didn't realize such a thing was allowed. I thought cases were supposed to be assigned to judges at random. But that's what Judge Scheindlin did.

Suddenly, the Center for Constitutional Rights was back with a whole new set of plaintiffs and the same old set of arguments against the NYPD street stops. They put their complaint again in starkly racial terms and purported to speak for all minority New Yorkers. The new case was called *Floyd v. City of New York*. This time, I was among the defendants, along with Mayor Bloomberg. The plaintiffs were several black and Latino people, including an African American man named David Floyd, who claimed he had been stopped and searched without any reasonable suspicion that he was committing, had committed, or was about to commit a crime.

On February 27, 2008, Floyd and another man were outside a building in the Bronx, trying to unlock a basement apartment. As they tried one key after another, three police officers walked up, asked the two men what they were doing, asked to see identification, and conducted a light pat-down.

The officers testified later that they thought the two men were committing a burglary, that there had been a pattern of burglaries in the area at that time of day, and that Floyd's behavior made them suspicious. They had filled out the appropriate UF-250, noting that the suspected crime was burglary.

In a preliminary ruling on August 31, 2011, Judge Scheindlin found that the police officers did, in fact, have reason to be suspicious and therefore the stop was legal, but that wasn't the end of the case. She said the plaintiffs' class-action suit could continue anyway. "There is a triable issue of fact as to whether the NYPD leadership has been deliberately indifferent to the need to train, monitor, supervise, and discipline its officers adequately in order to prevent a widespread pattern of suspicionless and race-based stops."

That was ridiculous. Our street stops weren't race-based. They were based on the presence of suspicious activity that was closely connected to crime. If there were more stops in some neighborhoods than others—and this was always the case—that was because those neighborhoods had more criminal activity.

*   *   *

The number of stops had been growing. At least, the numbers being counted had, though it was hard to say how much was the result of more activity and how much was the result of better record keeping.

In 2002, the first year of the Bloomberg administration, the police department recorded 97,296 street stops, though in those pre-*Daniels* days, certainly many stops went unrecorded. When I was making street stops as a young patrol officer, we only filled out a form if there was a problem or a complaint. Oversight and review were far less stringent in those days.

In 2008, the year *Floyd* was filed, the street-stop number crossed half a million. The peak year was 2011, with 685,724 stops. Overall, in about 12 percent of the cases, people were charged with some offense or crime. In other cases, people were sent on their way. Weapons were found in about 2 percent of the stops. You can't measure the amount of crime that wasn't committed.

But here's some context: the NYPD has twenty-three million citizen contacts a year, twelve million calls to the 911 system, four hundred thousand arrests, five hundred thousand summonses. Is 685,274 street stops a big number in a city with record-high population of 8.4 million people? Compared to everything else the department does, not really. It's more like business as usual. Here's what that number adds up to: less than one stop per patrol officer per week, and less than one limited pat-down every two weeks. With averages like those, it's hard to call the practice an egregious overuse.

On a per capita basis, the NYPD wasn't stopping people dramatically more often than other big-city police departments. When you normed for population, the number of stops was actually lower than in Philadelphia or Baltimore. Chicago's stop-question-and-frisk rate was four times New York City's. If you factored in the relative size of the cities, the Los Angeles police stopped the equivalent of 560,000 a year in New York City numbers.

But that didn't mean someone couldn't turn this into a political issue, even beyond the dispute in federal court. Soon enough, someone did.

* * *

In early June 2012, a group of black and Latino lawmakers met with attorneys at the Justice Department in Washington, complaining about stop-and-frisk. A big protest was planned by Al Sharpton's National Action Network for Father's Day, June 17, in which several thousand people, including NAACP president Benjamin Todd

Jealous and hip-hop executive Kevin Liles were expected to march down Fifth Avenue from Harlem to the mayor's town house on East Seventy-Ninth Street. The mayor wanted to get in front of that. So the Sunday before, he rode out to Brownsville, Brooklyn, to address the congregation at the First Baptist Full Gospel Church. I went along, as did schools chancellor Dennis Walcott and two deputy mayors, Howard Wolfson and Caswell Holloway. That was a large entourage for a church drop-in.

Though far safer than it had been a decade earlier, Brownsville still had some of the highest violent-crime numbers in the city—and therefore also one of the highest numbers of street stops. It was a perfect neighborhood for a review of our crime-fighting techniques, their effectiveness, and their fairness.

Bloomberg was eloquent.

"We are not going to walk away from a strategy that we know saves lives," he said from the pulpit that Sunday as the people listened in rapt attention. "At the same time, we owe it to New Yorkers to ensure that stops are properly conducted and carried out in a respectful way."

Racial profiling was banned at the New York City Police Department, he assured the congregation. "We will not tolerate it." But any effort to fight crime, he said, must go where the criminals are—regardless of where that is. It made no sense, he said, to insist that the people the police encounter precisely mirror the population at large. Women make up slightly more than half the city's population, the mayor pointed out. Does that mean half the people stopped for suspicious behavior have to be women? That made no sense at all. "If we stopped people based on census numbers, we would stop many fewer criminals, recover many fewer weapons, and allow many more violent crimes to take place," he told the congregation.

"We will not do that," he vowed. "We will not bury our heads in the sand. By making it 'too hot to carry,' the NYPD is preventing guns from being carried on our streets. That is our real goal—preventing violence before it occurs, not responding to the victims after the fact."

I couldn't have said it better myself.

*   *   *

Judge Scheindlin conducted a two-month bench trial—no jury—in the spring of 2013, already into our final year in office. From the questions she asked, the evidence she admitted, and that which she kept out, it was very clear to me that she was going to rule against the city, no matter how the evidence came in.

She took extensive testimony from a professor at Columbia Law School, Jeffrey Fagan, purporting to show that the stops were flat-out racist. Nonsensically, his criteria for determining whether racial profiling was happening revolved around census data. Taking his argument to its logical conclusion, half of the stops would be of females. His position involved something called "indirect racial profiling," which I am still not sure anyone understands.

He and his research assistants had reviewed something like four million police stops over the years. They contended that about 6 percent of those—just 6 percent—were based on questionable circumstances. In other words, 94 percent of the police stops met Constitutional muster. For the case, they chose nineteen examples, presumably the most egregious they could find, ten of which were ultimately found to have been acceptable under the Constitution and the law.

The lawyers for the city countered that the police department had been living fully within the limits established by *Terry v. Ohio*, the *Daniels* settlement, and state and federal law, calling the street stops perfectly legal and routine—not remotely racial profiling.

Some of the points I wanted to see pushed were never brought to the fore, and others were kept out of evidence by Judge Scheindlin. Was it really plausible that the most diverse police department on earth, with officers hailing from 106 different countries and representing every imaginable race, would engage in a massive conspiracy to conduct street stops to deny minorities their Constitutional rights? How would such a policy be disseminated? How would it be enforced? How could it possibly be kept secret? In fact, we had done exactly what we said we were doing. We went where the crime was, whatever color the perpetrators turned out to be.

At the police-officer rank, the department was already "majority minority." The recent academy classes were solidly so. The number of African Americans had dipped slightly, but so had the percentage of black residents citywide. The numbers of Latinos, Asians, and other nonwhites in the department were way up. This was an extraordinarily diverse police force, serving an extraordinarily diverse city—and proud of it. Was this department really engaged in wholesale racial profiling, making street-level decisions based on factors other than the demands of fighting crime?

I thought it was important to bring some objective measurement to the issue. Otherwise, the debate would be an endless exchange of conflicting slogans and little else. Without reliable data, who could ever know: Were the NYPD street stops built on prejudice, profiling, and preconception—or simply the realities of confronting actual street crime?

I asked the New York City Police Foundation to hire the RAND Corporation to study this in 2006. The consultants' first order of business: finding the right metric to compare the stops against. What's the proper benchmark for determining if police stops are fair?

Again it was clear why census data wasn't the right comparison. With slightly more than half the population being female and the vast majority of street crime being committed by young men, no one could expect crime and criminals to mirror the population at large. The RAND researchers rejected arrest reports as well.

The department controls those statistics by deciding whom to arrest. Arrest numbers could be as biased as the street stops.

So what did that leave?

In their report, "Analysis of Racial Disparities in the New York City Police Department's Stop, Question, and Frisk Practices," the researchers laid out a very sensible idea. They said we should use the descriptions of suspects provided to police by the victims of violent crime. More than any other measure, that should mirror the population that is actually committing crimes. The government doesn't create those numbers. The police don't craft those descriptions. Crime victims do. According to that data, the perpetrator descriptions over time in New York City are about 69 percent black. On average, 53 percent of the people stopped by the NYPD have been black. By that data-driven analysis, we were proportionally *under*stopping African Americans— not overstopping them. To quote the RAND report: "We found that black pedestrians were stopped at a rate that is 20 to 30 percent lower than their representation in crime-suspect descriptions." The judge would not admit the report into evidence.

Chapter Seventeen

Running Against the Police

Bill de Blasio didn't only run against the other candidates in the race to replace Mike Bloomberg. He also ran against the police.

Which seemed a little strange at first, given the Quinnipiac poll's 70 percent approval rating for the NYPD and 75 percent approval for me. That was in January 2013, just as the campaign was getting started.

But as the campaign revved up, one thing seemed almost certain: After twenty years of Republican-endorsed winners—two terms for Giuliani, three for Bloomberg—the election was the Democrats' to lose. With a six-to-one Democratic registration advantage and no well-known Republican or Independent in the race, the winner of the Democratic primary on September 10 would very likely be moving into the mayor's office on New Year's Day, 2014. There was certainly no shortage of candidates. The crowded field reflected almost every identifiable subset of New York Democrats. Looking back, it's almost harder to remember who wasn't in the race.

City council speaker Christine Quinn was there. She hoped to be the city's first female and first openly gay mayor. John Liu, the ambitious young city comptroller, was campaigning hard, dreaming of being the first Asian American mayor. Former city comptroller Bill Thompson was running too. He'd been beaten by Bloomberg four years earlier but still envisioned himself as the city's second African American mayor, after David Dinkins. The candidate list went on. There was a street-smart former city councilman from Brooklyn named Sal Albanese and a left-leaning political satirist named Randy Credico, whose big issue was legalizing drugs—but those two were total long shots. Rounding out the top tier were Anthony Weiner, a scandal-scarred former congressman from Brooklyn whose wife was a top Hillary Clinton aide, and Bill de Blasio, a media-savvy former Hillary campaign manager who'd become the city's public advocate, a job with very little actual power except for the right to call press conferences and complain about things.

As the campaign heated up around Memorial Day, support was so splintered, there was no way to know which candidate would come out on top. The early polls were all over the place. In June, Weiner and Quinn traded the lead, with Thompson just behind them. Then in July, Weiner got snared in a second round of his messy sexting scandal. He was calling himself "Carlos Danger" and posing for Twitter selfies in his underpants. Understandably, city voters had trouble shaking that image out of their heads. As Weiner's poll numbers tumbled and Thompson failed to catch fire, Quinn became the woman to beat. The veteran council speaker had worked fairly effectively with Mayor Bloomberg. She had solid support from gay and lesbian groups and the editorial board of the *New York Times*. A group of left-leaning labor unions and Democratic activists who didn't have their own candidate but considered her too close to Bloomberg were pledging to spend $1 million on an "Anyone but Quinn" campaign. But as the summer rolled on, the biggest question seemed to be: Could Quinn grab at least 40 percent of the primary vote, enough to avoid a runoff with the number-two finisher, whoever that might be? Five weeks before primary day, de Blasio was still polling fourth or fifth.

Then the race was turned upside down.

De Blasio's campaign manager, Bill Hyers, carefully parsed

the New York Democratic electorate, slicing and dicing the various ethnic, racial, and political groups. He knew that in an off-year like 2013, voter turnout was almost certain to be light, a tiny fraction of the city's total population. The most likely Democratic primary voters, he concluded, would be political liberals, and a high percentage of those voters would likely be African Americans, Latinos, and Asian Americans, many of them outer-boroughs residents.

What would these voters respond to? Hyers decided to strike two emotional chords: he would emphasize de Blasio's own multicultural Brooklyn family—his African American wife and their two biracial children—and portray the New York police as almost cartoonish villains. The star of this show—both the profamily and antipolice parts—wasn't going to be the candidate himself, a white, fifty-two-year-old, six-foot-five public official who'd grown up in Cambridge, Massachusetts, and changed his name twice—from Warren Wilhelm Jr. to Warren de Blasio-Wilhelm (in 1983) to Bill de Blasio (2001)—and had been knocking around New York politics for two decades already. The star, Hyers decided, would be the candidate's teenage son.

On August 9, the de Blasio campaign released its first television commercial. This wasn't a typical issues ad or even a slam at the other candidates. Talking straight to camera from beneath a large Afro, fifteen-year-old Dante de Blasio declares that his father is "the only Democrat with the guts to really break from the Bloomberg years." The Brooklyn Tech student mentions some familiar progressive planks—building affordable housing and raising taxes on the wealthy to pay for prekindergarten and after-school programs. Then, in explicitly racial terms, he touts his father's outspoken opposition to the NYPD's crime-fighting methods, singling out stop-question-and-frisk. "He's the only one who will end a stop-and-frisk era that unfairly targets people of color. Bill de Blasio will be a mayor for every New Yorker, no matter where they live or what they look like, and I'd say that even if he weren't my dad."

When that commercial hit the air, you could almost forget everything you thought you knew about the dynamics of the 2013 mayoral race. The Dante commercial spoke straight to the thin slice of left-leaning Democratic voters Bill Hyers and his candidate were trying to reach. De Blasio immediately began climbing in the polls.

I bristled at the implications of de Blasio's false narrative, the idea that our policies had been targeting people based on skin color and exacerbating racial tensions in New York. I knew the truth, that our policies targeted reported crimes—we didn't target people based on their skin color. I knew we had played a crucial role in making life better for law-abiding New Yorkers of all backgrounds. I knew that in all our policing strategies, we'd been guided by crime reports and other factual data—not prejudice, presumption, or broad demographic categories like race, religion, or ethnicity. To fight crime, we had gone where the crime was, simple as that, and the results spoke for themselves: violent crime in New York was lower than it had been for half a century, not to mention that we'd gone a dozen years without a single successful terror attack.

And who'd benefited most from our successes? The very people the de Blasio campaign was purportedly speaking for, young minority males especially. By the end of the Bloomberg Administration 9,500 lives would be saved, compared to the previous dozen years, many of them the lives of young African American and Latino men.

*   *   *

On August 12—three days after the Dante commercial hit the airwaves, and just over four weeks before primary day—U.S. district judge Shira Scheindlin presented her long-awaited ruling in

Floyd v. City of New York, the class-action stop-question-and-frisk case. It was a wonderfully targeted gift for the de Blasio campaign. In a sweeping 195-page decision, complete with charts, graphs, argumentative quotations, and some extremely pointed language for a sitting federal judge, she found the department's procedures unconstitutional on at least two fundamental grounds and demanded the department's practices be altered immediately. Judge Scheindlin didn't explain the curious timing of her decision. Whatever her intention, the decision was a huge boost to the de Blasio campaign, which was focusing more and more on the police.

In her decision, the judge found that the department had demonstrated a widespread disregard for the Fourth Amendment, which protects against unreasonable searches and seizures by the government, as well as the Fourteenth Amendment equal-protection clause. Blacks, she wrote, are "likely targeted for stops based on a lesser degree of objectively founded suspicion than whites." The police department, she said, had a "policy of indirect racial profiling" that illegally increased the number of stops in minority communities. That had led to officers' routinely stopping "blacks and Hispanics who would not have been stopped if they were white."

She didn't exactly say stop-question-and-frisk was itself unconstitutional. How could she? The U.S. Supreme Court had settled that decades ago in *Terry v. Ohio*. But she did the next best thing, from the perspective of the plaintiffs, their attorneys, and the de Blasio campaign: she ripped the "NYPD's practice of making stops that lack individualized reasonable suspicion."

That did not reflect the facts as we knew them to be. We had worked mightily to ensure the opposite. We kept voluminous records, which the plaintiffs tried to use against us. We ran extensive training programs. But the judge didn't seem to have noticed any of this. She said we had not done nearly enough to take the corrective action ordered in the *Daniels* case. Racial discrimination, she said, was "standard operating procedure" at the New York City Police Department.

She didn't stop there. She ordered a whole array of changes in department policy. She demanded a pilot program in which officers in at least five precincts across the city would wear body cameras. She called for a series of community meetings—a "joint remedial process," she called it—to solicit public comments on how to reform the department's tactics. And finally, she appointed an "independent monitor" to guide the department's reform, naming Peter Zimroth, a former city corporation counsel now practicing law at the Washington-based firm Arnold & Porter LLP.

When the judge's decision came down, I went straight to the Blue Room at city hall, where Mayor Bloomberg, Michael Cardozo, and I met the media.

I termed the decision "disturbing" and "highly offensive" and flatly rejected the claim that our officers had engaged in racial profiling. "That simply is recklessly untrue," I said.

I was angry, and so was Mayor Bloomberg. Accusing the judge of denying the city a fair trial, he announced that the city would immediately appeal. "You're not going to see any change in tactics overnight," the mayor said, striking an almost defiant tone. "I wouldn't want to be responsible for a lot of people dying.

As the mayor and I stood together at the podium, answering the reporters' questions, Cardozo was off to the side. I got the distinct impression he didn't want to be there at all. There was so much not to like about this decision. What really burned me up, though—one of many things—was that from a tiny number of incidents, cherry-picked from millions, Judge Scheindlin had painted the whole police department as a racist institution. It was bad science, bad judgment, bad policy, and, on a human level, personally wrong. This wasn't justice or fairness by any definition of those words. This was the product of a transparently cynical collaboration among an agenda-driven academic, a crafty plaintiff's attorney, and a judge who'd already made up her mind.

The only solace we got that afternoon was from our own strong confidence that once an appeals court got a look at Judge Scheindlin's reckless decision, it wouldn't stand for long.

*   *   *

Even as de Blasio rose in the polls of likely Democratic voters, the NYPD—and I personally—maintained our high approval ratings with the public at large.

It was almost like there were two separate populations in New York in the second half of 2013, the people in general, and the ones who would be voting in the Democratic mayoral primary on September 10. To break out of the candidate pack, de Blasio didn't need to reach the average New Yorker or even that many New Yorkers. He just needed to do well among the narrow slice of people who'd be voting that day—and somehow get his head above the crowded Democratic field. Yes, the Dante ad and de Blasio's similar comments in interviews and at public forums were a ridiculous caricature of the NYPD and our crime-fighting techniques, but here's the maddening part of the Hyers–de Blasio combination of identity politics and antipolice rhetoric: it worked.

The other candidates seemed almost helpless. One by one, they watched as their core supporters drifted toward de Blasio.

On primary night, de Blasio stood before a wildly celebratory crowd at the Bell House, an event venue in the Gowanus section of Brooklyn. To wild applause he sounded his divided-city theme. He warned against "powerful interests who benefit from the status quo." They might still try to stop him, he said. Then he summarized what had happened in the past few weeks. "You have made this campaign a cause," he said.

When the Democratic votes were finally counted, de Blasio

got 282,344, or 40.8 percent of the 691,801 cast, just enough to avoid a runoff. Bill Thompson came in second with 26.1 percent. Christine Quinn was far back at a disappointing 15.7 percent. Given the dominance of the Democrats, those 282,344 de Blasio voters—barely 3 percent of the city's 8.4 million people—really did effectively elect the next mayor of New York.

That same night, Joe Lhota, a former MTA chairman and deputy mayor under Rudy Giuliani, easily defeated billionaire supermarket magnate John Catsimatidis for the Republican nomination. De Blasio still needed to get past Lhota in the general election on November 5.

*　　*　　*

It was Halloween day that we got the legal news we'd all been waiting for. It was a stunning ruling from the Court of Appeals for the Second Circuit, blocking Judge Scheindlin's sweeping decision in the *Floyd* case and removing her permanently from having anything to do with the street-stop litigation. In a ruling that shocked the legal community and put a smile on my face, appellate judges John Walker, José Cabranes, and Barrington Parker declared that Scheindlin "ran afoul of the Code of Conduct for United States Judges," compromising the "appearance of impartiality surrounding this litigation." As a result, she was yanked off the case, and all her ordered remedies were put on hold. The ruling also postponed the operations of the new monitor who was going to oversee reforms of stop-question-and-frisk.

I was sitting in the conference room on the fourteenth floor when I got the news. Douglass Maynard, our general counsel, came into the room with a huge grin on his face. He and I just sat there, poring over the decision—not surprised exactly, just deeply, deeply gratified. The federal appellate court had agreed with what we'd felt all along: Judge Scheindlin had no business being on this case.

Scheindlin's "impartiality might reasonably be questioned," they concluded.

The appellate panel faulted Judge Scheindlin for suggesting to the plaintiffs' lawyers in 2007 that they file a new "related case" rather than extending the 1999 *Daniels* settlement, as well as for "a series of media interviews and public statements" to prominent outlets such as the *New Yorker*, the Associated Press, and the *New York Times* while the case was pending before her.

It was a stinging rebuke of a sitting federal judge—a personal embarrassment, really—especially for a judge as senior as Scheindlin in a jurisdiction as prominent as the Southern District of New York.

For his part, Bill de Blasio said he was "extremely disappointed" in the appellate panel's ruling. He was still dead set against the street stops. "We have to end the overuse of stop and frisk," he said, "and any delay only means a continued and unnecessary rift between our police and the people they protect." But all this back-and-forth didn't really matter anymore in the mayor's race. De Blasio headed into the general election with a commanding lead in the polls. His one remaining opponent, Joe Lhota, never had a chance.

The "practical Republican," as Lhota called himself, was a talented administrator with some fine ideas and credentials, but he didn't have the resources. With the Democrats' registration advantage and the momentum of de Blasio's come-from-behind primary win, Lhota faced a steep uphill climb. On Election Day, de Blasio easily rolled past him, 73 percent to 24 percent, to become the 109th mayor of New York.

In a race with record-low turnout, the lowest since World War I, de Blasio's 795,679 votes were almost exactly three times Lhota's 264,420, though numbers like that in a city so large could hardly be called a mandate.

What's the message there? It's obvious: vote.

*   *   *

Just because the new crowd won the election didn't mean they had to end the campaign. New Yorkers got a vivid preview of things to come even before the new mayor was officially sworn in.

I didn't attend Bill de Blasio's inauguration on the steps outside city hall. It had been twelve years since I'd had a vacation. Veronica and I were leaving that afternoon for Europe. I did watch a playback on YouTube, though I was immediately sorry that I had. Mayor Bloomberg was there, sitting gamely at the front of the stage, arms folded, staring glumly ahead as speaker after speaker denounced his legacy and mine.

Harry Belafonte went first. I'd always liked the eighty-six-year-old singer and activist. I thought he had a nice voice. Well, I couldn't believe what he was saying now. He attacked the Bloomberg administration for all manner of social ills we had absolutely nothing to do with—America's crowded prisons and the nation's "deeply Dickensian justice system." Really? The Reverend Fred Lucas Jr. of Brooklyn Community Church delivered a prayer that turned into an extended slavery metaphor. Apparently we were to blame for slavery, as well. "Oh God, oh God, oh God!" he wailed to the Almighty. "Break every chain, break every chain, break every chain!" As I listened to Reverend Lucas, I tried to calculate how many lives our anticrime policies had saved in his congregation's Fort Greene neighborhood.

Belafonte and Lucas were fiery. But it was the city's new public advocate, Letitia James, who really let loose on us. She called the Bloomberg years "a gilded age of inequality" where "decrepit" apartment buildings stood in the shadows of multimillion-dollar condos. Then she lit into stop-question-and-frisk. "Stop-and-frisk abuses," she said, "have been touted as 'success stories' as if crime can only be reduced by infringing on the civil liberties of people of color."

I'm not sure I'd ever heard a policing policy so mischaracterized in so few words.

Thank goodness for Bill Clinton. The ex-president had agreed to administer the oath of office. But before he conducted the formal swearing-in, he made a valiant attempt to dampen the nasty rhetoric, ad-libbing some lines of praise for the outgoing mayor about how Bloomberg, who "committed so much of his life to this city" was leaving office with New York "stronger and healthier than he found it." It was just a few nice words amid thousands of harsh ones, but they stood out as much for their contrasting tone as for their easy eloquence.

Bloomberg, who'd been sitting quiet and stone-faced for more than an hour by then, finally reacted. He nodded his head and mouthed two words: "Thank you."

The pile-on was so egregious, when de Blasio finally stepped up to the podium, even he felt compelled to address it. "Please," he told his people, "let's acknowledge the incredible commitment of our mayor."

Then, speaking to his predecessor directly, the new mayor said: "To say the least, you led our city through some extremely difficult times. And for that, we are all grateful. Your passion on issues such as environmental protection and public health has built a noble legacy."

It was a weird, uncomfortable display all around, especially for a new mayor's first public event. No one could credibly argue that Michael Bloomberg, who became mayor three and a half months after 9/11, hadn't done a terrific job.

It turned out I wasn't the only one who felt that way. *Classless* was a word a lot of people used. Even the *New York Times* editorial board, not always the Bloomberg administration's biggest booster, felt a need to weigh in with a withering assessment of the event. The inaugural ceremony, the paper wrote, was loaded with "backward-looking speeches both graceless and smug."

But as things turned out, the de Blasio inaugural was more a precursor than an aberration. The members of the new administration had barely unpacked their boxes when they turned their attention to "stop and frisk." On January 30, 2014, when the new mayor had been in office almost exactly a month, his new corporation counsel, Zachary Carter, filed papers in the Second Circuit Court of Appeals, abandoning the city's appeal in *Floyd v. City of New York*. It was an amazing surrender, given how the Second Circuit had so dramatically stayed the ruling, publicly questioned Judge Scheindlin's impartiality, and taken the extraordinary action of removing her from all aspects of the case.

We had, essentially, won in court. The stay was in place. The appellate judges of the Second Circuit had left little room for doubt about how they would ultimately rule. Victory, as a practical matter, was ours. And the new administration walked away from it, allowing politics—not law—to pull the rug out from under a policing strategy that I am convinced had already saved thousands of lives. De Blasio shrugged and walked away from a routine and useful policing tool, snatching law enforcement defeat from the jaws of legal victory. People will lose their lives as a result.

CHAPTER EIGHTEEN

Onward

Twelve years is a long time to be New York City police commissioner, the longest by far that anyone has ever served in the job. And that's not even counting the year and a half I was commissioner in the early 1990s. It's been an incredible honor, leading the world's premier police department through such challenging and important days. I am immensely grateful to those who joined me and hugely proud of what we have been able to achieve.

I have to keep saying "we." I didn't do any of this alone, any more than I ever acted alone in the half century I have spent in the military and law enforcement. These were not solo endeavors. They required smart, talented, and dedicated teammates every step of the way. I have been blessed with great people in all these organizations, none surpassing the remarkable men and women of the New York City Police Department.

When Mayor Michael Bloomberg appointed me police commissioner in those fragile post-9/11 days, I divided the task ahead into three main categories—the three Cs, I called them—counterterrorism, crime fighting, and community relations. All three, I knew, would require energy, creativity, and constant vigilance, more even than I imagined, as things turned out. In all three areas, I am proud to say, we saw tremendous successes.

The terror fight had so many different facets. It required a huge commitment and great creativity on our part. The creation of a real NYPD counterterrorism division, the expansion of the intelligence divisions, buttressing the Joint Terrorism Task Force with New York City police detectives, stationing other NYPD detectives overseas, hiring analysts from some of the top colleges in the country, bringing experts with heavy federal experience, enacting Operation Hercules, putting critical response resources onto the street, building vast new data and technology components—no one could possibly say we didn't throw ourselves into the fight.

We relied constantly on the FBI, the CIA, the Department of Homeland Security, and other agencies—local, state, federal, and international—as well as people from the private sector. We took help and guidance wherever we could find them and recruited some of the nation's top counterterror experts to join the NYPD. When we arrived at the start of 2002, you couldn't find anyone who thought the terrorists were through with New York City. After the deadly and spectacular results of 9/11, further attacks were considered a near certainty. Well, they tried. Relentlessly. Thankfully, we were ready for them.

We knew that no one would protect New York like New York would. We knew our city would always be a prime target for terrorists. We vowed we wouldn't let our guard down. We never forgot the importance of robust information gathering. We understood that our tactics always had to be a step ahead of the tactics we were guarding against. We recognized that a lull, even a long one, didn't mean we were safe for good.

The threat of terrorism is likely to be a permanent fixture of modern living, in New York City and elsewhere. The vigilance we established must continue indefinitely. But am I proud to say that, working together with our partners inside and outside the NYPD, we kept New York City safe after 9/11 and gave its people a dozen uninterrupted years without a successful terrorist attack.

At the same time, we pushed crime to an all-time low. After

the declines of the late-Dinkins and early-Giuliani years, most experts thought we'd be lucky just keeping crime where it was. We didn't accept that notion. We launched a series of crime-fighting strategies: keeping the cops constantly active, questioning people on the street when appropriate, finding creative new uses for data and technology, addressing special challenges with Operation Impact, Operation Crew Cut, the Real Time Crime Center, and many other initiatives. It wasn't any one thing that kept the crime rate falling. It was all those things done together and repeatedly. In the daily battle against crime and criminals, the police must never let up. There are many ways to measure our success fighting crime and violence. None is more gratifying than that often quoted homicide statistic: in the twelve years beginning with 2002, 9,500 fewer people were murdered in New York City than in the previous twelve years. Those 9,500 people, alive today, bear eloquent witness to what our efforts achieved. That gave us the lowest murder rate by far of any major American city.

As crime kept dropping, we were also building stronger relationships in the many diverse communities that make up New York City. By the end of the Giuliani administration, things had grown increasingly tense in this regard. So we devoted greater resources to community relations than the NYPD ever had before—inviting citizens into the local station houses, getting our officers to mix more casually in the community, encouraging precinct commanders to get to know people in the neighborhoods where they served, and making sure the police were helping to solve local issues long before they grew into violence or crime. At the same time, we kept improving the diversity inside the department. With robust populations of blacks, Latinos, Asians, Muslims, gays, and just about every other group represented on the job, we benefited from a level of cultural sophistication unmatched anywhere in law enforcement. I'm certain there is no other police department on earth that can boast that it has officers born in 106 different countries, the result of aggressive and sustained recruiting efforts on our part.

We took some tragic casualties and lost some very good people along the way. One of the toughest duties of a police commissioner is also one of the most crucial—being there when one of our people is badly hurt or killed. Police work can be dangerous. Everyone understands that. But when the worst does happen, the NYPD comes together like a close, caring family, doing everything imaginable to show support and ease the grief. In times of trouble, this is a culture that rallies around its own. It is impressive to witness, even more so to be part of. As commissioner, it was my job—and my honor—to be present for the worst possible moments, connecting personally with our people and their loved ones and doing what I could to help. I got to know many injured officers and the family members of those who paid the ultimate price.

Many of those memories are forever seared into my heart. Time and again, standing with the loved ones of those killed on 9/11 and those who died subsequently from Ground Zero–related illnesses, I am inspired by their strength, awed by their perseverance, and saddened by the terrible burdens they are forever forced to carry as they bravely press on with their lives.

Being in the emergency room at Bellevue Hospital in January 2012 as doctors pulled a bullet from the head of Officer Kevin Brennan, who'd been shot while arresting a suspect at the Bushwick Houses in Brooklyn. Miraculously, Brennan left the hospital, returned to the job, and was promoted to detective and then to sergeant and assigned to the Intelligence Division. The baptism of his child in St. Patrick's Cathedral was one of the happiest celebrations I have ever attended.

Keeping vigil at Kings County Hospital with Tatyana and Leonid Timoshenko while doctors tried to save their twenty-three-year-old son, rookie officer Russel Timoshenko. He and his partner, Herman Yan, were both shot in 2007 after pulling over a stolen BMW in Crown Heights. Timoshenko, who was shot in the face and throat, died five days later.

Escorting the mother of Detective Patrick Rafferty into a room at Kings County Hospital so she could see the body of her son. He and his partner at the Sixty-Seventh squad, Robert Parker, were both shot and killed on September 10, 2004, questioning an ex-convict they suspected of stealing his mother's car.

Going to Staten Island with Mayor Bloomberg and notifying Maryann Andrews and Rose Nemorin that their husbands were dead. Detectives Rodney Andrews and James Nemorin were both shot in the head on a deserted block during a 2003 firearms sting. They were posing as firearms traffickers planning to buy a TEC-9 submachine gun.

Getting to know Leslyn Stewart, whose husband Dillon Stewart was killed in 2005. He was pursuing a driver in Brooklyn when five shots were fired into his radio car, one of which slipped above his bulletproof vest and into his heart. Despite being shot, he kept driving for blocks in pursuit of the gunman.

There were countless stories of heroism, valor, and courage. But unfortunately there were many that involved tragedy and loss. The officers and their families were truly inspirational. Their stories stay with you. Steven McDonald was shot in 1986, long before I was commissioner, while questioning a suspected bicycle thief in Central Park. The three bullets left him paralyzed from the neck down. His wife, Patti Ann, and his son, Conor, have never left his side. I had the honor, as commissioner, of promoting this brave officer to first-grade detective and having Conor wear my former shield, number 15978, when he joined the NYPD in 2010.

We ask so much of these people. We must give them everything in return.

It matters when the police commissioner shows up, for our own people and for those we are privileged to serve. I spent countless hours attending worship services, visiting hospitals, going to public meetings, marching in parades—making sure I was plainly visible, especially in parts of the city where police brass was rarely seen except in the aftermath of some horrific disturbance or crime. It was far better, I believed, to build personal relationships in calmer moments. Then, at the very least, we'd have open lines of communication when the next crisis occurred. All these efforts together didn't mean we eliminated all tensions between the police and the people we served. We'll always have some of those, I am sure. But we had far fewer than in any recent city administration, and we tried to address them openly, frankly, and quickly when questionable cases arose.

*   *   *

The challenges were obvious from day one. But it was only in hindsight that I could see how so many factors collaborated to bring the past twelve years to life. The city, the threat, the mayor, our partners, some quirks of history, and my own personal experience all came together at this unique moment in time, and thank God they did.

Some of this was where I came from. My four-plus decades at the NYPD meant I knew the place well—its strengths, its characters, its far-off corners, its weaknesses—far better than any outsider possibly could. I knew where to go looking for sharp, hidden talent, and I knew who and what best to avoid. The fact that I'd been police commissioner during the last terror attack in 1993 was an added bonus. I had a clear idea of how such incidents were traditionally dealt with. And I had direct personal knowledge of how much the NYPD's top job entailed. The short answer: a lot.

My experience outside the NYPD was valuable as well. Having led U.S. marines in combat in Vietnam, I learned some things about motivating people and the tools of crisis management, especially the importance of effective teamwork when the stakes are highest. My education at Manhattan College, St. John's, NYU, and Harvard gave me critical insights into management and the law and set me off on a lifelong quest for learning. The time I spent in federal law enforcement as undersecretary for enforcement at the U.S. Treasury Department and as U.S. Customs commissioner was immensely helpful. It gave me a keen understanding of Washington's contribution to America's safety as well as a healthy skepticism. It certainly taught me a lot about navigating Washington's sprawling bureaucracies. I respected the federal agencies, but I certainly wasn't cowed by them. I knew we could enter some of the same arenas and perform at the highest levels. And my time with the police monitors in Haiti showed me vividly the human goodness that can rise even in abysmal circumstances and what can happen when social order really breaks down.

Had I not had this four-decade journey before saying yes to Mike Bloomberg, I'm not sure my experience as New York City police commissioner would have been remotely the same.

The uniqueness of our circumstances must not be understated either. When I returned as commissioner, the NYPD had a set of challenges and opportunities unlike anything that had existed before.

The horrors of 9/11 were fresh in everyone's mind. That gave us the leeway to make dramatic changes that, at a calmer moment, would have faced far greater opposition inside and outside the NYPD. In Mike Bloomberg, I had a boss who gave us extraordinary freedom to operate as we thought best. Without the mayor's faith and trust, we never could have gotten nearly as much done.

We also had a federal government that, despite its power and reach, really hadn't done that much to protect New York and America's other major cities from terrorism. Since terror fighting had become part of the national agenda, Washington had focused mostly on securing the transportation system, air travel especially, and taking the terror fight abroad. The field of urban counterterrorism was largely open to us.

And New York in the time after 9/11 was extraordinarily situated to answer that call. The city was large enough and the NYPD was staffed enough to benefit from real economies of scale despite operating with six thousand fewer police officers than in the previous administration. We could assign a thousand people on counterterror duty and still get the rest of our work done. What other police department could do that? We also benefited from the fact that, thanks to Mayors Giuliani and Dinkins, traditional street crime wasn't wildly out of control. If this had been 1985 or 1990, when homicides were soaring, it is hard to imagine we could have justified all the resources we needed to fight the war on terror. People would have been screaming too loudly about homicides in South Jamaica and East New York.

All these factors came together in a way they never had before and I'm not sure they ever will again.

We had a threat that everyone could understand and get behind. The basic job of policing was getting done. We had the scale to afford the resources and the talent inside and out. I had experience inside the NYPD and a broader view that came from working in Washington. I could say, "We're going to do things differently now"—and mean it. And with Mike Bloomberg's support, we actually got it done.

*　　*　　*

The lessons go far beyond New York City.

Other parts of America aren't quite the terror magnet that New York is, but the terrorists can turn their attention anywhere. Doubt that? Just ask the people of Boston or Oklahoma City. No one can say for certain which city or town will be targeted next time. So a certain level of wariness is justified everywhere. I don't expect every small police department to establish its own full-scale counterterror operation. That's just not possible. Our efforts at the NYPD consumed a large commitment of finite resources—dollars and people alike—far beyond the budgets of all but the largest law enforcement agencies. Still, local communities need to confront these threats, whether that means aligning with neighboring communities, working with state and federal agencies, or dreaming up fresh, creative approaches that work for their towns. The dangers are out there. No one can afford to simply ignore them.

At the same time, the daily challenges of regular policing never go away. Fighting crime. Maintaining order. Protecting people. Maintaining good relations with local communities. Someone has to do it, and no matter where you live, that someone will almost always be the local police. Our experiences in New York and my almost half century in law enforcement hopefully offer some valuable insights.

As I write this in 2015, our nation's police departments are facing enormous scrutiny. Though crime remains low by historic standards, controversial police shootings aren't just sparking protests and lawsuits—in some places, they provoked riots, looting, and massive violence in the streets. From Ferguson, Missouri, to North Charleston, South Carolina; from Baltimore, Maryland, to Staten Island, New York, many Americans feel intensely aggrieved at the behavior of some police officers. There is too much anxiety, too little trust, and far too much misunderstanding on all sides. Each specific case is different. From place to place, the blame can be apportioned in a variety of ways. Some complaints are legitimate. Others are overblown. Some reactions are justified. Others are just excuses for looting and criminality. But one thing is certain already: We've had more than enough sloganeers on all sides of these issues. It's time for smart people who understand the complexities to start making some key distinctions here.

First, there's no need to panic. Today's police overall are more professional, better educated, better trained, more diverse, and more restrained than ever before. It is simply not true, statistically speaking, that American police are on a murderous rampage.

New York City, of course, is the case I know best. In 1971, the NYPD killed ninety-three people in the course of policing New York City. In 2013, my last year as commissioner, our officers killed eight, the lowest number ever recorded since reliable record keeping was instituted in the NYPD. It was also the lowest per capita of any big city in America. We had the fewest nonfatal police shootings as well. I wish all these numbers were zero. But this could not be called an explosion of police violence. Quite the opposite. While other cities may not have had declines as dramatic as ours, many have also seen significant drops.

Many other lessons of policing we have learned in New York have also been learned elsewhere. That police officers need to stay active and engaged. That the biggest beneficiaries of lower crime rates are those who live in the most crime-prone neighborhoods. How data and technology can be valuable tools in focusing police attention. How diversity almost always makes policing easier. But some big problems do remain. Some important issues are not being adequately addressed today. We must address them, ideally without discarding the hard-won gains that have undeniably been made.

There is no denying we've had a rash of controversial cases of police officers killing unarmed civilians. Just in late 2014 and the first half of 2015, the reports seem to be everywhere. On Staten Island, Eric Garner died gasping for air as he was grabbed around the neck while being arrested. In Ferguson, police officer Darren Wilson shot and killed teenager Michael Brown. In North Charleston, Officer Michael Slager shot and killed a fleeing Walter Scott. Freddie Gray ended up dead with a broken spine in the back of a Baltimore police van. In apparent retaliation for the deaths of Brown and Garner, Ismaaiyl Abdullah Brinsley shot and killed New York City police officers Rafael Ramos and Wenjian Liu, who were sitting in their radio car in Brooklyn's Bedford-Stuyvesant neighborhood.

The Garner and Scott deaths were caught on cell phone cameras. Part of the Brown encounter was captured on a voice mail recording. All received extensive media coverage.

I have no firsthand knowledge of any of these cases beyond what I've learned from others' investigations. But the South Carolina case—an unarmed, fleeing man shot in the back by a police officer after a traffic stop—was shockingly unjustified. The video of Eric Garner's death—"I can't breathe...I can't breathe," the Staten Island man pleads repeatedly to the officers arresting him—is difficult to watch. It was in my first tour as police commissioner that choke holds were declared to be a violation of NYPD regulations, a rule that has remained in force. Though the Staten Island grand jury did not indict any of the officers, I certainly would have preferred that the testimony in the case had been released in its entirety. That way, people could have independently judged the evidence presented by the Staten Island district attorney, Dan Donovan.

It's hard to know exactly what happened inside that police van in Baltimore. So far, I have not seen a thorough accounting for how Freddie Gray ended up with a broken spine and dead. In Ferguson, by contrast, the evidence seems clear: Michael Brown's shooting was tragic but legally justified. It's never good when an unarmed civilian ends up dead at the hands of a police officer. But there is strong evidence in this case that the teenager confronted the police officer in a highly aggressive fashion, clearly justifying the officer's response. Brown's DNA was found on Officer Wilson's collar and gun.

There was an additional irony in the Brown case. Though Officer Wilson was not charged, the shooting did highlight severe problems inside the Ferguson police department: hostile relations with the community, an abysmal diversity record, unwise strategies on the street. The police in Ferguson handled the Brown incident terribly. They failed to release information in a timely fashion. As a result, Michael Brown's companion became the de facto spokesperson and, as it later turned out, was not telling the truth. They then had far too many officials talking to the media, delivering confusing and conflicting reports. They left Brown's body in the street for hours. All that contributed to the rush to judgment against Darren Wilson.

I just wish that amid all the media coverage of the department's many faults, there'd been a full day devoted to Officer Wilson's thorough exoneration by the U. S. Justice Department. His behavior can be confidently defended. The city of Ferguson's cannot.

Together, these cases were seen by a significant portion of the community as suspicions confirmed. Many people believe that such practices are a common part of policing in America. To be clear—police abuse does occur. Sometimes with tragic results. Those cases must be investigated and, if necessary, prosecuted aggressively, and victims should be compensated. But as a law enforcement professional with over four decades of experience, I can say that police abuse is a distinct aberration, not a systemic problem.

These cases do not represent typical police work. They are aberrations, not the rule. Police professionals should not—and must not—tolerate anything less than true professionalism.

*   *   *

This is a watershed time for modern policing, and those of us who care about the future of America need to respond accordingly. We have to take the challenges of the moment and mold them into long-lasting improvements. That's how we as police get better. That's how we as Americans build a better society for everyone.

The phenomena of cell phone cameras is a perfect opportunity. Everyone over ten years of age carries a camera now. That has undeniably altered the relationship between the community and the police. Whether police officers are evil-spirited ogres or have the best of intentions at all times, there is no denying this much: virtually every one of their actions can now be captured on a camera—a security camera, someone's cell phone, or some other device. After I saw the brutal killing of Walter Scott in North Charleston, I became a believer in police officers wearing cameras. You would have to believe that no one required to wear a camera would commit such a dastardly act. That was a game-changer for me. Police officers should wear cameras, I am convinced.

The police are being photographed anyway. They often have little control over how those videos are used. In the long run, police are better off with their own records of how they have behaved. Plus, universal body camera use will help restore confidence and respect among the public and provide some balance too, reminding everyone that the worst cases of police behavior are not typical ones. I guarantee this: Those body cameras will record far more acts of selflessness and heroism than of official abuse. The good far outweighs the bad in police work. Let's record it.

Role-playing exercises can also be helpful. They can become a larger part of training at the NYPD since a new $1 billion police academy was built during the Bloomberg administration. Police officers can act out challenging scenarios and learn from them.

On-the-job diversity will also help. Diversity isn't a panacea. It won't automatically make everyone get along. Minority cops can be bad cops just like white cops can. It's always a mistake to judge an individual on an arbitrary factor such as skin color. That said, diversity makes the job easier. Life on the street is almost always smoother when the police roughly resemble the makeup of the community. It opens the department to fresh perspectives and new ideas. It shakes up the old ways of thinking. It makes the police seem less like an occupying army and more like a part of daily life. It also increases the chance that the people in uniform will actually know the people they are sworn to protect and to serve.

Since the 1960s, when people started discussing diversity and policing, some critics have warned that greater diversity would lead to lower standards, that a less white police force would be a less educated one as well. In New York City, we have found the opposite to be true. On average, the nonwhite candidates have arrived with more college credits, to use one standard, than the white candidates. You can speculate about why that might be. Do we attract different strata of different communities? Perhaps. But the fact remains that our minority candidates are pulling the education levels up—not down.

Some diversity may be obtained by consolidating smaller departments. There are simply too many police departments in the United States, many of them quite small. The majority of the departments in America have fourteen or fewer officers. That's just too small, insufficient to afford much-needed specialized units and offer proper promotion opportunities.

For example, St. Louis County, where Ferguson is located, has ninety municipalities and fifty police departments. Surely higher professionalism and greater diversity could be attained by merging some of those little police departments. The federal government should encourage and facilitate such moves.

In the 1990s, New York's independent Transit Police and Housing Authority Police were merged into the much larger NYPD. There was resistance at first. People in the two smaller forces liked running their own shops and, in some cases, were eager to protect their own power bases. But the results have been almost entirely positive: greater flexibility in staffing, fewer communication slipups, more training opportunities, wider career paths, deeper leadership expertise, less administrative duplication—the benefits are simply undeniable.

When major events happen in small jurisdictions, those

departments must rely on mutual assistance from neighboring law-enforcement agencies. This can result in uncertainty over authority, rules of engagement, capabilities and accountability. We saw that confusion on display in Ferguson and in the apprehension of the Boston Marathon bombers. More joint training should be undertaken before the moment of need arrives, and the federal government ought to help pay for it.

Police departments everywhere should also be largely demilitarized. In 1994, with the best of intentions, the U.S. Department of Defense began dispersing surplus military equipment to police agencies across America. It was vehicles at first, Jeeps and Humvees, even a few armored weapons carriers. Once the program got started, the variety of equipment kept expanding. No one forced the police to use this stuff. But human nature being what it is, a Humvee sitting in a police station parking lot is extremely unlikely to remain there long. The optics were terrible. All that heavy hardware divided the police from the community.

In times of emergency—major storms, massive street disorders—the equipment can still be made available through state armories. But it shouldn't be used on day-to-day patrols or in anything less than the direst of circumstances. And certainly not when common sense tells us it will only exacerbate tensions.

Police also need better education. I've been pushing for that since I got an inside view of the system in the Police Cadet Corps during my college days. Law enforcement and education do mix.

Serious thought should be given by major departments to requiring a four-year college degree for all police officers. Few departments require this today. It should be a basic, universal standard of policing. The job is different now—more complex, more subtle, more legalistic, more closely watched, more culturally diverse.

A four-year college degree is the very basic requirement for teachers across America. Many are expected to earn master's degrees. Why should policing require any less? If that means we need to raise police salaries, so be it. The job of policing has become much more demanding with the use of technology, changing court decisions, and greater diversity. Departments should commit themselves to far more preemployment testing of applicants' social interaction, particularly in the area of bullying. What is the psychological impact on candidates who have been bullied or have engaged in bullying? This may help departments identify potential problem officers.

Finally, law enforcement agencies have to be open to asking for help. Police need support from communities, from the street corners to the executive suites. If the police are going to be a part of the people—not just among the people or on top of the people—we need to engage productively with everyone. Briefings of community leaders before engaging in tactical operations can be an effective way of obtaining needed support. Involving community leaders in the development of programs and initiatives from the very beginning can also be helpful.

I was deeply heartened by the broad community support we got during my time at the NYPD, and I'm not just talking about the flattering poll numbers. I mean the casual comments and the stray remarks. The advice and the suggestions. The calls to the tip lines and the information on the street. The invitations to speak to community groups and the honest give-and-take when I got there. All of it said to me that we were in this together: the police, the people, everyone.

Police need that everywhere.

The causes of both terrorism and crime are undeniably complex. Terror comes from ancient hatreds merged with accessibility to modern weapons of destruction. Crimes often bubble out of social realities that go far deeper than policing. Many go back generations, even centuries. Poverty. Too few jobs. Too little education. Fractured family structures. Substance abuse. We have to address all those root causes, however far back they go. But I am not naive. That won't happen tomorrow, and we cannot just wait around. We can't simply shrug our shoulders and avoid the hard, daily decisions. What will prevent someone from being shot tonight? We need everyone to help.

We need rappers and sports stars sending out nonviolent messages—not glorifying criminality or committing crimes of their own. We need clergy organizing their congregations and preaching peace in the streets. We need business leaders providing jobs for the young getting started in careers. We need brilliant academics generating fresh ideas for fighting terrorism and traditional criminality. We need it all.

Law enforcement leaders are in a period of soul searching. They know that, as a profession, we've had some remarkable achievements countering terrorism and fighting crime. But they see the media's coverage and hear all the debates, and they can't help but wonder, *Is that really what we're doing as a profession, oppressing the people we are here to serve?*

The answer is no, we aren't. All around the country, fine police departments are doing the job they are supposed to. But all of us have to be careful that in the political swirl that surrounds us, we continue doing what we all do well.

We can't, as some politicians are insisting, use this time to lighten up or tolerate more crimes and violations. The problem isn't proactive policing. The problem isn't that more of our resources are necessarily focused in certain neighborhoods where the crime is. The people in those neighborhoods are the ones who call us. They are the ones who need us most.

We have to continue doing what works best against the criminals, making sure we do it respectfully, thoughtfully, and legally. That's a prescription for moving forward, not for giving up.

If we ease up on the things that made us successful, if we bow too much to the political pressures of the day, we are going to see more young people dying, more young lives lost before they've had a chance to live.

The sheer size of our mission can be daunting. At the NYPD, we calculated that we had twenty-three million citizen contacts per year. If even one-tenth of one percent of those contacts goes bad, that's still a dramatic number. The activists and the media are always ready to pounce.

But we must not let our hearts grow weary. We must not pull back from the fight. We can't withdraw to avoid the possibility of complaints. We can never send up the white flag of surrender in such important fights. Nothing less than the future of our country and our way of life is at stake.

Acknowledgments

A book about my life and career was a natural thing to do after leaving the public sector as the thirty-seventh and forty-first commissioner of the New York City Police Department. But putting my many experiences into a book and making some larger sense of it all was far more difficult than I expected it to be.

I've had a great journey: more than four decades with the NYPD, wartime service in Vietnam, various high-ranking federal positions, an amazing adventure in Haiti, and certainly no shortage of stories to tell. I had a loving childhood and a remarkable education at some of the country's most revered institutions of learning. I have been blessed with an excellent marriage and a very supportive family. How could I possibly pack all that into a book?

Pulling it all together in a readable form was a monumental task, and I depended greatly on the talent and expertise of Ellis Henican. His patience, guidance, great sense of humor, and understanding were incredible. He is a true professional and, I hope, a friend for life.

My publisher, Hachette Books, was helpful in many ways. Publisher Mauro DiPreta and senior editor Paul Whitlatch, along with Michelle Aielli, Betsy Hulsebosch, Christopher Lin, and Lauren Hummel, moved the project along with insight and efficiency and helped me meet all the deadlines. Ellis's crew— Peter McGuigan, James Gregorio, Larry Kramer, Janis Spidle, and Roberta Teer—were immensely helpful.

But thinking back, as a story of one's life demands, I want to acknowledge my family: my mother, Elizabeth, and my father, James; my brothers Leonard and Donald; my sister, Mary; and my late brother, Kenneth. I was always surrounded by love, good humor, good music, and a keen understanding of the importance of hard work.

Since Veronica and I started dating so young, the Clarke family had a tremendous impact on me. Believe it or not, I had my first really good Italian meal at the Clarke table. Veronica's mother, Helen, and her father, John, loved the beach at Island Park, and that's where Veronica and I met. I worked as a lifeguard with her late brother, Jim, and sister Ellen. After 9/11 her brother Martin's New York apartment was a perfect place for me to crash. Theresa, her younger sister, has always been the first to call with support and good wishes no matter the event.

The Marine Corps had an enormous effect on my life. Virtually everything I know about leadership I learned in the Corps.

The NYPD, America's largest and the world's best police department, provided me with a career more exciting and fulfilling than anything I could have imagined. Being named commissioner by David Dinkins and by Michael Bloomberg are two of my proudest days. I am indebted to both mayors for their confidence and faith in me.

I am also grateful to President Clinton and Treasury Secretary Bob Rubin for appointing me as undersecretary for Treasury and U.S. Customs commissioner.

The multitalented Paul Browne, who worked by my side at the NYPD, in the federal government, and in the private sector has been a steadfast and loyal friend. Mike Farrell and I have worked together often over the last thirty years. His counsel and knowledge of the world and government have been tremendously helpful.

When New York and America needed them most, David Cohen and Frank Labuti stepped up, joined the NYPD, and helped to meet the new threats of terrorism. All New Yorkers owe them thanks. Later, Michael Sheehan, Richard Falkenrath, and Richard Dadario also joined the department and helped to turn our counterterror commitment into tireless reality. Jim Waters and Tom Galati, uniformed members of the department, were major contributors in this effort.

Steve Hammerman, Andy Schaefer, Doug Maynard, Katherine Lemire, and Jessica Tisch provided world-class legal advice to the NYPD and to me in a very demanding environment. Charles Campisi was an ideal chief of internal affairs, a man of solid judgment and unquestioned integrity.

As police commissioner, a security unit is a must. A team of dedicated police professionals under the leadership of Brian Burke made certain that things went as smoothly as possible.

Bob Barnett has been my legal advisor since I left the police department and has helped greatly in navigating the private sector.

Anne Reingold of HL Group has become my go-to person in all manner of things. I am grateful for her help, her guidance, and especially her friendship. And Valerie Salembier provided outstanding leadership for the New York City Police Foundation during my time as police commissioner.

My sons, Jim and Greg, have been extremely helpful and supportive with this project, as they always are. Their extraordinary recall clarified many dates and details. Their input has been invaluable. I am very proud of both my sons. They are my best friends.

Veronica has been my wife for more than fifty-one years. During that time she managed to become a registered nurse, join the Coast Guard Reserve, and have a successful, twenty-year career as an award-winning sales representative of a Fortune 500 corporation. Despite all that, my sons and I always came first for her. She has been incredible. She is smart. She is funny. And I learn something new from her every day. Without Veronica's help, support, and endless love, my life simply would have no meaning.

Together with her the journey continues.

Index

10-15
d
5-23-16 12